ALWAYS UNDER PRESSURE

Malcolm Fuller,

Lesler Gus Museum, 7/7/88

DONALD M CONDON JR

Always under Pressure

A History of North Thames Gas since 1949

Malcolm Falkus

Professor of Economic History
University of New England, New South Wales

MACMILLAN
PRESS

First published 1988

Published by
THE MACMILLAN PRESS LTD
Houndmills, Basingstoke, Hampshire RG21 2XS
and London
Companies and representatives
throughout the world

Typesetting by Footnote Graphics, Warminster, Wilts

Printed in Great Britain by
Camelot Press Ltd,
Southampton

British Library Cataloguing in Publication Data
Falkus, Malcolm
Always under pressure: a history of North
Thames Gas since 1949.
1. North Thames Gas–History
I. Title
338.7'6657'09421   TP733.G72L6
ISBN–0–333–46819–8

Contents

List of Maps and Figures

List of Tables

List of Illustrations

Preface

This history of North Thames Gas was originally planned in 1982 and a version was ready by 1985. However, in the wake of the Government's decision to return the gas industry to private enterprise it was decided to delay publication so that the story of North Thames Gas as a nationalised enterprise between 1949 and 1986 could be covered in its entirety. This delay has given me the opportunity not only to bring the text up to date but also to see in perspective the significance of the events of 1979–83, and so to appreciate the various recent reforms introduced under John Gadd's chairmanship.

One or two points should be made clear at the outset. I am very much an 'outsider' to the gas industry. Indeed, prior to being asked to write this history my view of the gas industry was coloured largely by the arrival of gas bills, the non-arrival of fitters, and by childhood memories of being dragged to the Torquay and Paignton Gas Company where the smell of the sulphurous discharge was supposed to induce sickness and cure whooping cough. As an outsider, I have not attempted to write a technical history, and would not have been competent to do so. Nor have I been able to give as much space as I would wish to many of the divisions and component parts of what has always been a very large and dispersed organisation. Instead, I have concentrated on what appear to me to be the most fundamental aspects of North Thames's story: the peculiar difficulties and responsibilities which arose from supplying gas to the nation's capital; the traditions inherited from pre-nationalisation days; and the technical and administrative responses to changing market and technological conditions which unfolded during the period and which have revolutionised the entire gas industry.

Although I have received the fullest help and co-operation from North Thames, the book presents entirely my own view of the subject. North Thames Gas is in no way responsible either for the topics covered or for their interpretation. Any shortcomings and errors are mine alone.

It is a pleasure to acknowledge the help I have received from many quarters. I am sincerely grateful to the present and former officials and employees who took the time and trouble to give me information, answer queries, locate material and check parts of the manuscript. These personal contacts have been the more important since, sadly, much archival material was destroyed at the time of the move to the new headquarters at Staines in 1977. I should like especially to record my debt to John Gadd (Chairman until 31 January 1988), and to Derek Dutton, Head of Public Relations, who conceived the project and encouraged it throughout; to former chairmen Sir Michael Milne-Watson and George

xi

Cooper; to Janet Welch, formerly in the Public Relations Department and an unfailing source of help in the early stages of the project; and to John Barnes, Laurie Bartlett-Rawlings, Reg Bloom, Tony Brown, Nigel Bruce, Dr Jim Burns, Philip Carpmael, Leslie Clark, John Osbon, Ken Scrine, Alan Webster and Tom Welch.

MALCOLM FALKUS

1

North Thames Gas: History and Tradition

North Thames Gas has several histories. On one level it is the history of a once distinct, autonomous, and many-sided undertaking, which gradually lost that autonomy and many of its activities, becoming in 1973 a 'mere' region of British Gas. In the process the number of employees has fallen sharply, from some 25000 in the 1950s to only some 8000 today. Change has, indeed, been immense. Before 1973 the Chairman, Deputy Chairman and the Board members were all Ministerial appointments. The Board was in turn responsible directly to the Minister and submitted to him its own financial accounts. Each individual Board was then responsible for its own tariffs, capital investment projects, customer service, sales initiatives, internal organ-isation, and so on. The Boards' activities included then gas production as well as gas distribution and sales. Today North Thames makes no gas. Now, throughout the country, all is central and similar, from the colours of the vans to the layout of gas bills. Even the financial performance of an individual Region is buried in the anonymity of British Gas's aggregate accounts. But, even if North Thames is now just a Region of British Gas, there still remains a distinctiveness which has survived centralisation and privatisation, just as it survived nationalisa-tion. The comment 'North Thames is different' is heard still throughout the industry, and it is a uniqueness founded on deep roots. It derives from a long history and from the special character that has evolved from supplying gas to the nation's capital. It would seem that no amount of purely organisational change, whether from within or without, can take that away.

At another level the story of North Thames Gas is the history of the achievement of the gas industry itself. This achievement has seen the industry grow dramatically from a position of relative unimportance (in 1949 gas supplied only about 4 per cent all useful energy and this 4 per cent was concentrated overwhelmingly in the domestic cooking market) and struggling for survival in an increasingly competitive world, to that of a giant among the energy industries. In 1964 gas still supplied only 6 per cent of Britain's energy requirements, but by 1978 the figure had reached over 25 per cent and in 1986 was nearly 45 per cent. Large sectors of industry now had turned to gas, and from the 1960s new markets were expanding in all directions. By the late 1970s, however, the period of rapid expansion was over, and following the second oil crisis in 1979, came a challenging time in which North Thames and the other Regions came under urgent pressure to reduce costs and improve efficiency.

At yet another level the story is one of technological advance, without which none of these successes would have been achieved. North Thames has been very much to the fore in these developments, which have seen the industry develop along a path from almost total dependence on coal, through the manufacture of gas from various oil-based feedstocks and through the importation of liquefied natural gas, to the present era of North Sea natural gas. The fortunes of the industry and technical change were closely linked. Broadly speaking, the 1950s – the coal era – was a time of stagnation and anxiety; the 1960s saw a radical improvement, founded on cheaper, oil-based gas and on ever-increasing domestic sales; and the 1970s marked the natural gas era, with sales rapidly expanding not only to domestic but also to commercial and industrial consumers.

There has, too, been the history of North Thames as an organisation, concerned with such matters as its overall performance and with its relationship with its customers. Here, paradoxically, the story is almost the reverse of the picture gleaned from output figures and technological advance. At its inception North Thames was undoubtedly the leader among the Boards, the most advanced, efficient and integrated and also the largest in terms of the number of consumers and, sales. Today the Region is only third in sales and consumers, and by the end of the 1960s the period of expansion was exposing many fundamental weaknesses in the Board's structure. The early 1970s, at the height of conversion to natural gas, was a nightmarish period of mounting customer complaints and internal frustration, of critical public scrutiny and falling standards of service. Only slowly, from the middle of the decade, did recovery set in.

And finally, at another level, is the history of the people who have worked at North Thames and who have made its history. They include, of course, the chairmen (only four before privatisation, each of whom has left a distinct stamp on the organisation) and the other chief officers. But they include also the thousands of employees 'on the district', in Divisional and District offices, in showrooms, depots, stores and manufacturing stations. In their time gas workers have formed distinct local communities, especially those based on gas-making plants. Beckton Works, for example, in its heyday employed 4500 gas workers of all grades. Beckton had its own railway station, and houses in several streets were owned by the Board and rented to its engineers and other key employees. Beckton's world, with its works' pub, churches, shops, post office, sports days and other social activities, was very much a self-contained community. Now the community has disappeared, and less than 100 employees are left at the site which was once the largest gasworks in the world. At the other end of the scale was a works like Ascot, a rural station employing in the 1950s only some fifty workers; yet even here the sense of community was deep-rooted, and long service and family tradition were maintained. Indeed, one of the more striking features of North Thames has been the strength of family tradition and the long-service records which have seen clusters of 40- and even 50-year service awards handed out each year.

Selecting which strands to develop from this variegated historical web is not an easy task, nor made easier by the destruction of so many records which took place in the 1970s at the time of reorganisation and the acquisition of a new central headquarters. Nevertheless, this story is about North Thames, not about the gas industry generally or about other Boards and Regions. Hence, it will focus on the problems and achievements of North Thames, and in doing so will help to bring out those features which have given North Thames such a distinctive role in the history of the gas industry.

Early in 1948 Hugh Gaitskell, Minister of Fuel and Power, introduced a bill into the House of Commons to nationalise gas undertakings in Great Britain. The bill received its Royal Assent in July of that year and on 1 May 1949, twelve Area Gas Boards, covering the entire country, came into being. The North Thames Gas Board was thus a creation of the post-war Labour Government, and state control of the gas industry was just one part of its large-scale nationalisation scheme, which included the other major fuel and power industries – coal and electricity – as well. Gas was, in fact, the last to be nationalised; the National Coal Board was taken into public ownership at the beginning of 1947 and the Electricity Authority commenced operations in 1948.

Among the twelve new Boards, North Thames was unique in that it already had a history, the history of a company incorporated 137 years previously as the Gas Light & Coke Company. Inevitably the Board's story has been coloured both by its role as a nationalised enterprise and by its part in the gas industry generally, but it has been coloured also by this inherited tradition. On vesting day in 1949, twelve separate undertakings, covering more than 1000 square miles, were merged to form the North Thames Gas Board. Some four-fifths of all the Board's sales, its customers, its mains, and its employees, were taken over from one company: the Gas Light & Coke Company. From top management at headquarters to fitters 'on the district' the traditions of the Gas Light & Coke Company held sway and the organisational structure of the new undertaking was largely that inherited from the Gas Light. In no other Area was a single company so dominant. For North Thames, the new territories which were added to the Gas Light more or less consolidated and 'filled in' an area already delineated before the Second World War. Indeed, of the eleven undertakings merged with the Gas Light, only two, the Romford and the Commercial, were independent companies, for eight had already been associated with the Gas Light through a holding company. Thus, from north to south and east to west the territorial structure of the new Board, with its attendant pattern of gasworks, distribution systems, regional offices and so on, was already established (see Figure 1.1). This was a far cry from, say, the adjacent Eastern Gas Board, which acquired some 100 separate undertakings, none of them very large, with 92 gas manufacturing stations covering more than 7000 sq. miles of territory. Even the Coat of Arms of the Gas Light & Coke Company, granted in 1932 and bearing the not very forward-looking motto *Stet capitolum fulgens* (Bring Light to the Capital), was taken over by the North Thames Gas Board in 1949. It was hardly surprising, therefore, that the first post-nationalisation issue of the Board's monthly 'house magazine', then still called the *Co-Partner's Magazine* as it had been since 1911, headed its editorial 'Business as Usual'.

There can be no doubt that the traditions of the Gas Light & Coke Company have played, and to some degree still play, a part in shaping the attitudes and policies of North Thames. In many ways, indeed, the Gas Light & Coke Company survived not until 1949, but until the internal and industry-wide reorganisation of the early 1970s. In this opening chapter, therefore, we shall look at some aspects of this heritage as well as surveying the state of the gas industry on the eve of nationalisation. A full history of the Gas Light & Coke Company is well outside the scope of this book, and in any case has been excellently told by Stirling Everard. Nevertheless, the shape, character, problems and policies of the new Board cannot be understood without reference at least to some of the principal background events, for the heritage of the Gas Light & Coke Company forms an integral part of the story of North Thames Gas.

By the outbreak of the Second World War the Gas Light & Coke Company was remarkable both for its antiquity and for its size. The Company was the first and therefore the oldest gas company in the world. It had been formed as long ago as 1812, at a period when England, just entering the Regency period, was still at war with Napoleonic France. The Company started in London, its first offices in Pall Mall, and its first permanent gasworks in Great Peter Street, Westminster. The Great Peter Street site, fronting on to Horseferry Road, later (in the 1870s) became the site of the chief offices of the Company. London was then expanding apace, and already contained

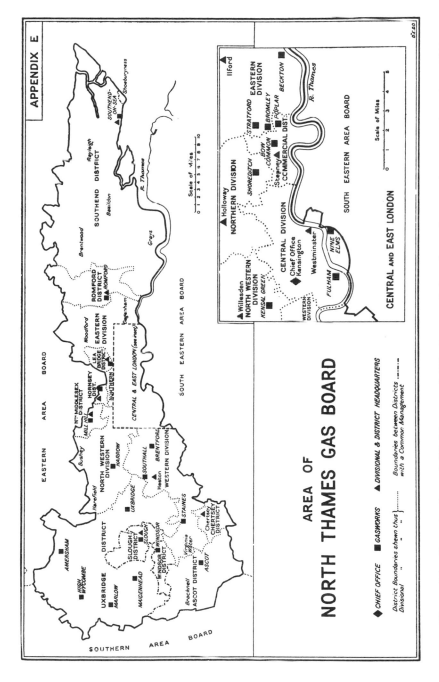

Figure 1.1 Organisation of Divisions and Districts, and location of gasworks at vesting day, 1949

nearly 1 million inhabitants. To the west the villages and townships of Kensington, Chelsea and Fulham were being devoured by the urban mass, and to the north the fields around Bloomsbury were being laid out in fashionable squares and terraces. The most densely populated areas were still in the City, which then housed some 130 000 people, compared with only 5000 at vesting day in 1949. In these early days gas was a novelty and gas undertakings were risky and speculative. It was largely due to the perseverance and enthusiasm of surely the most flamboyant of all Britain's early entrepreneurs, a German called Frederick Albert Winsor, that the Gas Light & Coke Company was founded. This was no easy task and was the culmination of five years of pamphleteering, exhibitions, lectures and successive abortive attempts to start such an undertaking. As part of his campaign Winsor had lit Pall Mall with gas lamps in 1807, an event which caused a minor sensation and brought throngs of incredulous spectators. But the company which started life in 1812 was very far from Winsor's early grandiose vision; the untold riches he had foreseen (which were to pay off the entire National Debt) did not materialise, and the Company paid no dividend until 1817; the national scale of enterprise he envisaged was cut down to a more modest territory, comprising parts of the City of London and Westminster; and the capitalisation of £1 million was lowered to £200 000 (though still colossal by the standards of the times). Moreover, the Company's directors soon ousted Winsor himself from any say in the fortunes of the concern, his technical competence falling a good deal short of his flair for publicity.

For the first few years the survival of the Gas Light & Coke Company was very much in doubt. No one before had grappled with the problems of supplying gas to consumers from central stations, although some factories and other large institutions were already producing their own coal-gas. Every process, from heating coal in retorts, to purifying and distributing the resultant gas, and then burning the gas in gas lamps, had to be developed from experiment and experience. Nonetheless, gaslight was such a superior illuminant compared with guttering candles and smoky oil lamps, especially for such purposes as lighting streets and large buildings, that the prosperity of the Company rapidly improved. The Company was fortunate to employ a number of brilliant engineers, none more so than Samuel Clegg, who joined the undertaking in 1813, and who is remembered as one of the great pioneers of the gas industry.

Partly by accident, the state of company law being then very uncertain, the new Company had established itself by Royal Charter as well as by Act of Parliament. In consequence, rather like the great trading companies, or the Bank of England, it was dignified with a governor and a court rather than with a chairman and a board of directors, and the Company was often known simply as 'The Chartered'.

By the middle of the nineteenth century the gas industry was firmly established, not only in Britain but in many countries overseas too. By now every town of any size had a gas company. In London, the threat of self-destructive competition had been met after 1860 by 'districting': the allocation of particular areas to individual companies. Elsewhere competition between rival companies had almost ceased and most towns were served by just one undertaking exercising a natural monopoly, usually with some form of statutory restriction to protect the consumer. In some towns gas companies were being taken over by municipal authorities, although this movement was relatively weak in the south of England and non-existent in London. And gradually the gas industry assumed the mantle of respectability, a secure outlet for the small investor, a 'public utility' industry paying a regular dividend, and with an assured and growing demand for lighting as the population grew both in numbers and in wealth.

Until the 1880s gas was used almost entirely for lighting, but from that decade competition from electricity began to make itself felt. Gas undertakings were forced to develop new outlets for their product, such as cooking and water heating. At the same time the rapid development of prepayment (coin-in-the-slot) meters opened up a whole new area of gas demand among working-class consumers. Moreover, the industry was fortunate that just at that time an Austrian chemist, Carl Auer, Baron von Welsbach, developed the incandescent gas mantle, which greatly improved both the quality and the convenience of gas lights and gave to gas lighting a new lease of life, alongside the still-experimental and unreliable electric light bulbs.

The Gas Light and the South Metropolitan companies dominated London's industry during the last three decades of the nineteenth century. This was a period of vigorous amalgamation, with the Chartered absorbing no fewer than eight smaller companies in inner London between 1870 and 1883 and hence becoming the largest of Britain's many gas companies. On the production side, the Company had begun the construction of a gasworks in 1868 which was to become the world's largest. This was at a site in Barking Creek, named 'Beckton' in honour of the then Governor, Simon Adams Beck (1860–76). On the commercial side, the Company developed the first gas showrooms from 1881 to exhibit gas appliances, and from 1898 sought sites in busy shopping centres where offices and showrooms could be combined. Cooking demand grew apace, and by 1896 some 36 000 cookers had been hired out by the company, compared with only 7000 four years earlier. Slot meters also spread rapidly – in 1910 alone over 226 *million* pennies were gathered by the Company's 136 collectors. By the outbreak of the First World War the Chartered had nearly 700 000 consumers, more than

1 Part of Beckton Gasworks in 1949. The largest gasworks in the world, it
processed some 4500 tons of coal a day, had a total capacity of 119 million cu ft
gas/day (one-third of the Board's total) and employed over 4000 workers.

double the figure of the second largest company, the South Metropolitan, and the Company's eight stations had a maximum daily capacity of
more than 150 million cubic feet (m. cu ft), over half of which was
supplied from Beckton alone.

When we turn to the years between the outbreak of the First World
War in 1914 and the start of the Second World War in 1939, we enter a
period where competition posed ever-increasing problems for the gas
industry as electricity continued to make inroads into traditional
lighting markets. These years saw the Gas Light & Coke Company, and
the gas industry generally, with its back to the wall as it endeavoured
to meet the threat.

In some respects the inter-war period was an era of expansion and
success for the Gas Light. In terms of sheer size, for example, the
Company became even more dominant. This was primarily the result of
yet another series of amalgamations. Between 1910 and 1932 the
Company expanded from its inner London base both to the east and to
the west. Particularly significant was the amalgamation in 1926 with the
old Brentford Gas Company, for this move increased the area served
from 134 to 265 square miles at a stroke, added five new gas-making
stations and brought one-third more consumers. The Brentford Com-

pany had also made a number of amalgamations during its long history. One, in 1915, was with the Staines and Egham District Gas & Coke Company, so that the Brentford amalgamation in 1926 brought Staines within the Company's area exactly fifty years before that town became the new headquarters of North Thames Gas. In 1932 the Company took the decision to expand no further by amalgamation and when, the following year, gas was brought to the hitherto unsupplied Canvey Island, the total territory extended to 547 square miles, including a nearly continuous line north of the Thames from Old Windsor in the west to Southend in the east.

There were several reasons for these amalgamations. The then Governor, Sir David Milne-Watson, was certainly not averse to seeing the power and influence of the Gas Light & Coke Company spread far and wide. But there were commercial considerations also. As competition from electricity grew, gas suffered acutely and increasingly from its antiquated image. Milne-Watson felt that the existence of small-scale, inefficient and backward undertakings within the Company's territory, or in close proximity, was unhelpful to the image the industry was trying to portray. Fundamental also was the policy pushed vigorously by the Chief Engineer, Thomas Hardie, to concentrate production at the most efficient works (especially Beckton), to construct there the most up-to-date manufacturing plant, and to link the entire territory into an integrated grid system. Large-scale plants, especially the new coke-oven batteries which were planned at Beckton, were capital intensive and inflexible in operation, although relatively cheap to run. They required, therefore, an extensive base load in order to justify a sufficient scale of operation. There was thus a significant engineering impetus behind the spate of amalgamations in these years.

In other fields, too, progress was made. The far-sighted programme of technical development improved the Company's ability to produce gas not only more cheaply but of better quality. Much emphasis was laid on research, and the period between the wars was notable for the founding of the No. 1 Laboratory at Fulham (1923) and the Watson House Research Laboratory (1926). The Company sought out science-trained university men and also took steps to expand and develop the apprenticeship schemes which had been started before 1914. On the commercial side, the Company for the first time sought to use vigorous marketing methods, promoting cookers, water-heaters and other appliances which would diversify the load in the face of falling lighting sales. A great deal of effort was put into promoting and extending showrooms. As part of its advertising campaign the company introduced its 'Mr Therm' symbol in 1931 – a symbol later to be adopted throughout the industry and surviving at North Thames into the 1970s. On the welfare side, much progress was made through the Co-

Partnership Committees, while sports activities were fostered with the acquisition of large sports grounds in Acton and East Ham in the 1920s.

Much of the credit for the Company's standing, in both size and prestige, must belong to Sir David Milne-Watson, who guided the undertaking throughout this difficult period. He was Governor and Managing Director from 1919 until the Second World War, having joined the Company in 1897 and reached the position of Managing Director in 1916. He only laid down the reins of governorship in April 1945, shortly before his death. A lawyer by training, he was the first non-engineer to achieve a leading position in the gas industry, and throughout the inter-war period his stature as leader not only of the Company but also of the national industry was unrivalled. Sir David's interest and involvement covered all aspects of the Company's activities: production and sales of gas, purchases of coal and disposal of by-products, administration, organisation, and many other fields, as well as taking an active role in social welfare measures for the 25 000 employees (the Company was then one of the six largest industrial employers in the country). He was especially involved in the Company's

2 Started by Sir David Milne-Watson in 1931, subsidised holiday camps for boy employees remained an annual event (except for the war years) until 1958. This group in 1953 had their holiday in Ashdown Forest.

Co-partnership scheme, begun in 1909, which gave members both job security and a small bonus out of profits each year, the bulk being allocated to a pension fund. Personal visits to all stations and depots; unfailing attendance at the great annual sports 'Gatherings', for which each employee was given two entry tickets and a free railway pass; keen support for the 'Rangers' Territorial Battalion, composed largely of Company employees and of which Sir David was Honorary Colonel; annual camps for boy apprentices; a 'Chairman's fund' for special hardship cases among employees; individual interviews with all salaried staff who qualified for a rise in pay ... these were the hallmarks of the man who has been well described as 'the last of the autocratic Governors'. Sir David (he was knighted in 1927 and received a baronetcy in 1937) was also a leading figure in attempts to organise various national gas bodies. He was, for example, the first Chairman of the National Gas Council (from 1919 until 1943) and of the National Joint Industrial Council (from 1919 until 1944), and helped set up national bodies for the sales of by-products.

Alongside Sir David Milne-Watson, a number of other key figures influenced the shape of the Company in these years. The Chief Engineer for many years was Thomas Hardie. He worked hard in liaison with the scientists at Watson House and with appliance manufacturers to improve the performance of gas in order to meet successfully the new markets for space and water heating. We have noted already that as part of the productivity drive production was concentrated as far as possible in efficient plants, and the Beckton grid was extended to embrace nearly all the Company's territory. By 1930, for example, all the stations in the Brentford territory were included in the Beckton grid. Another dominant figure was R. W. Foot, perhaps one of the most able but least known of Britain's leading industrial managers. He became General Manager in 1929 and from then until 1940, when he left the Company to become Director General of the BBC at the request of the Ministry of Information, he was closely involved in many of the most important administrative developments. These included detailed negotiation of the amalgamations, the handling of parliamentary legislation, and the organisation of the South Eastern Gas Corporation, a holding company set up by the Gas Light & Coke Company in 1934.

The dominance of the Gas Light & Coke Company among Britain's gas companies, statutory and municipal, achieved under Sir David Milne-Watson was overwhelming. On the eve of the Second World War the Gas Light produced about one-eighth of the entire gas output in Britain and no other undertaking approached it in size. The Company then had a capacity of some 250 m. cu ft gas/day. Next came the South Metropolitan with a mere 80 million, Birmingham with 75 million, Glasgow with 42 million and Sheffield with 41 million. Moreover, the companies of the South Eastern Gas Corporation, managed by the Gas Light & Coke Company, jointly had a capacity about equivalent to the Glasgow figure.

But expansion and progress were only on the surface. Long-term trends were moving against the gas industry. The rise of electricity meant not only the capture of the domestic lighting load but also an increasing threat even to the cooking market. In 1920 only one house in seventeen was wired up for electricity; in 1939 the figure was two in three. And in the years 1930–35 alone, sales of electric cookers trebled. Although the number of customers served by the Gas Light & Coke Company grew steadily throughout the inter-war years, the average consumption per consumer fell at the same time, making it sometimes uneconomical to connect a gas supply to a domestic dwelling for the small amounts consumed. By the end of the 1930s prepayment customers formed about three-quarters of the total consumers, and their average consumption had declined from 96 therms in 1920 to only 77 therms, reflecting the very small loads that new business was attracting. The depressed years after 1929 were especially bad, and overall the demand for gas was stagnant during the 1930s, growing at a little over 1 per cent per year, compared with electricity's expansion rate of 20 per cent annually. Although there was some gain in industrial and commercial business (overall the proportion of domestic sales in the total slumped from 80 per cent to 65 per cent in the inter-war years), these could do little more than prevent total sales from falling.

The failure of demand to rise as had been hoped and the immense problems caused by the absorption of so many new companies in the period between 1926 and 1932 produced a crisis in the Gas Light & Coke Company. Insolvency actually threatened, and it was at the insistence of one of the Company's leading creditors that a radical reorganisation of affairs took place. The Company found itself obliged in 1932 to call on the management consultancy services of a City firm of chartered accountants, Barton Mayhew and Company. This move was a prelude to a gradual revival in fortunes. Edgar Sylvester, brought in to head the consultancy team, was appointed Comptroller of Finance in 1934, and he, together with Milne-Watson and Foot, undertook some major changes in operations. First, a number of commercial departments were reorganised, including Rental, Gas Sales, Stores, and Stove and Meter, and Sylvester formed a new Budget and Audit Department. Efficiency and economy became the order of the day, being necessary counterparts to the huge sales drive which was now under way to promote cookers, fires, water-heaters, refrigerators and other appliances. Milne-Watson decided that aggressive selling and advertising of gas and gas appliances was the best way to build up sales. These years saw the Company's finances put on a much sounder footing, with the setting up of a reserve fund for planned expansion and the modernisation of gasworks and showrooms.

The most fundamental organisational changes involved those sections dealing with customer service. The new developments brought in the concept of 'territorialism' rather than 'departmentalism', and involved a large measure of decentralisation based on territorial divisions in place of the old system of district offices, sub-offices and showrooms controlled from the centre. The first of the new Divisions was the Western Division, set up in 1937 with headquarters at Heston. By 1941, when the Central Division was established with headquarters at Westminster, the whole of the Company's territory had been grouped into six Divisions, with all consumer affairs being the responsibility of the Divisional Manager within his area. As well as the Western and Central there was the North Western served from Pound Lane, the Northern from Seven Sisters Road, the Eastern from Ilford, and the South Essex from Southend.

By the middle of the decade the need for a new chief office was becoming increasingly apparent and in 1935 the Court decided to erect a modern office block at Horseferry Road. Already a number of departments had overflowed into nearby buildings and most of the headquarters' staff were now housed in temporary accommodation in Vincent Street. Finally, in 1937, the old offices, including the Court Room, were demolished in preparation for the new headquarters, but sadly, war intervened. The Horseferry Road site was requisitioned by the Government and the deep tanks of the old gasholders became one of the fortified meeting places for the wartime Government leaders. The search for a new headquarters site was later to become one of the most intractable problems faced by North Thames Gas.

War broke out with the Company in the midst of its reorganisation and efforts to modernise. Of course, these years formed a dramatic period in the history of all of London's gas companies. Every one of the Gas Light & Coke Company's gas-making stations suffered bomb damage, over 200 bombs falling on Beckton alone. There was extensive damage to mains and service pipes, most of the attacks being concentrated in the blitz of 1940 and during the rocket and flying bomb attacks in 1944 and 1945. The worst attacks came on 'Black Saturday' – 7 September 1940 – when hundreds of German aircraft attacked London's docklands and put the gasworks at Beckton, Bow Common, Bromley-by-Bow and Stratford out of action. Beckton's ten holders were each hit by enemy bombs and gas production ceased there for a fortnight. The history of the war years could fill a book in itself. There were countless acts of heroism in the face of extreme danger by the Company's employees, and over 160 bravery awards were made to individuals. Yet throughout these years London was somehow supplied with gas for all but the briefest of interruptions. The succession of emergencies and crises, and the shortages of labour, coal and materials of all kinds made the running of the Company very much a day-to-day affair, with little prospect for long-term development planning. A great deal of responsibility in these years necessarily fell on the shoulders of the Divisional Managers, who were often obliged to make instant decisions at times when communication with headquarters was impossible. The labour problem was especially acute, with over 7000 of the Company's employees, nearly one in three, on active service (the Company guaranteeing their jobs at the end of the war). Labour shortages, together with the scarcity and low quality of coal supplies and the widespread damage to plant and mains, made the manufacture of sufficient gas supplies a constant struggle. It was perhaps fortunate that total gas demand fell as London's wartime population declined, and the lack of appliance sales and the blackout combined also to lessen sales. On average, sales of gas were some 17 per cent lower during the war and actually declined to 40 per cent less during the blitz in September 1940 at the height of the evacuation. Though fortunate in one way, lower sales and rising costs led to financial difficulties. Although the Government permitted price rises of some 44 per cent, coal costs rose by 100 per cent and wages increased by 57 per cent, and the Company paid no dividend in 1940 or 1941. Nevertheless, the careful husbandry of the 1930s and improved market conditions after 1941 enabled the Company to end the war in a relatively sound financial position.

The return of peace in 1945 saw in some ways considerable changes from pre-war days. Above all David Milne-Watson was no longer at the helm. Ill health had obliged him gradually to lay down his Company and industry-wide responsibilities, and in 1944 Edgar Sylvester, who had become joint Managing Director alongside Sir David in 1942, became sole Managing Director. In April 1945 Sir David finally relinquished his Governorship, being succeeded by Sylvester, and in October of that year he died at the age of 76, mourned not only by the Company but by the gas industry throughout Britain and beyond.

Under Sir David's long leadership the Gas Light & Coke Company had evolved a tradition quite unique among Britain's business enterprises. The combination of co-partnership, paternalistic management, and the very real progress and initiatives undertaken by the Company produced a close-knit community and a pride in the Company's achievements. During crisis periods, in the two world wars and in the 1926 General Strike, for example, the Company 'never failed London'. Long service and family tradition were encouraged and extolled in the pages of the monthly *Co-Partner's Magazine* (one example was the Mercer family, whose three generations had contributed over 450 years of service at Beckton by the year Sir David died). The great Annual

Gatherings on the sports fields, the pioneering social welfare measures (a form of health service had been introduced as early as 1877) and the fact that the Gas Light & Coke Company was at the forefront of nearly all new technological and commercial developments in Britain's gas industry had all contributed to the Company's image, both to its employees and to the outside world. The Second World War was naturally a severe and testing time, but the strong traditions of the Company continued into the post-war era.

One significant change after 1945 was in the market situation. During the inter-war years, and again in the 1950s, the problem was to find new markets in the face of stagnant or declining demand. But in the immediate post-war years prevailing shortages and rationing (coal and coke were rationed, but gas and electricity were not) meant the problem became one of providing sufficient supplies. After the war the average domestic consumption per consumer rose steadily from under 80 therms in 1945 to over 130 therms annually on the eve of nationalisation. During the war itself industrial sales had doubled and they continued to expand in the immediate post-war years. In each post-war year until nationalisation there were pressure reductions at peak times as this growing demand outstripped the Company's capacity at a time of extreme shortages of many materials and labour. Indeed, the enforced lack of investment and replacement of plant during the war, and the immense amount of damage to plant and distribution systems which had often been only temporarily patched up left a huge backlog of work to be done to restore capacity to pre-war levels. In 1945, although total consumption was now a little above the pre-war level, the total capacity had fallen by some 35 m. cu ft gas/day. Reconstruction programmes were constantly threatened by labour shortages, high labour turnover, and by lack of steel and coal. In addition there was a dearth of gas appliances of all kinds, and the many thousands of obsolete 'black' cookers which had existed at the start of the war were still in service at the end.

One of the criticisms of the programme of nationalisation announced by the post-war Labour Government was that the necessary delays between announcement and implementation would create a climate of uncertainty in which essential investment would not be undertaken. There was anxiety that some companies, fearful of investing shareholders' money for what might prove inadequate compensation, would hold back the necessary reconstruction of plant. Such an attitude did not influence the Gas Light & Coke Company at all. Massive reconstruction plans were put in hand at once. Delays arose not by intention but from shortages and external circumstances. Work on a new battery of coke ovens was started in November 1945 and by the end of 1946 projects for additional plant costing some £7 million had been approved by the Court. This work included new coke ovens, water-gas plant, vertical retort installations, and gasholders, as well as repairs and modernisation to existing plant. In addition, the Products Works at Beckton was to be rebuilt, five new colliers ordered, and a programme of mains construction authorised, which included bringing Southend within the Company's grid. The Company seems to have taken the threat of nationalisation very much in its stride; even early in 1949 the normal five-year time horizon for planning plant capacity was still being invoked, while in November 1948 the Production Committee was already laying plans for extending mains in the Romford region in anticipation of the merger with that company on vesting day.

After 1945 the finishing touches were put to the reorganisation of the Company which had been initiated before the war. During Sylvester's brief Governorship, from April 1945 until ill health forced his resignation at the end of 1946, some significant developments took place. Gas-making stations were divided into four regional groups, each under a Group Engineer, who was responsible in turn to the Chief Engineer and his deputy. The management was streamlined, with responsibility for routine affairs concentrated in four committees – Production, Commercial, Staff and Accounts – while the Court could turn its attention to wider issues of planning and policy. At the same time the lines of direct responsibility were strengthened by the appointment of functional heads, mostly termed Controllers, under the joint Managing Directors, Michael Milne-Watson (Sir David's son) and Falconer Moffat Birks. Among important appointments were S. G. Aberdein as Controller of Divisions (later renamed Commercial Manager), N. Willsmer as Chief Engineer in succession to Birks, W. K. Hutchison as Controller of By-products, Dr H. Hollings as Controller of Research, W. S. Gooch as Staff Controller and R. N. Bruce as Controller of Industrial Relations, while Brian Wood continued as Secretary to the Company. On Sylvester's resignation the Governorship passed to Michael Milne-Watson, only thirty-seven years of age and the second youngest Governor in the history of the Company. Birks now became Deputy Governor and Hutchison was appointed Managing Director.

Overshadowing the affairs of the gas industry in the post-war years was, of course, the prospect of nationalisation. Oddly, nationalisation was not a particularly controversial issue for the gas industry. This was largely because the inadequacies of the existing industry had long been recognised by all interested groups, by the major political parties, by independent reports and government inquiries, and even by the gas industry itself. Reorganisation was felt to be not only inevitable but desirable and, to some extent, it could be said that the gas industry was anxious to be nationalised. The basic inadequacy of the gas industry was its fragmentation and variety. There were in 1948 over 1000 separate gas undertakings in the United Kingdom of many shapes and sizes. The biggest, of course, was the Gas Light & Coke Company, with some one-eighth of total national output. It had a payroll of 21 250, owned 13 gas stations, and possessed 65 locomotives, 19 colliers, 626 road transport vehicles and 55 horses. But at the other end of the scale were many minute enterprises, often too small to be efficient in production or to provide adequate sales and service. The Shipston-on-Stour Gas Light, Coke & Coal Co. (1921) Ltd supplied just 132 customers, for example. Some two-thirds of all enterprises were private companies, the remainder being municipally owned. Reflecting this variegated pattern was the multitude of differing calorific values (CV) of the gas produced. For example, in 1947 gas was supplied at twenty-six different calorific values, ranging from 200 to 600 BTU (British Thermal Units), and there were many hundreds of different tariffs charged throughout the country.

Various reports, including one by the British Gas Federation in 1943 under Edgar Sylvester, had analysed the structure of the gas industry and suggested improved arrangements. All these inquiries advocated measures of centralisation and some even of central control. The most influential was the Heyworth Committee, set up by the National Government in 1944 under Sir Geoffrey Heyworth, which reported in 1945. The Committee advocated overall public ownership as the best solution to the industry's problems. The report urged strongly the necessity for large-scale operations on technical grounds. Although it stopped short of suggesting a national grid, it recommended instead the setting up of ten autonomous Area Boards, one of which would serve the London area – a huge Metropolitan Board. This report formed the basis of the nationalisation plan eventually contained in the 1948 Gas Act, and which came into effect on vesting day, 1 May 1949.

The Heyworth Committee had been set up under the National Government before Labour came to power and could hardly be accused of political bias therefore. Moreover, one-third of the gas industry was already under some form of public ownership and the existing statutory companies operated under many forms of parliamentary restriction and supervision, including dividend limitations. During the war, government control was extended, covering gas prices, coal and coke allocations, timber and steel supplies and much else. With the Labour Government returned by a landslide in 1945 and with the new Government's clear determination to nationalise the fuel and power industries (coal nationalisation was announced in the King's Speech in May 1945), opposition from the gas companies would be futile. Although formally expressing opposition, the Gas Light & Coke

Company co-operated fully with the Government's plans and directed its energies to securing the best compensation terms for its share holders that it could.

The nationalisation scheme contained in the 1948 Gas Act differed in some important respects from the recommendations of the Heyworth Committee. There were to be twelve Area Boards, not ten, and the large Metropolitan Board serving the whole of Greater London envisaged by Heyworth was split (partly for civil defence reasons). This meant in practice that the new North Thames Board was to a large extent the territory of the Gas Light & Coke Company. Although twelve undertakings were merged, over 80 per cent of the customers, the output, and the mains network were taken over from the Gas Light.

In another important respect the nationalisation Act differed from Heyworth's recommendations. This was in the setting up of a central body, which Heyworth had not thought necessary. The new British Gas Council was composed of a Chairman and Deputy Chairman, appointed by the Minister of Fuel and Power, and of the twelve Area Board Chairmen. Not initially a powerful body, the Gas Council had overall responsibility for research, education and training undertaken by the Area Boards, and was to establish machinery at national level for the negotiation of terms and conditions of employment within the industry. The Council could borrow money to finance approved capital expenditure by the Area Boards and had a general advisory role to the Ministry of Fuel and Power. But the autonomy of the Area Boards was not at this stage undermined, although there were those in 1948 who foresaw in this central body the seed of an organisation which would eventually take over the powers of the regional Boards.

Under the 1948 Gas Act, the twelve Area Boards were charged with the following three basic duties:

1. To develop and maintain an efficient, co-ordinated and economical system of gas supply for their areas and to satisfy, so far as it is economic to do so, all reasonable demands for gas within their area.
2. To develop and maintain the efficient, co-ordinated and economical production of coke, other than metallurgical coke.
3. To develop and maintain efficient methods of recovering by-products obtained in the process of manufacturing gas.

Despite the changes in market conditions, the place of gas in the nation's energy industries was still very much what it had been before the war. Cooking still dominated the total gas load and in other markets the gas industry's penetration was limited. Solid fuel was pre-eminent for both domestic and industrial heating and still accounted for some 80 per cent of the domestic load, while gas and electricity supplied only about 10 per cent of this market. A report published in 1946 drew particular attention to the supremacy of the coal fire, and pointed out that 'the area of the house properly warmed for comfort during the winter is probably smaller in England than in any other civilised country'. For domestic water heating, too, solid fuel still led the way, with over three-quarters of the market, while gas took only a 10 per cent share.

Despite a fierce rearguard action, gas had lost the domestic lighting load between the wars, with only a few pockets of resistance surviving into the 1940s. This loss posed a dilemma for gas suppliers. Since electricity now had a lighting monopoly, it was often a problem to get gas supplied at all to new houses, and the 'all electric' household threatened gradually to take over. Negotiations with builders and local authority housing officers were to become a major preoccupation after the Second World War, but at least, thanks to an Act of Parliament promoted by the Gas Light & Coke Company in 1933, gas companies had the right to supply gas to any consumer requesting it. Gas had been much more successful in keeping the public lighting load and half of London's streets were gas lit in the immediate post-war years. The reason here was a mixture of long-term contracts, low prices, and

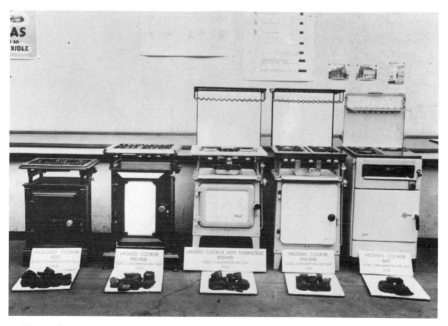

3 Typical cookers 1900–47. Domestic cooking was the backbone of North Thames's gas demand at the time of nationalisation. Note how cooker development in the period covered in this picture resulted in a 40 per cent improvement in efficiency.

inertia, but one may question the wisdom of the Gas Light & Coke Company in clinging so tenaciously to this load at prices which were usually well below cost. It was felt by the Company that the advertising benefits would more than offset the costs, but while the soft, yellow-green glow of the lamps and the nocturnal rounds of the lamplighters doubtless produced an atmosphere of nostalgia and quaintness, it could hardly have helped the gas industry to rid itself of the antiquated and old-fashioned image from which it was suffering.

So, to all intents and purposes, gas was essentially a domestic cooking fuel, despite all endeavours to develop other markets. Two-thirds of total gas sales by the Gas Light & Coke Company in 1949 were to the domestic market, two-thirds of this for cooking, and overall some 75 per cent of domestic sales went to prepayment customers. This was the nature of the enterprise that became the nationalised North Thames Gas Board.

4 A scene on the Chelsea Embankment in 1951, as the gas lamps, refitted by the Board, were relit for the first time since the war as part of the Festival of Britain illuminations.

2

The New Enterprise

It was with a sense of profound relief that the Gas Light & Coke Company, both court and employees, learned of the Government's nationalisation plans, which unfolded during 1948 and in the early part of 1949. The Gas Bill, introduced in the House of Commons in January 1948, outlined the areas each of the 12 proposed new Boards would serve and indicated the powers the Boards would have. From this Bill it was at least clear that the North Thames Gas Board would consist very largely of the Gas Light & Coke Company, with the addition of territory in Essex supplied by the Romford Gas Company, some areas in the City and to the north of London, and a large area of Buckinghamshire and Berkshire, running north to south from Amersham to Ascot and east and west from Uxbridge to Maidenhead. Almost half the territory and over four-fifths of the new Board's customers and plant were taken over from the Gas Light & Coke Company and, in many ways, the additions were a rational development of the process of amalgamation which had stopped in 1932. Indeed, the Gas Light & Coke Company had long cast envious eyes on the 'Romford Corridor', which split its territory, but the Romford Company had staunchly repulsed all overtures. With the publication of the Gas Bill the threat of Heyworth's large 'Metropolitan Board' disappeared. Nevertheless, the core of North Thames's area of supply lay very much in London. Although less than one-third of the total area, Greater London held 84 per cent of the total population served by the new Board.

Not only did the Company's area remain largely intact, but the powers vested in the new Board were substantial. As mentioned already, responsibility for research and development and for labour relations at national level became centralised under the new Gas Council, but such matters as gas tariffs, coal purchases, coke sales, investment in plant, and internal organisation were left very much to the individual Boards, subject only to their matching expenditure with revenue, 'taking one year with another'.

A third element of relief was that all the employees of the constituent undertakings were taken over by the new Boards, while the chief officers of the Gas Light & Coke Company became the chief officers of North Thames Gas almost to a man. Thus, Michael Milne-Watson became the first Chairman and Birks the Deputy Chairman. Hollings

21

5 The chief office of the new North Thames Gas Board, 30 Kensington Church Street, c. 1950. Still carrying its former name, the building was originally opened by the present Queen Mother, then Duchess of York, in 1926. The showrooms and offices became the Gas Light & Coke Company's headquarters during the war.

became Controller of Research, Aberdein the Commercial Manager, Bruce the Staff Controller, Wells the Chief Accountant, Gooch the Controller of Services, and Burns the Chief Engineer (on the retirement of Willsmer). There were a few significant losses, caused principally by the promotion of Gas Light men to posts elsewhere. Thus, Hutchison (Managing Director) and Johnson (Controller of Services) left to become Chairman and Deputy Chairman respectively of the South Eastern Gas Board. But, with few exceptions, throughout the length and breadth of the Board, whether Divisional Managers, Group and Station Engineers, Coke Manager, Coal Officer, Solicitor, Labour Relations Officer or in any of the multitude of offices big and small, the Gas Light men stayed in place and simply continued their work as before.

All this was, of course, a tremendous vote of confidence in the Gas Light & Coke Company. With the Company forming the basis of North Thames, the biggest of the Boards, with ex-Gas Light men at the helm of the second largest, the South Eastern, and with Sylvester as the first Chairman of the Gas Council, there was something of a family feeling to

6 Meeting of the Chairman and Chief Executives in the Board Room, 1949. The Chairman, M. Milne-Watson, is seated directly under the clock. On his left is the Secretary, B. Wood; then come F. M. Birks, Deputy Chairman; J. Burns, Chief Engineer; H. Hollings, Controller of Research; L. H. Harden, Public Relations Officer; W. S. Gooch, Controller of Services; O. W. Wells, Chief Accountant; R. N. Bruce, Staff Controller; and S. G. Aberdein, Commercial Manager.

the new public enterprise. It says much for the spirit of goodwill and co-operation existing at the time that so many individuals who had publicly taken a stance against nationalisation (Milne-Watson and Sylvester among them) were entrusted by the Labour Government with the task of leading the new public enterprise. Five of the new Boards had chairmen brought in from outside the gas industry and no other undertaking, statutory or municipal, retained such a large share of its former identity after 1949.

It is worth emphasising too, that in many ways nationalisation, oddly, liberated the gas industry. All the old restrictions on tariffs, dividends, and so on, which had severely hampered development before the war, were now swept away. New capital projects could be embarked upon with ready acquiescence from a 'tame' Gas Council and a co-operative Government. The Boards had both the will and the means to modernise themselves.

There remained some aspects of public ownership which were contentious, however. The question of compensation for shareholders was fixed in much the same way as it had been for other nationalisation schemes, namely on the market value of shares at a given date (for gas, shareholders were given a choice of years betwen 1943 and 1945). Compensation for municipal owners was naturally calculated on a different basis, while the many private companies whose shares were not actively quoted had also to be dealt with differently. But for Gas Light & Coke Company shareholders the terms of compensation were relatively straightforward. They were paid compensation during 1949 and 1950 in 3 per cent Gas Stock at an amount which was not ungenerous, although a severe financial crisis in September 1949 raised interest rates and caused a sharp decline in the value of the stock.

Another problem was what to do about co-partnership schemes. The Gas Light & Coke Company's scheme had existed since 1909 and included the great majority of the Company's employees. Under the scheme, co-partners received a small annual bonus related to gas sales, two-thirds of which was held in Company stock and went into a pension fund, while one-third was paid in cash. The gas industry had pioneered co-partnership. Indeed, the Gas Light's scheme was started two decades after the first had been promoted by the South Metropolitan. At its best, co-partnership gave workers a share in the undertaking they worked in, a guarantee of employment and a pension upon retirement. In 1949 about one half of all gas workers were covered by some form of co-partnership scheme, including most of those in the undertakings forming North Thames Gas. Sir David Milne-Watson had been a great champion of co-partnership and an unfailing attender of Co-partnership Committee meetings, of which he had been Chairman. However, it must be admitted that by the 1940s many aspects of co-partnership were no longer appropriate in an age of increasing social welfare legislation and trade union involvement. Co-partnership was not abandoned immediately, but after negotiations between unions and the Gas Council it was ended finally in March 1951, with Boards agreeing to pay co-partners a sum equivalent to their last bonus for a period of fifteen years.

Another difficulty was the terms of appointment of Area Board Chairmen, Deputy Chairmen and other Board members (that is, the members of the actual 'Board', analogous to a Board and Directors. Whether the term 'Board' refers to this group, or to the whole undertaking, should be evident from the context.) As in the case of co-partnership and stock compensation, this was an industry-wide rather than simply an Area matter, which had to be settled in relation to other nationalised industries and which involved all sorts of political as well as purely financial considerations. After a great deal of debate the Government decided that the appointments for the Chairmen and Deputy should be initially for five-year periods, renewable thereafter, and part-time members would be appointed for three years. Salaries for the Chairmen and Deputy were fixed at £5500 per annum and £4000 per annum respectively, although this was significantly below those formerly paid by the Gas Light & Coke Company. The Government agreed to some supplementation, but a difficulty remained about pensionability. Initially, the Government thought that the positions, theoretically short-term as they were, should not carry pension rights. However, strong representations from the gas industry were successful in reversing the decision in 1953. Milne-Watson, for example, forcefully argued that the top positions should be open to ambitious employees and that these positions should be part of an established career pattern.

The part-time members of the Boards of nationalised industries were in a somewhat anomalous position. Their appointments were intended to bring a wide range of experience and opinion and to prevent the new nationalised enterprises being dominated by technical experts. However, many have considered that the part-time members (whose payments were initially a derisory £500 a year) could not fulfil the functions they were supposed to. Kelf-Cohen, for example, who was Under-Secretary to the Ministry of Fuel and Power at the time of nationalisation, has written that 'with the best will in the world their grip of the numerous and complex problems facing their industry must be slight compared with that of the full-time members ... It would be surprising if part-time members can be of great value to a Board of a nationalised industry. Their influence can be no more than marginal. The public are misled if they assume that the presence of three or four part-time members of a Board makes any difference to the policy of a nationalised industry.' However, this has not been the experience at North Thames. Successive chairmen and other chief officers have been unanimous in acknowledging their debt to the part-time members of the Board throughout its twenty-three years of existence. North Thames was singularly fortunate in the composition of its Board, and the appointment of part-time members by the Ministry of Fuel and Power brought together a team which was notable for its breadth of interest and wide experience in the fields of labour relations, finance and consumer affairs, as well as in the gas industry. The members also co-operated well together and they proved of great value to the Chairman and Deputy and other officers in formulating broad policy decisions. Part-time members attended the monthly Board meetings and were represented on the three principal committees – Production, Commercial and Staff. Also, 'supervision visits' to various works and districts – a continuation of Gas Light & Coke Company practice which lasted throughout the Board's existence – always included at least one part-time Board member.

A brief glance at the composition of the first Board demonstrates clearly the range of experience and expertise brought by the part-time members. Dr E. V. Evans had been General Manager and Managing

Director of the South Metropolitan Gas Company. His experience of the
gas industry was vast, having joined the South Metropolitan at the turn
of the century and having later become its first Chief Chemist. Dr Evans
was President of the Institution of Gas Engineers in 1942 and was the
first Chairman of the Gas Research Board from 1939 to 1947. L. C.
Hansen was a leading official of the Transport and General Workers'
Union, with nearly thirty years' experience of union work. He had
already served as a member on both the South Eastern and the London
Regional Gas Industrial Councils and was in 1949 Secretary of five Joint
Industrial Councils. G. D. Dillon was a partner with the Chartered
Accountants, Barton Mayhew and Company, a firm which already had
a long and close association with the Gas Light & Coke Company.
Dillon had a particular interest in the gas industry, having been
involved previously in organising new methods of marketing gas by-
products. Mrs I. T. Barclay had the distinction of becoming in 1922 the
first woman Chartered Surveyor. Subsequently she had much experience in housing matters and was Housing Manager for several housing
associations. The Earl of Verulam, at thirty-nine the youngest member
of the Board, was an industrialist with wide experience as well as being
Chairman of the Association for Planning and the author of works on
planning and industry. He was also active in various charity organisations and before the war had organised a co-operative scheme for the
unemployed in South Wales. The sixth part-time member was Edwin
Bayliss, who was appointed to the Board ex officio in his capacity at first
Chairman of the North Thames Gas Consultative Council. Consultative
Councils were set up as part of the nationalisation programme to serve
and safeguard the interests of consumers. They were to deal not only
with specific complaints but also with matters of general concern for
consumers, and under the 1948 Gas Act it was the responsibility of Area
Boards to keep the Councils informed of their general plans and
arrangements. Despite the many potential sources of disagreement,
relations between North Thames and its Consultative Council were
marked always by a cordial spirit of close co-operation. Not least among
the reasons was the friendly spirit maintained between the chief officers
of the company and Edwin Bayliss, who served on the Board for a long
period. After 1970 such a spirit of co-operation was maintained also
with his successor, Christopher Higgins. Bayliss brought to the Board
some thirty years of distinguished public service. In 1949 he was
Chairman of the General Purposes Committee of the London County
Council and had already served on several government bodies and had
been a founder member of the British Legion.

The new North Thames Gas Board in 1949 covered an area of 1059
square miles from Southend-on-Sea in the east to Bracknell, Marlow
and High Wycombe in the west. The Board served the whole of London

north of the Thames and small pockets south of the river; it supplied, too, nearly the whole of southern Middlesex and Essex, South Buckinghamshire, the eastern part of Berkshire, the Richmond, Egham and Chertsey districts of Surrey and a few areas in Hertfordshire. From the twelve vested undertakings the Board acquired thirteen gasworks belonging to the Gas Light & Coke Company, five from the Uxbridge, Maidenhead and District Gas Company and one each from eight of the other constituent companies (the two remaining made no gas of their own).

The total work-force of the new Board was almost exactly 24 000, making North Thames the largest employer among the twelve Area Boards. Of this number, no fewer than 18 000 were manual operatives. The majority of operatives (some 10 000) were employed among the twenty-six gas stations and the Products Works. There were additionally some 3000 gas fitters and plumbers, nearly 1000 drivers and other transport staff, about 700 meter readers, and over 3000 'other operatives', including apprentices. The remaining 6000 or so employees were the technical, administrative and clerical staff, who worked in the showrooms and district offices, in the various headquarters departments, and in the engineering, reseach, training and other technical sections.

The early tasks of the new Board were to integrate the twelve constituent undertakings into a cohesive unit, to continue the post-war work of reconstruction and modernisation, and to lay plans for future development. Integration of the work-force, plant and management of the vested undertakings was facilitated by the dominating role of the Gas Light & Coke Company, with its well-developed distribution grid and internal organisation. Of the undertakings merged, only three, the Gas Light, Romford, and Commercial, had been independent statutory companies; the minute Shoeburyness undertaking was municipally owned, while the remaining companies were already associated with the Gas Light through the South Eastern Gas Corporation holding company. Indeed, the Beckton grid already supplied gas to a number of these companies, including Shoeburyness and Chertsey, and also sold bulk supplies to the gasworks at Uxbridge and Slough. On vesting day the Gas Light & Coke Company supplied 83 per cent of the total gas sold and the undertakings in the South Eastern Gas Corporation contributed a further 12 per cent. The Gas Light territory formed just over half the total area, while the Beckton grid already extended to twelve of its thirteen stations and a link to the last, at Southend, was under way. The integration of the Board's area was thus well on the way to achievement at the very outset.

Some details of the twelve undertakings are given in Table 2.1. The outstanding position of the Gas Light & Coke Company is, of course,

Table 2.1   North Thames Gas, 1949

Companies merged	Founded	Area (sq. miles)	Consumers	Mains Miles	Output 1948[1] (m. cu ft)
Ascot District Gas and Electricity Co.[2]	1883	78	8 000	122	445
Chertsey Gas Consumers Co. Ltd[2]	1837	17	7 000	67	309
Commercial Gas Co.	1839	7.5	64 000	224	2 279
Gas Light & Coke Co.	1812	547	1 433 000	6 400	56 674
Hornsey Gas Co.[2]	1857	4	28 000	109	879
Lea Bridge District Gas Co.[2]	1853	10	43 000	156	1 656
North Middlesex Gas Co.[2]	1862	11	33 500	212	1 365
Romford Gas Co.	1847	43.5	43 000	292	1 593
Slough Gas & Coke Co.[2]	1866	21	14 500	108	1 104
Shoeburyness (Southend Corporation)	1866	1.65	2 200	12	55
Uxbridge, Maidenhead & District Gas Co.[2]	1861	234	64 000	552	3 056
Windsor Royal Gaslight Co.[2]	1827	10	6 000	29	316

[1]Includes gas 'bought'.
[2]Member of the South Eastern Gas Corporation.
Source: North Thames Gas.

obvious and contrasts strangely with the tiny municipally owned Shoeburyness works, which served an area of under two square miles through some twelve miles of main. Each of the merged undertakings had, of course, a tradition of its own, and retained some of that distinctiveness even under nationalisation. Shoeburyness, for example, had a long military tradition and gas had first been supplied there by the War Department in 1866. Subsequently, a private company was formed to serve the town and this, in turn, was taken over by the Shoeburyness Urban District Council. In 1933 control passed to the Southend Corporation and Shoeburyness was thus the only municipally owned undertaking to be absorbed by North Thames, although in the country as a whole about one-third of all gas undertakings were municipally owned before nationalisation. It was something of an anomaly that although the Southend Corporation owned the Shoeburyness gasworks, the town of Southend itself lay within Gas Light & Coke Company territory. In 1939, the Corporation found it more convenient to buy gas for Shoeburyness direct from the company and gas making at Shoeburyness then ceased.

At the other end of the territorial scale was the Uxbridge, Maidenhead and District Gas Company, serving a large, sprawling and mostly rural territory which was principally in Buckinghamshire, though extending into Middlesex and Berkshire. Its area amounted to about half that of the Gas Light & Coke Company, although serving less than 5 per cent of the number of customers. The Uxbridge Gas Company had started operations in 1861 and subsequently amalgamated with Eton in 1916, High Wycombe in 1920, Marlow in 1922, and Maidenhead in 1924. This company possessed a number of scattered works throughout its territory, some of them rather out of date and inefficient. The main works was at Uxbridge, with further plants at High Wycombe and Taplow and with two small works, still with hand-charged retorts, at Marlow and Amersham.

A near-enclave within the Uxbridge Company territory was the small Slough Gas & Coke Company, with a territory of twenty-one square miles. This company served Slough, Langley, Stoke Poges, Datchet and Farnham Royal. Founded in 1866, the Slough Gas & Coke Company remained a very small undertaking until its development was transformed by the development of the Slough Trading Estate after the First World War. This encouraged the town's population to quadruple between 1920 and 1950, and by 1949 the company served about 14 500 consumers.

The Commercial Gas Company was another whose territory had been eyed longingly by the Gas Light before the war, but which had retained its own independence and character. The company had started life in 1839 and its main territory lay in the heart of London's docklands. In 1850 the Commercial absorbed the Poplar Gas Light Company and later took over works belonging to the British Gas Light Company (1852) and the Ratcliffe Gas Light & Coke Company (1875). Its seven square miles of territory covered the boroughs of Poplar and Stepney, together with parts of West Ham and Bethnal Green. The war had dealt harshly with this strategically located region, the boroughs of Stepney and Poplar losing about one half of their population through bomb damage and evacuation. Nevertheless, in 1948 the company still supplied over 60 000 consumers from its works at Poplar, and among its largest customers were the Royal Mint and the Port of London Authority.

The Lea Bridge, Hornsey and North Middlesex undertakings were all small companies on the northern borders of the North Thames area and all had been associated with the Gas Light & Coke Company through the South Eastern Gas Corporation before the war. The Lea Bridge

District Gas Company supplied the Borough of Walthamstow and part of Leyton. The original works, in Lea Bridge Road, had been built by the South Essex Gas Light & Coke Company in 1853. The first company survived for only five years and its successor managed only a further eleven. Finally, in 1869, the works passed to Lea Bridge Gas Company which survived as an independent concern for over sixty years until it joined the South Eastern Gas Corporation. The Hornsey Gas Company had started in 1857 and served a compact residential area in North London. In contrast to Lea Bridge, whose industrial sales amounted to some 42 per cent of the total, Hornsey's industrial sales were only 4 per cent. The North Middlesex Gas Company had started in 1862 and from its works at Mill Hill the company served an area of eleven square miles, which covered Finchley, Hendon, Mill Hill, and parts of Golders Green.

Of the other companies, the Chertsey Gas Consumers Company Limited had been formed in 1864, although the town had been served by a gas company from 1837, the year of Queen Victoria's accession. The entire area of this company, of course, lay south of the Thames. From 1936 gas-making at Chertsey ceased and gas was then bought in bulk from the Gas Light & Coke Company. Also south of the Thames was the territory served by the Ascot & District Gas & Electricity Company. This covered an area of some seventy-eight square miles in Berkshire and Surrey. The company had started in 1883 and the electricity side of the company's activities had already passed into public ownership in 1948.

The oldest of the amalgamated undertakings, apart from the Gas Light & Coke Company itself, was the Windsor Royal Gas Light Company. This had been founded in 1827 to supply Windsor Castle and the surrounding districts, strictly known as New Windsor because the village of Old Windsor lay within the Gas Light & Coke Company's territory. The Romford Gas Company was the third of the independent statutory companies within North Thames Gas. This served a large wedge of territory which ran right across the area of the old Gas Light & Coke Company, and for a long time the Gas Light had tried to acquire it. But the Romford Company had vigorously maintained its independence against all overtures. Indeed, when the Governor and Deputy Governor met the Romford officials before vesting day in their new guise as future Chairman and Vice-Chairman of the North Thames Gas Board, they noted an air almost of capitulation, as if the Gas Light & Coke Company had finally won. In their turn, Milne-Watson and Birks tried hard to be, or at least to look, consoling and magnanimous. The Romford Company had started in 1847, when an undertaking was formed to buy up a small private gasworks. A century later the company supplied an area of over forty square miles from a works in Romford, which extended to some twenty-five acres and which was later to be in the forefront of the new technology developed by North Thames Gas during the late 1950s and 1960s.

Although North Thames was the smallest of the Boards in area (one-third the size of the South Eastern, the next smallest) it had more customers, greater sales, more consumers per mile of mains and more employees than any of the others. The new Board comprised all the land, buildings, works, equipment, showrooms and offices of the twelve vested undertakings. In all, there were 26 gas stations, 2 Tar and Ammonia Products Works (at Beckton and Southall), 87 showrooms (61 formerly within the territory of the Gas Light & Coke Company), 45 depots and 75 stores. In devising its immediate organisational structure the Board wisely maintained the identity of the vested undertakings by continuing the divisional structure within the territory of the Gas Light & Coke Company and by constituting the other undertakings as separate Districts. This meant that for a time the former commercial organisation of the various undertakings could be continued. One by one the Districts were gradually either absorbed within the existing Divisions or new Divisions were created. This allowed the Board to achieve the separation of production (under the Chief Engineer) and sales (under the Commercial Manager) already entrenched in the organisation of the Gas Light & Coke Company.

By the beginning of 1956 restructuring was completed when the Romford and Southend Districts were constituted as the Mid-Essex and East Essex Divisions. (see Figure 2.1) Most of the key divisional appointments went to Gas Light men, although A. R. Shirley, Secretary of the former Romford Company, became the new Divisional Manager of the Mid-Essex Division. By this time the customer service and marketing side of the Board's activities was organised in eight territorial Divisions (subsequently reduced to six by amalgamations), with an additional Headquarters Division to handle industrial sales, local authority contracts and other matters requiring a more centralised administration. On the production side the existing hierarchy of stations grouped under Group Engineers and responsible to the Chief Engineer was maintained, and the new works added to the Gas Light & Coke Company's nucleus were allotted among the existing groups on a territorial basis.

The Board's total gas-making capacity and its distribution among the various works are shown in Tables 2.2 and 2.3 respectively. Early meetings of the Board were concerned with considering reports by the Engineering, Commercial and other important committees in order to draw up medium-term plans for development. The Board decided to continue with all those major new construction developments already authorised or under way by the Gas Light & Coke Company. However, proposed new plants at Romford and Hornsey were abandoned, while it

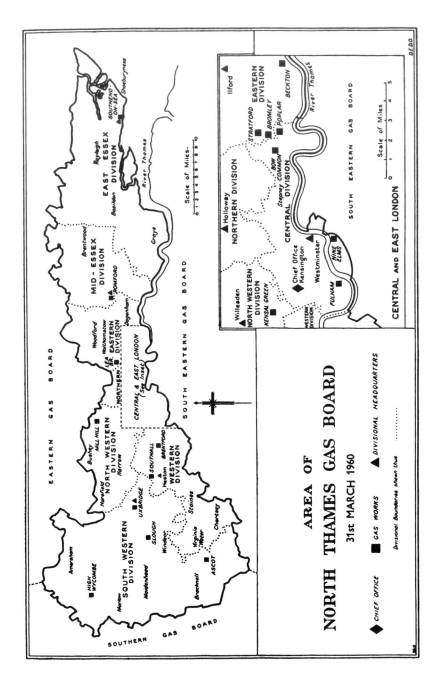

Figure 2.1   Divisional structure and location of gasworks, 1960

Table 2.2 North Thames Gas Board – gas-making methods and capacity at 1 May 1949

Method	Total capacity (m. cu ft gas/day)
Coke ovens	22.50
Horizontal retorts	106.99
Vertical retorts	94.61
Carburetted water-gas (CWG)	122.15
Oil-gas	0.75
Blue water-gas	7.50
Total	354.50

Source: North Thames Gas.

Table 2.3 North Thames – gas-making stations and capacity at 1 May 1949 (m. cu ft gas/day)

Station	Capacity	Station	Capacity	Station	Capacity
Beckton	119.12	Stratford	9.00	Harrow	3.28
Fulham	32.50	Kew Bridge	8.65	Ascot	2.66
Bromley	30.65	Southend	7.75	High Wycombe	2.60
Nine Elms	27.70	Mill Hill	7.55	Staines	1.30
Southall	20.25	Slough	6.00	Maidenhead	1.15
Kensal Green	16.30	Shoreditch	5.75	Windsor	0.85
Brentford	15.30	Romford	5.25	Marlow	0.15
Poplar	11.10	Hornsey	4.95	Amersham	0.09
Bow Common	10.50	Uxbridge	3.90		

Source: North Thames Gas.

was considered that the existing works at Hornsey, Maidenhead and Windsor 'were approaching the end of their useful lives' and should be closed down. It was proposed to extend the existing grid to all the gas-making stations within the Board's area as soon as possible and to concentrate production in a few major gas stations as far as it proved practicable to do so. This would result in further closures of smaller, uneconomic works and in this way the Board would get the benefits from large-scale units and could also choose those sites which were the most efficient and convenient. The Board therefore decided to concentrate production principally at those stations which lay on the River Thames, for here coal could be delivered relatively cheaply in the Board's own fleet of colliers. In turn, other works would be either closed down or used primarily for peak-load output. The key plants in this plan were Beckton, Nine Elms, and Fulham, because it was to these gasworks that sea-borne coal could be brought directly from the ships. Other stations at Brentford, Bromley, Southend, Staines, Poplar and Uxbridge, obtained their coal from barges loaded from ships berthed at Beckton, or occasionally at Nine Elms or Fulham. In the case of Staines and Uxbridge the coal arrived by road from convenient up-river wharves. Elsewhere, sea-borne coal could not be used, and these works relied on coal brought by rail.

The counterpart to the policy of developing the river stations was that the fleet of colliers was strengthened. The Board immediately confirmed orders for new colliers placed by the Gas Light & Coke Company and the fleet continued to be managed by Stephenson Clarke Ltd, as it had been since its establishment in 1912. All the loading and distribution of coal was controlled by the Coal Department. The launching in 1954 of the *Thomas Goulden* and the *John Orwell Phillips* (both recalling famous names in the annals of the Gas Light & Coke Company) completed the programme of twelve new colliers ordered by the Company in 1946 and confirmed by the Board, and brought the collier fleet to its maximum of twenty-six vessels.

At the outset also the Board decided to modernise the distribution system in Buckinghamshire, the most important step being a new trunk main from Fulham to Slough via Richmond and Twickenham. This was put in hand at once and was constructed at a cost of £1.2 million and opened by Sir John Maud, Permanent Secretary to the Ministry of Fuel and Power, in 1955.

7 The gasholder at the Fulham Works, in use until the 1980s, photographed in 1951, was erected by the former City Gas Company in 1830. Its capacity was 250 000 cu ft gas, at a time when few holders were larger than 40 000 cu ft.

8 The m.v. *Falconer Birks*, last of the North Thames Gas Board's fleet of colliers, leaves the River Tyne on 23 January 1970 to make her final delivery of coal to Nine Elms Gas Works, London. In the background are the ruins of Tynemouth Priory, burial place of the brothers John and Ralph Clarke, who founded the Stephenson Clarke company in the eighteenth century. This company became part of the Powell Duffryn Group which managed the North Thames Gas Board's collier fleet.

At this early stage demand for gas was still rising and plans for further plant capacity made in 1951 were based on the assumption that sales would rise by about 2 per cent annually. The Chief Engineer, Jim Burns, estimated that by 1960–61 total sales would be about 489 million therms and that some 5.4 million tons of coal would be carbonised. Only from about 1954 was it clear that these forecasts were over-optimistic and, in fact, total demand ceased to rise at all. In the event, the figures reached by 1960–61 were to be an output of only 388 million therms, and the carbonisation of 3.7 million tons of coal.

The post-nationalisation plans for the modernisation of existing plant and the rationalising and concentration of gas production at the most economic stations bore considerable fruit in the five or six years after 1949. Some stations, notably Beckton, Bromley, Fulham, Kensal Green and Nine Elms, were developed and enlarged, while a number of smaller works were shut down. The scale of reconstruction was massive and all the more commendable because it took place against a background of continual post-war shortages of both labour and materials.

9 View of the Brentford Works in 1951. The works occupied a site of some nine acres across the river from Kew Gardens and the capacity then was 17 m. cu ft gas/day. Gas was first made on the site in 1821 from a works constructed by the old Brentford Gas Company.

Notable landmarks included the opening of a large modern carburetted water-gas (CWG) plant at Beckton in 1952, which added more than 20 m. cu ft gas/day to total capacity. Also, in the same year a new jetty and coal handling plant were completed at Nine Elms. In 1953 the Board's largest gasholder, capable of holding some 8 m. cu ft gas, was brought into operation after a lengthy programme of reconstruction from wartime damage. In 1954 came the opening of the new No. 3 Retort House at Kensal Green, and this year also saw the completion of a new type of CWG plant at Southall, which could produce the cheapest gas in the country. Edwin Bayliss, officially opening the plant, noted that 'several steps into the unknown were taken when it was designed as a co-operative effort between the Board's engineers and the contractors, Messrs Humphreys and Glasgow'. Incidentally, Humphreys and Glasgow was the same firm which had designed and built Britain's first CWG plant in 1891 for the Gas Light & Coke Company. Michael Milne-Watson, in his speech at the Southall ceremony, drew attention to the growing use of oil in gas-making which the new plant demonstrated, and added that 'the Board is today turning its mind more and more to alternatives to coal, which is pricing itself out of the gas-making market'. In fact, when in the following year the large new retort house was opened at Bromley, bringing capacity there to nearly 40 m. cu ft gas/day and establishing that works as the Board's second largest (and the third largest in the country), this was to be the last additional gas-making plant carbonising traditional coals installed by North Thames. After this additions to carbonising capacity were simply replacements for obsolete plant.

The early 1950s also saw an extensive scheme for the complete reconstruction of the Products Works at Beckton, and many improvements were made in gas distribution, welfare facilities and the transport fleet. Indeed, few, if any, areas of the Board's operations were untouched by modernisation and rationalisation.

The casualties were the small, high-cost gasworks, where the expense of transporting coal made it cheaper to supply these areas from the grid. The grid itself was finally completed in 1955 when Ascot was brought within the system. Already, by the end of 1954 the number of gas-making stations had been reduced from the vesting day level of twenty-six to twenty, although total capacity, through the opening of new plant and economies in existing operations, had increased by some 15 per cent. The stations closed were at Amersham, Marlow, Harrow, Shoreditch, Windsor and Maidenhead, while in 1957 Hornsey was added to the list of closures. The total capacity of the closed works was little more than 20 m. cu ft gas/day, and their demise was inevitable in the existing economic circumstances. All the stations had, of course, a lengthy history and tradition of their own. The layout of the Shoreditch

10 Early morning scene in one of the Beckton loco sheds, c. 1953. Some of the famous old squat 'Jumbo' engines, specially designed to run right into the retort house coke holds, can be seen.

11 The Chairman, Michael Milne-Watson, with the Duchess of Kent during the inauguration of new plant at Nine Elms in May 1952. Also in the picture are (left to right): W. E. Davies, Station Engineer; H. C. Smith, Chairman of the Gas Council; and the Mayor of Battersea.

Works, for example, had originally been planned in 1820 by Samuel Clegg, one of the pioneers of the early gas industry, and the gasworks there had served for many years as one of London's principal stations. Both the Harrow and Hornsey Works had been producing gas for nearly a century, the former partly on the initiative of Dr Vaughan, headmaster of Harrow School, who wished to introduce gas lighting to his school. After closure, each site was retained as a holder station and sometimes as a depot or for other purposes. In this way some employment was maintained and the Board was able to find jobs elsewhere for all displaced employees who wished to continue working for North Thames.

Concentration of gas production meant a similar concentration of coke output. Coke was, of course, a by-product of major importance as long as gas manufacture was based on coal carbonisation. Every ton of coal carbonised produced roughly half a ton of coke for sale and in the first half of the 1950s coke sales formed between a fifth and a quarter of total revenue.

Indeed, the gas industry should properly be thought of as a two-product enterprise, manufacturing and selling coke as well as gas. Beckton alone produced some 700 000 tons of coke annually in the 1950s. Coke grading and sales were the responsibility of the Coke manager, whose department was based at Vincent Street, Westminster. Coke was sold both directly and through merchants, the bulk of it going to domestic and commercial consumers in the Board's own area. Additionally, some coke was exported to Scandinavia, maintaining a traditional sale from Beckton which had started in the 1880s.

Coke sales remained buoyant for much of the 1950s, although towards the end of the decade demand fell away and an embarrassing rise in stocks occurred. From this time coke gradually declined in importance as coal carbonisation itself declined and market conditions turned against solid fuels. After 1966 the Board ceased to make coke deliveries direct to customers, marketing its rapidly diminishing supplies solely through local fuel merchants. The fall in coke production after the mid-1950s can be seen in Table 2.4.

Table 2.4 Coal carbonised, and coke and Cleanglow for sale

	Coal carbonised (m. tons)	Coke/Cleanglow for sale (m. tons)
1951–52	4.8	2:0
1955–56	4.8	2.3
1959–60	3.6	1.6
1967–68	1.7	0.3
1969–70	0.4	0.2

Source: North Thames Gas.

In addition to coke, North Thames sold a range of other by-products from the carbonisation of coal. Coke customarily accounted for around three-quarters of the gross revenue from sales of all by-products, but the other products were a valuable addition as long as gas manufacture continued to be based on coal carbonisation. They consisted primarily of tar, pitch, benzole, ammonia and of the enormous variety of refined chemicals made from these substances at the Products Works. Most of the tar was sold to contractors, but until the mid-1960s the Board also ran its own fleet of tar-spraying lorries, undertaking road spraying for public authorities. Tar was exported to many countries, reaching as far afield as New Zealand.

Table 2.5 shows the relative contribution made by the various components of total income for the year 1956–57, and it can be seen that by-products other than coke accounted for nearly 10 per cent of revenue.

Table 2.5   Gross income from sales, 1956–57

Source	Income (£000)	Share (%)
Gas	35063	50.5
Coke and breeze	19010	27.4
Tar and tar products	3710	5.4
Benzole and benzole products	1513	2.2
Other by-products	900	1.3
Appliance sales	4848	7.0
Meter rentals	1040	1.5
Appliance rentals	1147	1.6
Miscellaneous	2142	3.1
Total	69373	100.0

Source: North Thames Gas.

As we have seen, North Thames had taken over from the Gas Light & Coke Company the large Tar and Ammonia Products Works at Beckton and the smaller one at Southall. These works, which employed some 1000 people in the 1950s, were under the Controller of By-products, whose department looked after both the preparation and the sale of the products. North Thames was almost alone in processing its own by-products instead of disposing of them in an unprocessed state (although the South Eastern Board had inherited a large works from the South Metropolitan Company at East Greenwich). An early decision was to modernise both Products Works, and the total reconstruction and layout of the Beckton Works was put in hand at once. By 1957 nearly all the by-products from the Board's various carbonisation plants were being processed at Beckton or Southall.

The Products Works, especially Beckton, produced and sold a very large variety of specialised products derived from tar, ammonia and benzole. Many of them provided important raw materials for the synthetic chemicals industry and a substantial export trade to many countries was maintained. Specialised chemicals, such as phenol, cresylic acid, naphthalene, toluene, tar bases and coal-tar spirits, found outlets among manufacturers of plastics, drugs, dyes, explosives, fertilisers and paints and were exported to countries in every continent.

Naturally, the quantity of by-products available for processing depended on the utilisation of coal and the subsequent production of tar and ammoniacal liquor. Until 1957 the throughput of the two works increased steadily. This was not only the result of more coal carbonised, but also of an increasing proportion of the resulting by-products going to the Products Works. In 1957 itself the utilisation of coal was unexpectedly large, as increasing oil prices in the wake of the Suez Crisis in 1956 dictated a greater emphasis on traditional carbonisation plant.

Table 2.6   Throughput at Products Works, 1950–59

	1950–51	1953–54	1956–57	1958–59
Crude tar distilled (000 tons)	227	235	265	217
Ammoniacal liquor treated (million 10-oz gall.)	111	126	136	114
Crude benzole (million gall.)	6.5	8.8	9.4	7.7
Spent oxide consumed (000 tons)	14.3	24.3	17.6	16.3

Source: North Thames Gas.

But thereafter there was a steady fall in throughput as the consumption of coal declined and new production methods reduced the supplies of by-products available for processing. Table 2.6 indicates the extent of this decline by the end of the decade.

The gross revenue from sales of chemical products, which had risen from £3.2 million in 1950–51 to £5.6 million in 1956–57, fell to £4.9 million in 1958–59 and, despite higher prices, to only £1.6 million in 1968–69. By this latter year, the last in which processing was carried out at North Thames, only 46 000 tons of coal tar were distilled.

As far as the establishment of uniform tariffs was concerned, North Thames was not faced with the same problems as elsewhere. The North Eastern, for example, inherited more than 500 separate tariffs, as well as many individual contracts with large industrial and commercial firms. For North Thames, the range and the number of tariffs were not great, although it is noteworthy that tariffs were not uniform even within the old Gas Light & Coke Company territory (termed the Gas Light District), as Table 2.7 shows. At vesting day flat rate domestic tariffs varied from

Table 2.7   North Thames domestic tariffs at vesting day, 1949

District	*(old pence per therm)*
Lea Bridge	14.4
Chertsey	15.0
Slough and Uxbridge	15.4
Gas Light (Central), Hornsey and North Middlesex	15.6
Romford	16.2
Gas Light (Grays Inner and Southend Inner) and Commercial	17.0
Shoeburyness undertaking	17.8
Ascot and Windsor	18.0
Gas Light (Brentwood, Canvey, Grays Outer and Southend Outer)	18.2

Source: North Thames Gas.

14.4*d*. (old pence) a therm to 18.2*d*. a therm and steps were taken immediately to bring prices into line and to remove anomalies. On 1 January 1951 North Thames became the first Board to achieve a uniform tariff rate, which was set as a flat rate of 16.1*d*. a therm, with concessionary block rates for large consumers.

Commercial development continued to be hampered for several years by constant shortages of coal and steel (although all coke restrictions were lifted from the beginning of 1950). Appliances, too, were in short supply. The Board continued as far as possible with the pre-war policy of replacing the 300 000 or so rented 'black' cookers which still existed in the North Thames area and by 1955 these had at last all been replaced, albeit that this was some thirty years after the development of enamelled cookers had made the cast-iron models obsolete. On the service side, emergency work was considerably improved with the opening in April 1950 of a radio communications station, Temgas, with a central control room at Vincent Street, Westminster, from where instructions could be radioed to mobile repair vans. Once again this development, the first of its kind, was based on a scheme already planned by the Gas Light & Coke Company. The Board also continued the various social and welfare schemes of the Gas Light Company. Medical services were co-ordinated with the appointment of a Chief Medical Officer in 1952, and in the next few years medical units were established at each works.

North Thames continued to manage and staff research laboratories both at Watson House and at the London Research Station. Until 1954, Watson House was maintained by subscription from all the Area Boards, but in that year (on the death of the Watson House Manager, G. Holliday, and the subsequent appointment of L. W. Andrew as Director of Watson House) North Thames agreed that the institution should become an activity of the Gas Council, though still administered by the Board. Both these research institutions undertook invaluable work during the 1950s in the development of more efficient appliances, better quality gas, and new processes of gas-making which were later to help transform the industry.

A word should be said about the financial state of the North Thames Gas Board at the beginning of its operations. As mentioned already, the Boards were individually responsible to the Minister of Fuel and Power, and each was obliged to match its expenditures with revenue, 'taking one year with another'. During the early years of operations North Thames was easily the most profitable of the various Boards and was successful not only in meeting its statutory obligations, but in increasing its reserves and paying for capital expenditures out of its initial liquid assets (£2 million) and war damage claims (about £4 million) without recourse to further borrowing. However, the amount of British Gas Stock allocated to North Thames, £62.5 million, was also

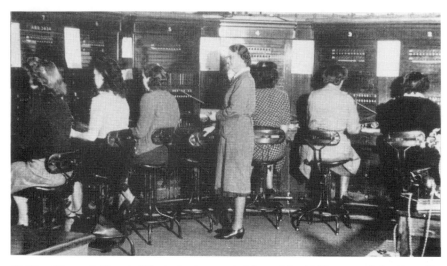

12 The Vincent Street, Westminster, switchboard in 1949, one of the Board's largest. The switchboard dealt with eighty exchange lines and could handle up to 2000 calls per hour.

the highest of any Board (the South Eastern coming next with £42.1 million), and this imposed an interest charge of some £1.8 million, which had to be met from the Board's revenue. This large sum reflected the relatively high compensation paid to statutory company shareholders (municipal compensation was significantly lower) and, together with the generally high cost of coal in the London area, was a major reason for the high price for gas charged by North Thames (and the South Eastern Board) in comparison with other areas of the country.

By about 1954 the first phase of the Board's operations may be considered to be over. The integration of the new undertakings had been successfully achieved within the organisational and administrative structure of the Gas Light & Coke Company; the grid had been extended to nearly the whole territory; the process of reconstructing war damage and modernising existing plant had been largely completed; and the plans for concentrating production in efficient plants and shutting small, uneconomical works was well under way. A further step in streamlining the organisation and improving efficiency resulted from the decision taken in 1950 to centralise stores and stocks of materials. A large new Central Stores and warehouse was established in Brentford on the Great West Road to replace the various offices and fourteen scattered stores and depots, which had been the result of wartime bomb damage to the Gas Light & Coke Company's old Central Stores at Nine Elms. Although partly operational in December 1951, the Brentford Stores was not finally completed until 1954. There was a new era dawning, too, in market conditions. From about 1953 competition from electricity and oil was increasingly felt as the nation's prosperity and productive capacity grew. Now each year attractive new appliances were tempting North Thames's customers to change from gas. Appliances become more plentiful and the post-war ban on promotional advertising was ended in 1952. Massive new housing schemes, many of them local authority developments, held out the prospect of an increasing proportion of non-gas households unless the Board's salesmen could successfully persuade consumers to choose gas. There was, therefore, an increasing concentration on marketing as it became recognised that the survival of the industry depended upon successful sales of appliances in order to maintain loads. In many ways the situation was reminiscent of the inter-war years, and a sign of the renewed emphasis on marketing was the reappearance in 1953 of *News*, the former sales and service magazine of the Gas Light & Coke Company, which had ceased publication upon the outbreak of war in 1939.

3

The Struggle for Survival

Knowing of the great expansion achieved by the gas industry during the 1960s and 1970s, it is hard to comprehend just how real appeared the threat to the continued existence of the industry during the first decade of nationalisation. Yet the threat was real enough. Milne-Watson recalled later how it seemed at one stage as though 'we were threatened by a competition so severe that it would eventually kill this great industry'; and R. S. Johnson also recalled that around the middle of the 1950s 'it seemed that our industry was doomed'. The problem for gas was one of price. Costs rose, especially coal costs. In consequence, gas became increasingly uncompetitive and it was difficult for the industry to maintain its traditional load let alone enter new markets. As a result, the total sales for North Thames stagnated throughout the 1950s and domestic demand actually fell. Far from the optimistic sales forecasts of the early 1950s there was now a desperate struggle to maintain existing levels as costs rose inexorably.

During the 1950s, of course, North Thames was still almost entirely dependent on coal and coke as feedstock for gas production. Some Boards, more favourably situated in industrial regions, could purchase cheap gas supplies from nearby coke ovens, but with the single exception of small quantities from Fords at Dagenham, no such gas was available to North Thames. Coal was the single largest element in production costs, accounting on average, for about 40 per cent of total costs. True, some half of any increase in coal prices could be recouped by corresponding rises in coke, but the succession of coal price rises which took place during every single year of the 1950s, usually without prior warning, imposed the severest of burdens on an industry whose role in the market-place was already insecure. The rising coal charges paid by North Thames can be seen in Table 3.1 – in all, the prices doubling between 1949 and 1959. The Board estimated that for each increase of 9s. (shillings) a ton, in the absence of greater efficiency of carbonisation or offsetting coke increases, the extra cost of gas would have to be 1d. a therm.

In addition to rising prices, there was a steady deterioration in the quality of coal, while in some years the Board was unable to purchase sufficient quantities of suitable coal at all and was forced to import expensive coal from overseas. Unlike some of the other Boards, North

Table 3.1 Average cost of coal carbonised, 1949–59 (year ended 31 March)

Year	Per ton s. d.	Year	Per ton s. d.	Year	Per ton s. d.
1950[1]	64 3	1954	86 2	1958	118 10
1951	65 9	1955	90 7	1959	123 11
1952	72 3	1956	100 11		
1953	80 7	1957	110 11		

[1]Average for 11 months.
Source: North Thames Gas.

Thames had to bring in all its coal from outside the region, and transport costs, adding some 25 per cent on average to coal costs, rose steadily, too. Most of North Thames's coal supplies, some three-quarters, came from the traditional Durham mines and was brought in the Board's colliers to the Thames-side gas stations. The remainder, from Yorkshire and the Midlands, came by rail and the cost here was more than double that of sea carriage, amounting to about 40s. a ton by 1960.

Labour costs also rose substantially. Wages and salaries were around 22 per cent of costs in the 1950s. The average payments to manual labour at gasworks rose by some 75 per cent during the decade, and there was often extreme difficulty in finding suitable labour for what was heavy and arduous work at a time of full employment generally. The impact of increasing coal costs was magnified by the differential charging scheme operated by the National Coal Board. This scheme was introduced by the Coal Board in 1951 and first put into effect in 1954. It meant that the gas industry would have to pay more for its coal than virtually every other class of industrial consumer. Despite strenuous attempts by Milne-Watson and Burns to persuade the National Coal Board to revise its decision, the new charges were maintained. Burns wrote to Milne-Watson, 'the National Coal Board are completely unmoved. They seem particularly proud of their scheme, having thought it up all by themselves.' Thus, between December 1951 and September 1961 pit-head coal prices to the gas industry were raised by 70 per cent, while to general industrial consumers the increase was 63 per cent and to the electricity industry only 45 per cent. No wonder the gas industry was worried, and Table 3.2 shows how the increased costs of gas were reflected in higher charges.

Inevitably, North Thames had to increase its prices. As we see from Table 3.3, the flat rate price of gas rose from 16.1d. a therm in January 1951 to 25.85d. a therm in August 1957. The Board had, indeed, been able to keep prices stable between 1952 and 1955 by its various economy measures and steps taken to improve productivity, but none the less the increase in a little over six years amounted to 60 per cent. By contrast,

Table 3.2   North Thames: Cost of gas, 1950–60 (*d.* per therm)

	1950–51	*1959–60*
Cost of gas	8.66	13.02
Distribution, administration, etc.	2.76	5.24
Depreciation	1.24	2.46
Interest (net)	1.24	2.13
Total	13.90	22.85
Average selling price	14.15	22.89

Source: North Thames Gas.

Table 3.3   Quarterly gas tariffs (domestic), 1951–60 (*d.* per therm)

Date	Tariff	Date	Tariff
1 Jan 1951	16.1	1 Oct 1955	21.85
2 July 1951	17.6	1 Aug 1956	23.85
1 Feb 1952	19.1	14 Aug 1957	25.85
1 June 1955	20.85	1 Aug 1960	25.35[1]

[1]Plus 7s. primary charge.
Source: North Thames Gas.

Table 3.4   Average price of fuels (domestic and industrial), 1950–60

	1950	*1955*	*1960*
Gas	100	135	173
Electricity	100	112	123
Oil	100	131	141

Source: Report from the Select Committee on Nationalised Industries, *The Gas Industry*, vol. 2 (1961) p. 613.

electricity prices to the domestic consumer rose by only 22 per cent in the 1950s (the same rate as the increase in the general level of retail prices), while domestic oil prices rose 12 per cent. It is hardly surprising, therefore, that gas found it so difficult to penetrate the domestic and commercial space heating markets, refrigeration, central heating and other fields where electricity and oil were able to compete so effectively. Table 3.4 reveals the relative price movements. Electricity even began to make significant inroads into the domestic cooking market, especially in new private housing developments. Before the Second World War about 90 per cent of families in the Gas Light Company's area had cooked by gas; by 1950 the proportion had fallen to about 85 per cent, by 1960 to 80 per cent and during the 1970s to 75 per cent. However, these

13 A District Office, c. 1952. This is the main office at Barking Road, in the Eastern Division. Here the District Clerks, Area Representatives and clerks in the Ordering and Rental Sections still worked by gaslight.

proportions have always remained higher than achieved by gas in any other area of the country. The very saturation of the cooking market already achieved in Gas Light Company days was, indeed, a problem, since it was virtually impossible to expand the market and only a vigorous sales policy which promoted new models of cookers could keep the load from falling. Also, there was a trend for average domestic cooking consumption to fall, for appliances were becoming more efficient, and changing social habits (the growing numbers of working wives, for example) lessened demand for cooked breakfasts and a midday meal.

Year by year during the 1950s manufacturers produced at least twice as many models of electric cookers, space heaters and refrigerators as they did gas. Installation and service of gas appliances tended to be a cumbersome and lengthy business; for example, each cooker had to be assembled by the fitter in the house of the purchaser, and losses from damaged enamel were estimated to lie between a quarter and a third of the value of the appliance. Gas cookers were slow to incorporate such devices as automatic ignition, while there were technical problems which delayed the introduction of freezer compartments into gas refrigerators. The old radiant gas fires were expensive to run, and could not compete effectively with electric fires or oil heaters (although it must be remembered that throughout the 1950s coal burned in grates continued to account for about three-quarters of living-room heating). It was not surprising, therefore, that during the 1950s the average consumption of each domestic consumer, whether prepayment (still in the vast majority) or credit, tended to fall. In 1949 the average domestic consumer burned 133 therms annually. By 1950–60 the total number of consumers supplied by North Thames had increased, but each now burned on average only 115 therms. Nor is it surprising that sales to domestic consumers should therefore form a smaller proportion of the total, so that the percentage of domestic consumption declined from 61 per cent at nationalisation to only 52 per cent in 1959–60. Another problem was that despite all the real improvements which were made in the purification of coal-gas, it remained sulphurous and toxic and often of uneven quality. Gas, in consequence, suffered by comparison with clean and odourless electricity.

Faced with the prospect of declining sales, the search for new markets to boost sales was further hampered by what was termed the 'load factor'. Demand for gas was not constant throughout the year. On average, sales during the winter months in the 1950s were some 40 per cent to 50 per cent greater than in the summer months, while the difference between the coldest day in February and the slackest in July was 70 per cent or more. Plant capacity had to be kept ready to meet this peak winter demand (plus a safety margin to ensure against exceptional weather or plant breakdown, a margin which was traditionally kept to meet the sort of load which might be expected with a 'one in fifty' winter) and, of course, the labour to man it. Running gas output at near full capacity was an expensive business. It meant that the most inefficient and high-cost plants needed to be brought into operation, while for slack periods of the year there were both plant and labour which were underemployed at the gas stations.

Gas engineers had a choice of manufacturing plant with which to meet the different kind of demands. Traditionally, the base loads were met with coal carbonising plants, which produced gas of about 500 BTU per cu ft (the standard calorific value adopted by the North Thames Gas Board in 1949) and from which such by-products as coke, tar, ammonia and other materials were obtained. Coal-gas could be produced from either horizontal or vertical retort plants but, because of the arduous labour conditions involved in the former, no new horizontal plant was planned or brought into operation after the Second World War. Additionally, Beckton possessed coke-oven capacity of 36 m. cu ft gas/ day, inherited from the Gas Light & Coke Company, which produced

14 Inside a Beckton retort house, c. 1950.

cheap, good quality gas but which did not yield coke for sale. Since coke sales enabled the Board regularly to recoup something like one-third of the cost of total gas manufacture, the output of coke was an important consideration.

Traditional coal-gas plant was expensive to install and required a great deal of labour. It was also inflexible in operation. For example, the horizontal retort houses at Beckton, employing over 300 men, had to be heated up for at least three weeks before being brought into operation, and they were slow to shut down. Once running, despite the rises in coal prices, they were cheap to operate. But high installation costs (during the war the cost of carbonisation plant had trebled, so that it was sometimes economic to keep old, inefficient plant in operation, rather than invest in new) and inflexible production made the plant unsuitable for peak-load output. Indeed, one calculation made in the 1950s put the cost of the 'ultimate therm', to use Milne-Watson's phrase, using coal plant at its maximum, at £3.10s. Producing at £3.10s. and selling at about 1s.6d. was not attractive.

In practice carburetted water-gas plants were used for peak periods. These plants were cheaper to construct and used less labour. Gas was produced by passing steam through white-hot coke – a technique practised at Beckton since 1889 – the resulting product being a 'lean' gas of about CV300. In order to enrich the gas it was sprayed with petroleum oil through a carburettor. The enriching process was expensive, but CWG plants had the advantage that they could be brought into full production in about eight hours and shut down in ten minutes. Moreover, the steadily widening gap between coal and oil prices, research into cheaper and more efficient enriching processes, and problems with disposing of coke which arose at the end of the 1950s made the use of CWG plants to supply base loads increasingly attractive to North Thames by the end of the decade.

Generally speaking, it was the space heating load which fluctuated with the seasons. Domestic cooking and water heating were spread evenly throughout the year, though not, of course, throughout the day or week: Sunday lunchtime was a regular peak period. Most of the industrial process load was also non-seasonal. Some case studies of individual loads were made by the Board in 1951. One domestic household, using a cooker and sink water-heater only, and having a coin meter, used 53 per cent of its annual gas between 1 October 1950 and 31 March 1951. A block of flats, Victoria Dwellings, using gas for lighting and cooking, took 56 per cent. Another household, paying on credit, with a cooker and four fires, used 69 per cent of its gas in the winter quarters, while an Islington block of flats, with cookers and fires, used 78 per cent. By contrast, ABC and Lyons Catering used 53 per cent and 54 per cent respectively. On average, the typical prepayment customer, paying at the domestic flat rate, used 55 per cent of annual consumption between October and March, while the large domestic customer, paying at the promotional two-part rate (a relatively small concession for large users), used 65 per cent; and for those – mostly substantial commercial establishments – paying the central heating and hot water block rate, the proportion was 72 per cent.

During the 1950s the load factor tended to worsen and was a severe constraint on the Board's marketing strategy. As long as peak production remained costly the development of large heating loads by the use of attractive tariffs was impossible. In consequence sales efforts for much of the 1950s were concentrated on maintaining cooking levels, especially, and successfully, by negotiating with local authorities to bring gas to new housing developments, and to develop load-spreading markets like refrigeration and water heating.

Throughout the 1950s domestic sales, the bulk of which went to prepayment customers, continued to predominate. On average, between 1955 and 1959 domestic sales formed 56 per cent of the total, two-thirds of which was bought by consumers with coin meters. A further 20 per cent went to industrial consumers, while about 25 per cent was bought by the large variety of commercial customers, such as shops, offices, restaurants and hotels. Gas lighting by now was an insignificant addition to revenue, producing less than 1 per cent of the total.

Faced with the problems of maintaining competitiveness and improving peak-load capacity, the Board's engineers cast round for solutions. All attempts to persuade the National Coal Board to change its policy had failed, so North Thames turned to other expedients. These included both new coal-based methods like the Lurgi process and total gasification of low-grade coals, and new oil-based processes, which will be discussed in the next chapter. It should be emphasised that although many Boards were engaged in similar exercises and that some developments, like the Lurgi process, were conducted with the Gas Council and several Boards together, North Thames took the lead in a great many fundamental research initiatives. Both Burns, the Chief Engineer, and L. J. Clark, the Development Engineer, realised that the survival of the gas industry depended upon engineering solutions to the problems of high-cost coal. Michael Milne-Watson was supportive throughout the numerous pilot schemes and experiments which his engineers put forward. Not all were successful, and the Board sometimes paid the penalties of a pioneer. But the role of North Thames engineers was a distinguished one, evidenced both by the numerous practical new developments in technology and by the succession of path-breaking technical papers published by the Institution of Gas Engineers, many of which received Gold Medal and other awards.

There was naturally a constant effort to improve efficiency in traditional manufacturing processes and, as we have seen, some small works were closed down and production concentrated in the most efficient plants. As a result of this, by April 1959 some three-quarters of the Board's capacity of 425 m. cu ft gas/day was concentrated at five major stations: Beckton, Bromley, Nine Elms, Fulham, and Southall. Gas produced from one ton of coal, despite its deteriorating quality, rose from 79.0 therms in 1949 to 82.1 therms in 1959, although even this latter figure was lower than that achieved before the war by the Gas Light Company from its superior Durham coal. The Board was also successful in developing a process which carbonised low-grade coal, yet which still produced a good quality reactive coke for domestic sale. This coke was launched in 1956 under the name 'Cleanglow', a resurrected brand name used by the Gas Light & Coke Company in the 1930s, and was an instant success. Produced from Midlands coal from continuous vertical retorts, its output was concentrated initially at the small Ascot and Lea Bridge works, the total produced being about 75 000 tons annually. By the winter of 1960–61 annual sales were over 250 000 tons and production was additionally based at Stratford, Kensal Green, and Bow Common.

The launching of Cleanglow coincided with the passage of the Clean Air Act. Public interest in cleaner fuels had grown in the wake of the terrible 'smog', which killed more than 4000 Londoners in the winter of 1952–53. Since the new fuel could be used in ordinary grates, it was highly suitable for those areas which became smokeless zones under the Act. After 1959 the spread of smokeless zones in the London area was rapid and Board representatives were quick to make personal calls on all consumers as soon as a local authority announced the decision to change. Visits were under the direction of the Coke Manager and until 1962 the main effort was directed towards inducing customers to change from coal to coke or Cleanglow. Thereafter, the steady decline in the availability of coke as coal carbonisation was run down led to a sales drive for gas fires. Many hundreds of new customers were won through these efforts and the part played by North Thames in London's environmental improvements should not be minimised. The change-over to oil-based gases made a dramatic impact. From calculations made in 1963 it transpired that to produce 1 million effective therms of heat from oil-gas plants some 2 cwt. of sulphur was released into the atmosphere. The pollution from an equivalent output from coal carbonisation plants (most of it produced by the secondary burning of coke by households) was 82 tons. And the equivalent heat produced by coal burning electric power stations flung no less than 208 tons of sulphur into the atmosphere. The autumn of 1962 saw the last of London's great smogs.

Another Board initiative was the marketing of 'Gloco', a high-grade domestic coke suitable for burning in gas-ignited grates. Sales of Gloco also expanded rapidly in the wake of the Clean Air Act and by 1960 three other Boards had followed North Thames in making Cleanglow and six were marketing Gloco.

Within the constraints permitted by the load factor, the Board steadily developed its commercial activities. Aberdein, Commercial Manager until 1959, was particularly concerned to see that gas was introduced into local authority housing schemes and, as we have seen, some notable successes were achieved here, with over 80 per cent of housewives in council houses opting to cook by gas. The Board ran many seasonal promotional and advertising campaigns, often in conjunction with adjacent Boards and with appliance manufacturers. In 1959, for the first time all twelve Area Boards combined with the Gas Council in a co-ordinated campaign to advertise the new convector gas fires. The Divisions, too, held their own campaigns and provided various incentives for those representatives who achieved target sales figures. The Board, through its commercial department, kept in close contact both with the manufacturers of appliances and with the appliance testing laboratories at Watson House and made numerous representations and suggestions for improvement. None the less, marketing activity was on the whole low key and muted for much of the 1950s. Promotional campaigns were complicated by frequent changes in hire-

Room Heaters are IN

THERE'S NO DOUBT ABOUT IT—convector gas room heaters are proving overwhelmingly popular. In fact, we are selling far more of them than of any other kind. The idea of two kinds of heat (convected and radiant) for the price of one is a big selling point. That is why we are emphasising gas room heaters in our current publicity, and why we are giving them this page to themselves.

BRAND NEW

HIRE PURCHASE PAYMENTS CAN BE SPREAD OVER THREE YEARS

Walmer (Bratt Colbran). Pewter and silver; gold. £19 14s. 8d.

Main 268. Bronze; gold; silver £15 9s. 9d.

Queen (Sugg). Gold and silver; silver blue. £12 1s. 5d. (with flash tube ignition £14 11s. 5d.)

271 Century (Main). Bronze; old silver; cream; guardsman red; £24 7s. 4d. (with thermostat £28 8s. 6d.).

GasMiser (Cannon). Cream; bronze lustre; pastel blue and cream; pastel green and cream. £24 2s. 10d. (with thermostat £26 19s. 4d.)

Rado Vecta (Radiation). Nubian and cream; mandarin red and cream; gold and pewter. £15 16s. 9d.

Kingsbury (Bratt Colbran). Gold and bronze; black and pewter; £24 1s. 9d. (with thermostat £29 10s. 0d.)

Conray (General Gas). Gold and silver; almond green and silver; light grey and silver £14 9s. 2d.

15 This range of new convector heaters appeared in *News*, the sales and service magazine of the Board, in September 1959.

purchase and purchase-tax rates, which were a feature of these years. During the decade the purchase tax on water-heaters was altered four times and hire purchase terms five times, while in 1956 the purchase tax on all gas appliances was suddenly increased by 20 per cent.

Despite ebbs and flows resulting from the activities of the seasons, campaigns, and governments, overall appliance sales were generally stagnant until the end of the 1950s. Sales of cookers and water-heaters, averaging about 140 000 and 50 000 a year respectively, declined somewhat after 1954, and there were substantial increases in sales of refrigerators and gas heaters, although from a very low base. Indeed, despite all endeavours to promote refrigerators as a way of load spreading, electricity always achieved more than 90 per cent of the sales.

The ways in which consumers acquired their appliances underwent some significant changes over the period. At the time of nationalisation and for several years subsequently, the hiring out of appliances, particularly cookers, owned and maintained by the Board, was carried out on an extensive scale. Until 1958 revenue from such rentals regularly brought in more than £1 million annually, but thereafter there was a substantial fall and North Thames soon ceased to open new rental contracts for domestic appliances. By 1960–61 revenue had fallen to about £500 000 and by the mid-1960s the figure was around £250 000. One reason for the fall was the growing variety and sophistication of appliances available, while rising levels of income brought such models within the budget of an increasing range of consumers. The hiring of appliances, pioneered by the Gas Light & Coke Company, had essentially aimed at a standardised, low-income market. Another factor was the expansion of hire-purchase, the volume of sales financed in this way growing erratically in line with budgetary manoeuverings. Thus, between 1950–51 and 1959–60 appliance sales by the Board for cash or on credit grew slowly and steadily from £1.3 million to £2.3 million. But hire purchase sales were £2.2 million in 1950–51, over £5 million in 1954–55, only £3 million in 1956–57, and nearly £6.5 million in 1959–60. During the following decade the fluctuations were less evident, and the proportion of appliances bought for cash or on credit rose steadily. By 1970–71 hire purchase sales stood at £5.2 million, whereas cash and credit sales had risen to £4.2 million.

Despite the difficult market conditions of the 1950s, the Board could look back on its first decade of operation with much satisfaction. By 1961 a total of over £73 million was invested in new capital projects, some £41 million of which had been found from internal resources, without recourse to borrowing. Integration of the various undertakings had been achieved, efficiency enhanced and the quality of gas greatly improved (the average sulphur content of gas was almost halved in this decade). In many ways, the end of the 1950s saw the end of an era, for it was from the closing years of the decade that a gradual turnaround in the fortunes of the gas industry can be discerned. Perhaps symbolically, 1959 saw the expiry of the last of the public lighting contracts and the period witnessed many such breaks with the past. Progress inevitably brings casualties, and one of them was the horse. During 1957 the last of the Board's stables at Brentford, where horses for coke deliveries had been stabled, was closed down. The Fulham stables had already been closed five years earlier. Over the years the Board's horses had built up a fine tradition of service and won hundreds of awards. Another break with former times came in 1958 with the closing of Beckton railway station to goods traffic, while in 1960 the traditional green and gold of the transport 'livery' was changed to two-tone grey.

From about 1955 the initial labour shortage had eased, if only temporarily. The Chief Engineer reported in this year that for the first time since nationalisation there was no undermanning at the principal works. Labour relations continued to be excellent, which carried on a tradition from pre-war days. Wages and salaries were, of course, negotiated nationally through various National Consultative Councils

16 The Pound Lane Divisional Warehouse in 1951. From this warehouse some 500 cookers and 400 other appliances a week were despatched in 1950 throughout the North Western Division.

and with the major trade unions involved. Between 1949 and 1959 average wages and salaries went up by about 70–75 per cent. At local level, conditions of work, bonuses and other matters affecting labour relations were negotiated through Area Joint Consultative Councils for employees of all grades. Nationalisation had given staff, as opposed to manual labour, strong representation for the first time. Increasingly, staff became unionised, with the majority of members belonging to NALGO (National and Local Government Officer's Association). Partly as a result of this development, wages for staff employees gradually improved relative to those of manual workers. Steady improvements were made in working conditions generally, helped by the closure of old plants and the development of new types of gas-making. In 1956 the principle of equal pay for female employees was adopted and by 1961 was operating completely. In 1960 a five-day week was introduced for all employees, except those on shiftwork or working in showrooms. At the same time the hours of shiftwork and day-work personnel were reduced from 48 hours and 44 hours weekly to a standard 42-hour week. There is no doubt that the strong sense of almost a family tradition helped preserve cordial industrial relations after nationalisation. The Board had always had a high proportion of employees with long service, despite the upheavals of war and post-war years. For example, in the seven years after 1952, 40-year service awards were given to 2138 employees, while nearly 9000 received their 25-year certificates. Rather like coal mining, there was also a strong tradition for generations of the same family to enter the Board's service, as they had the Gas Light & Coke Company. At one time in the middle of the 1950s, no fewer than eleven members of one family were on the payroll at the Southall Works.

During these years the Board also extended its training facilities. In 1949 a new training centre had been opened at Slough to add to the facilities at Watson House and Stratford, and by 1959 the numbers of apprentices undergoing basic training there had risen from 267 to 661. The numbers of apprentices trained in workshops also rose (from 68 to 173). Throughout this period these activities were looked after by R. N. Le Fevre. Le Fevre retired in 1962: he had served as Training and Education Officer for thirty-four years and in this capacity had not only selected and trained thousands of apprentices but had also taken a leading role in many adult education schemes. For many years he ran the traditional annual camps for boy apprentices, begun in 1931 and continued, except for the war years, until 1958. His many technical books and articles had earned him an international reputation and it was appropriate that the new training centre at Stratford, opened by Le Fevre himself three days before his retirement, should be called The Le Fevre Training Centre. Later, in 1969, the Slough Centre was closed

17 Apprentices under instruction at Watson House, Fulham, 1951.

down and a new larger one opened at Uxbridge. In 1958 the Board instituted a second university scholarship to add to the Milne-Watson Scholarship established in 1946. This new scholarship, to enable each year an able young employee to study a technical subject to degree level, was named after Falconer Birks. The Board's interest in improving the welfare and social facilities for its employees continued also. In 1957 a fine new pavilion was opened at the Acton Sports Ground, a project originally planned by the Gas Light & Coke Company in 1939 but delayed by the war and subsequent building restrictions. The pavilion was named after Brian Wood, Board Secretary and Chairman of the Sports Association.

Difficult market conditions which remained throughout the 1950s inevitably made progress slow. The most significant response to the competitive climate of the 1950s, and the one which after 1960 brought a transformation in the industry's prosperity, lay on the engineering side. With coal costs rising and efforts to build plant which economised on the use of coal disappointing, North Thames turned additionally to oil-based feedstocks. As a result of major technological advantages as well as the fortunate availability of cheap oil, the nature of gas-making was revolutionised. Coinciding with this was an even more adventurous experiment to import natural gas into Canvey, this in turn forming a prelude to the utilisation of Britain's own natural gas from the North Sea.

4

New Technology and New Markets

In the early 1950s few could have foreseen an era when coal would not form the basis of gas manufacture. In 1956 a report by the Chief Engineer, Jim Burns, on future plant requirements at Beckton still envisaged the necessity for new coal carbonisation plant into the foreseeable future. Even in 1960 the overwhelming bulk of North Thames gas was made from coal or coke. Yet, within the space of a very few years, the whole picture was transformed. New technology had made possible the use of oil feedstocks in revolutionary new types of plant, and by the second half of the decade coal was supplying a rapidly dwindling proportion of town gas. By this time, too, still further developments were under way with imported and domestic natural gas.

First oil and then natural gas saved the gas industry from the extinction threatened by rising coal prices. During 1955 the Board had been forced to raise its prices twice, and in 1956 once again; and each rise encouraged gas consumers to turn towards more competitive fuels. The dilemma caused by rising, and unpredictably rising, coal costs and by deteriorating qualities of coal caused an atmosphere of crisis and even panic. It was clear to all that something had to be done, but quite where the solution lay was not so clear. As we saw in the last chapter the engineers looked for solutions in many different directions. One obvious avenue was the development of carbonising plant to use cheaper grades of coal, and North Thames engineers co-operated with the Gas Council and other Boards in the development of Lurgi plants to carbonise low-grade coal. But such plants (two were constructed in the West Midlands and in Scotland) proved disappointingly expensive and difficult to operate. North Thames also constructed the country's first total gasification 'Gas Integrale' plant at Kensal Green in 1955, which could use cheap coal but produced no coke. To make room for this plant, incidentally, the oldest surviving continuous vertical retort installation in the country was shut down after more than a century of operation. Another experiment was the construction of a pilot plant at Bromley in 1960 for making gas from low-grade coal. This plant, using a total gasification process developed in West Germany, was operated by the London Research Station (which was managed and run by North

Thames) and it was able to start production in 1961. Elsewhere, new carbonisation methods were introduced at some works to produce Cleanglow from lower grades of coal.

The solution, however, was not to be coal or coke, but oil. Until the middle of the 1950s nearly all the oil used in gasworks had been gas oil to enrich the gas produced from coke in CWG plants. But during the 1950s the supplies of various kinds of oil products from oil refineries and chemical works increased dramatically. All sorts of new hydrocarbon fuels now became available, which opened up the possibilities for their use in gas-making. Massive research was undertaken both in the United Kingdom and abroad into a whole host of new processes, the result of which was a series of new oil-based plants which transformed the gas industry.

Two types of hydrocarbon which became available from the refineries were butane and propane, which could easily be stored at gasworks in liquid form under slight pressure. The very rich gas they produced (CV3000) could be reduced to the necessary calorific value for normal town gas by mixing with air in specially designed plants. These plants were ideal for peak-load production, since they were flexible enough to be brought into operation in a mere twenty minutes. Immediately following a spell of very severe weather in February 1956, which strained the Board's existing capacity (and during which capacity capable of producing 9 m. cu ft gas/day lay idle for want of labour), the decision was taken to build butane/air plants at Beckton, Bromley, and Fulham. These plants came into operation during 1957 and made a considerable improvement to peak-load production. Butane was also used as an enricher in CWG plants, which proved cheaper and considerably more efficient than gas oil and led to CWG plants being used for base-load production as well as for peak-load.

The most significant steps, however, were those which could provide a new source of base-load gas from oil, and here some fundamental technological developments in the 1950s and early 1960s, coupled with the new sources of supply, led to processes for manufacturing town gas from oil products. These gases were mostly produced in catalytic reforming plants, producing either 'rich' gases (with about CV650) which were subsequently reformed into town gas, or 'lean' gases (CV340), subsequently enriched by mixing with richer gases from a variety of sources.

North Thames experimented with many different processes in these years. In 1956 a small catalytic reforming plant was opened at Fulham to make town gas from heavy fuel oil. This was an Onia-Gegi plant using a process developed in France. The following year a similar works was installed at Romford and another small Segas heavy oil plant was opened at Uxbridge. But the first real breakthrough came with the

18 Part of Romford reforming plant by night, 1969.

purchase of refinery 'tail gas', which was a hitherto wasted by-product of oil cracking processes at refineries. The new era started in 1955 when negotiations commenced between the Board and Shell to purchase tail gas from the refinery at Shell Haven, near Tilbury on the Thames Estuary. A ten-year agreement was signed in June 1956, under which Shell agreed to supply at least 25 million therms of refinery gas (which was a rich gas, of about CV1500) each year to a specially constructed catalytic reforming plant at Romford. The Board planned a 17-mile high-pressure main to Romford, built by William Press and Sons Ltd, and in May 1958 the first unit of the plant was brought into operation. Hitherto, Romford had been among the Board's smaller works and had been capable of producing a maximum output of only some 5 m. cu ft gas/day. The new plant had a capacity of about 50 m. cu ft gas/day and Romford suddenly became second only to Beckton among the Board's gas stations, and hence one of the major gas producing works in the country.

During 1958 also, agreement was reached with the Mobil Oil Company to supply tail gas from Britain's newest refinery at Coryton, also to Romford. The first deliveries (guaranteed at 12 million therms annually) were received in 1959 and in that year the contracted supplies from Shell were increased to 30 million therms. But, in fact, the Board's purchases of these refinery gases always exceeded the guarantees: in 1960–61, 64 million therms were bought from Shell Haven and Coryton; in 1961–62, 74 million; and in 1962–63, 81 million. Most were reformed at Romford, but in 1959 a 6.5-mile spur from the Romford–Shell Haven main was linked to Beckton and reforming there began for the first time.

Side by side with the use of tail gases from refineries, North Thames engineers also investigated the possibilities of new types of direct oil gasification. This resulted in a new catalytic reforming process for liquid petroleum gas, LPG (butane/propane), and in 1961 another major step was taken when negotiations with Esso resulted in an agreement for the Board to buy liquid petroleum gas from the Esso Fawley refinery near Southampton. A large plant was constructed at Southall to convert the fuel into town gas and a 70-mile pipeline was laid to the refinery. This was a completely new type of plant devised by the Board's engineers, although similar processes were being developed independently. Unlike the Segas and Onia-Gegi processes, which were cyclical, the Southall reforming plant was continuous. Cyclic production was necessary where carbon affected the efficiency of the catalyst. Where no carbon was produced (generally with such feedstocks as liquid petroleum gas, naphtha or methane) the process could be continuous. The principal advantage of the latter was that such plants operated at high pressures, whereas cyclic reformers functioned at low pressures. Continuous production could result in lower distribution costs if an adequate high-pressure system existed. The Southall plant encountered a number of teething troubles and the contractors were late in their delivery date, but it eventually came into operation in November 1963 and was the largest catalytic reforming plant for LPG in Europe. The Southall capacity then, 60 m. cu ft gas/day, was equivalent to some 10 per cent of the Board's total capacity.

Around 1960 the Board became increasingly concerned at the threat posed by the direct marketing of bottled liquid petroleum gas to industrial consumers by oil companies. Several Boards had already begun to supply LPG in bulk themselves, although North Thames was not among them. By 1963 the Board estimated that North Thames had lost industrial loads totalling some 2 million therms annually through industries switching from gas to LPG or choosing LPG rather than gas when changing from solid fuel. The threat was real but short-lived. From about 1963 the economics of manufacture moved against LPG and the promise of cheap natural gas soon removed the threat altogether.

We have stressed already that North Thames engineers were among the leaders in pioneering new oil-based technology, but research was

19 Southall's revolutionary new catalytic hydrocarbon reforming plant, with a capacity of 60 m. cu ft gas/day, 1963. The plant reformed LPG from the Esso refinery at Fawley.

being carried out on both a national and an international scale. ICI, Shell, BP, the Gas Council, other Boards, and many foreign chemical and gas concerns were contributing to the new technologies. Particularly significant was a development in 1963 when ICI and the Gas Council developed a successful process for lean gas manufacture from the steam reforming of naphtha. The principle here was similar to that employed by North Thames at Southall, but naphtha was cheap and readily available and the ICI process was not subject to many of the teething troubles which North Thames had experienced at Southall with its LPG reforming plant.

The new Southall works was just one part in a major expansion plan decided upon at the beginning of 1960. By this time the success of the refinery gas projects was assured and in a far-reaching review of long-term strategy the Board took the major decision to phase out coal carbonisation, and to develop oil-based manufacturing plant, which would be concentrated in large units. The new replacement Retort House No. 4, which came into operation at Fulham in 1962 – of a design similar to No. 3 Kensal Green – was the last carbonisation plant to be installed by the Board. The fruits of the policy were seen in 1963 with the opening not only of the Southall plant, which served the western and central areas, but also of further peak-load LPG plants at Beckton and Bromley.

Another significant development was the installation of a new naphtha continuous reforming plant, using the ICI process, at Bromley. This plant, producing a lean gas enriched with butane or methane, had a capacity of 80 m. cu ft gas/day and began operations in June 1964. Two months later a pilot Gas Council catalytic rich-gas plant (CRG), the first in the country, was completed at Bromley, based on research conducted both by North Thames and by the Gas Council's Midland Research Station. The success of this plant led to the installation of larger works using this process at Bromley and Southall (each of 30 m. cu ft gas/day), and further new plants at Slough (80 m. cu ft gas/day) and Romford (120 m. cu ft gas/day) in 1967 also used the process as an integral part of their operations.

In all, various types of catalytic reforming plants were brought into operation at seven of the Board's works. In 1967 alone, plant with a capacity of 378 m. cu ft gas/day was installed, one-third of this at Romford, which represented half of the total capacity of North Thames Gas Board. In this year, oil-based gas output exceeded coal-based output for the first time and by 1968 some 85 per cent of all gas made by North Thames was produced from oil gasification and oil reforming plants. Among many other additions to reforming capacity at the time was another giant natural gas reforming plant at Beckton, brought into service in 1968, with a capacity of 100 m. cu ft gas/day. A similar natural gas reforming plant (capacity 50 m. cu ft gas/day) began operations at Southall during the same year. Both plants operated initially on LPG until natural gas from the North Sea became available. Yet another big plant was brought into operation at Southall in November 1968. This was a natural gas reforming plant with an output of 50 m. cu ft gas/day. During its first winter it similarly operated on LPG, until the following year when North Sea gas could be used.

By the mid-1960s the Board was facing increasingly urgent distributional problems as output, especially from the new continuous reforming plants, soared to meet the rising demand. To safeguard supplies to London it became essential to link the new plants in the east and west of the region with a new high-pressure distribution system, and during 1965 a major extension to the distribution was authorised. This was the 50-mile, 30-inch steel North Orbital high-pressure pipeline, linking Romford in the east with Staines and Slough in the west. To avoid central London, the pipeline was routed to the north of the Board's area, running for most of its length through the area of the Eastern Gas Board. Great care was taken to disturb the environment as little as possible; for example, when the pipe was laid through Epping Forest, oaks, elms, birches, sycamores and other trees were removed for storage in a peat mulch and then replaced. The pipeline was completed at the end of 1966 and gave a greatly improved and more rational system as the main centres of production were shifted away from former centres like Beckton.

The move to oil production brought with it the gradual cessation of coal carbonisation and after the mid-1960s the process of change gathered considerable pace, as Tables 4.1 and 4.2 illustrate. The initial measures of rationalisation and integration carried out by the Board in its early years of operation had brought one spate of closures; now the new technological conditions brought another. Elsewhere, coal carbonisation plant was phased out and the remaining works eventually, by 1970, relied solely on oil-based feedstocks for the manufacture of town gas. Between 1959 and 1965 coal carbonisation ceased at Ascot, Brentford, High Wycombe, Slough, Southall, and Mill Hill, and in the winter of 1959–60 four of Beckton's eight vertical retort houses were dispensed with. The closure of a works meant the ending of a chapter of history, and each event, inevitable as it was, was a sad occasion. Each works could trace its history back to the days of Queen Victoria or even earlier. For example, the Brentford Works, although redesigned and rebuilt in 1935, had a continuous history stretching back to 1821. The

Table 4.1   Gas capacity at North Thames 1952–69, capacity (m. cu ft gas/day) at 31 March

	1952	1961	1969
Coal carbonising plant	237.76	219.75	35.6
CWG	137.84	162.50	86.0
Reforming plant (including oil gasification)	3.00	55.20	816.4
Totals	378.60	427.45	938.0

Source: North Thames Gas.

Table 4.2   Gas feedstocks used by North Thames, 1960–69

	1960–61	1964–65	1965–66	1967–68	1968–69
Coal carbonised (m. tons)	3.7	3.0	2.5	1.7	0.9
Coke in CWG (000s tons)	314.4	213.5	193.0	176.2	93.8
Refinery gas (m. therms)	62.9	69.1	67.5	59.9	48.0
Imported natural gas (m. therms)	–	25.2	65.3	136.1	223.3
Light distillate in refining plant (000s tons)	4.0	130.1	160.2	376.2	595.8
LPG (000s tons)	–	174.6	228.9	264.1	214.7

Source: North Thames Gas.

Brentford Gas Company was one of London's earliest gas companies and it had contributed an unusual number of high-calibre staff who reached top positions with the Gas Light & Coke Company and with the North Thames Gas Board. The riverside location of the 8.5 acre works and its position on both sides of Brentford High Street had also made the station a prominent landmark.

In 1967, gas-making at Poplar and Stratford ceased. The Poplar Station had been built by the Commercial Gas Company in 1878. The first Joint-Engineers were a father and son team named Jones, the great-grandfather and grandfather of Sir Henry Jones, Chairman of the Gas Council at the time of the works' closure. The Stratford Works was even older, dating from 1845, and the only works of the West Ham Gas Company which had joined the Gas Light & Coke Company in 1910.

The series of closures brought a steady diminution in the Board's employment of manual labour. The extent of the decline was spectacular, as the data in Table 4.3 show. At the beginning of the 1960s the Board's works still employed some 8000 manual operatives and the total number of manual grade employees was around 15 000. These numbers still bore comparison with the vesting day totals when, it will be recalled, the works had employed about 10 000 operatives and the entire manual labour force totalled some 18 000. But by the beginning of the 1970s the situation had been transformed. In 1971, for example, North Thames employed a total of only some 7000 manual workers, little more than 1000 of them at the gas stations. The proportion of manual employees in the work-force, which had stood at about 75 per cent in 1949 and 1959, slumped, and in 1971 the proportion was only 43 per cent. By contrast, the number of office staff rose both absolutely and relatively in the 1960s. A consequence was the growing proportion of female employees among the North Thames work-force. In 1959 only 6 per cent had been female, but by 1971 the figure had risen to 21 per cent.

Table 4.3   North Thames personnel, 1956–71 (numbers at 31 March)

	1956	1959	1968	1971
Total employees	24848	24086	19448	16431
Production operatives	9316	8838	4626	1396
Appliance fitting and servicing	3561	3650	3264	3285
Distribution operatives	1814	1856	580	572
Consumer services and collection of arrears	4007	4021	4994	6185
Administration and general services	770	754	1114	1226
By-product operatives	1101	1073	156	14

Source: North Thames Gas.

Every works closure was made with the fullest consultation with the unions concerned and through the relevant consultative committees. In fact, most of the job losses were achieved through natural wastage and retirement, and where possible employees were offered jobs at other of the Board's works. Retraining became a major preoccupation, and a large number of former production workers beame fitters or trained for other suitable occupations. During 1968 the Board started special retraining courses at Stratford Training Centre for men displaced from the defunct works. Among the first to benefit were groups from the Beckton and Southall Products Works, who were retrained as conversion fitters.

The amicable and mutually beneficial way in which unions and management co-operated in the introduction of the revolutionary technological advances of these years was a major achievement and a striking contrast to the industrial relations experience of so many other nationalised enterprises. It surely derived from the long tradition of good labour relations within the industry and was exemplified at North Thames when the Chairman, Deputy Chairman, Chief Engineer, Chief Accountant, Staff Controller, and other chief officers made a visit to the minute rural Ascot works in April 1963 to make the first announcements of the impending closure. A meeting was held to explain the decision to shop stewards and other representatives and to detail the steps the Board would take to find alternative employment for its employees or to negotiate compensation in case of redundancies. These meetings were repeated in each case of closure.

The 1950s and 1960s saw a steady erosion among many of North Thames top management as they were recruited by other Boards. A high proportion of the chairmen and deputy chairmen of the Area Boards were from North Thames and in this way North Thames made a not inconsiderable contribution to the running of the national gas industry. On the other hand, the outward flow could not but have its effect within the organisation. Almost without exception the Board, following the tradition of the Gas Light & Coke Company, was able to fill leading positions from within North Thames. Only very rarely was it necessary to look outside and, indeed, the weight of tradition was against it. The result was a gradual but perceptible undermining of the organisation, as the loss of able men at the top and their replacement within the organisation produced a weakening which stretched back to Divisional and District Offices. The problem was that total employment was not expanding, so that the intake of new blood was limited. The Board tended to become inbred and introspective, and in some ways, oddly, the traditions of the old Gas Light seemed even to harden in these years. Total employment had reached its peak of some 25 000 in the early 1950s, and thereafter, as we have seen, the spread of new technology at the gas stations and various measures of internal rationalisation and centralisation led to a steady fall. Even so, by the late 1960s, North Thames, by comparison with other Boards, was heavily overstaffed and this in turn became one of the dilemmas of the 1970s.

Another point which needs emphasis is the extent to which engineering considerations dominated North Thames in these years. Perhaps this was natural, for the unhappy market situation in the 1950s was seen very much as an engineering problem. For more than a decade development of new processes and plant of all kinds appeared to offer the only way to an assured future for the industry. Although not themselves engineers, both Milne-Watson and Johnson were fully supportive of their engineers and before 1967 four of the first five Deputy Chairmen were all former Chief Engineers. Falconer Birks was the first, a distinguished Chief Engineer of the Gas Light & Coke Company, who had started at Beckton as early as 1921. His successor in 1956 was the former Staff Controller, R. N. Bruce. Bruce did not have an engineering background, but when he left to become Chairman of the South Eastern Gas Board in 1959 he was replaced until 1962 by the Chief Engineer, J. Burns. Burns had long been a dominant personality at North Thames and one of the country's leading gas engineers. He had joined the Gas Light & Coke Company in 1929 and was closely associated with the various technical developments which revolutionised the gas industry during the 1950s and 1960s. In 1962 he was appointed Chairman of the Northern Gas Board, and the new Deputy Chairman at North Thames was J. A. Hepworth, who had begun at Beckton as a Junior Assistant Engineer at about the same time as Falconer Birks and who had succeeded Burns as Chief Engineer. When Hepworth retired in 1964 he was replaced by his successor as Chief Engineer, Leslie Clark, who also has begun his career with the Gas Light & Coke Company (and whose father had helped establish the first Watson House). Later, in 1967, Clark also went to the Northern Board and L. W. Smith, another pre-war Gas Light & Coke Company man and Chief Accountant for twelve years, became Deputy Chairman. In this year, E. J. Edwards, Chief Engineer since 1964 and who had begun his career under Thomas Hardie in the 1930s, was made a member of the Board.

These various appointments illustrate vividly the three points made already: the role of the engineers; the drafting of North Thames men to posts elsewhere; and the strength of the Gas Light tradition. From 1949 to 1975 North Thames did not have a Deputy Chairman who had not started with the Gas Light & Coke Company in the days of Sir David Milne-Watson, and this highlighted the very special 'family' characteristic of the Board, analogous perhaps to the Great Western Railway, which continued for so long after nationalisation. It highlights also the exceptional difficulties which 'outsiders' faced when they entered the Board's top management after 1970.

To return to the new technological developments, from the Board's point of view, oil-based gases were better in nearly every respect. Not only were the plants cheaper and quicker to build than equivalent carbonising plants but they were much cheaper to run, they used much less space, and working conditions, and hence labour recruitment, were much better. The quality of gas was also significantly improved, being virtually free of sulphur and containing very little toxic carbon monoxide. Indeed, the gas produced from LPG was, according to the Chief Engineer, 'the finest ever to enter the Board's grid', being, for the first time, both sulphur-free and non-toxic.

The reductions in costs were striking. The Southall LPG reforming plant was erected at a cost less than one-sixth that of an equivalent carbonising plant, while total maintenance and operating costs were one-third lower, since the plant used one-third less labour. The overwhelming case in favour of oil convinced even a Labour Government naturally anxious to protect the coal industry. A White Paper on Fuel Policy in 1965 stated that 'the Government is satisfied that the trend of the gas industry towards petroleum should be accepted' and ruled out special measures to preserve the gasification of coal. The data in Table 4.4 illustrate clearly the cost advantage the new processes possessed over traditional methods.

To these revolutionary new processes the North Thames Gas Board added a still more imaginative project. This was the import of natural gas (methane) in liquefied form in special tankers to specially constructed terminals at Canvey Island. The scheme was very much a North Thames initiative and the successful arrival of the first cargo was a triumph for the Board's officers and especially for Michael Milne-Watson.

The practicability of importing liquid natural gas (LNG) on a

Table 4.4   Cost of gas by various processes, 1964

Process	Main feedstock	Cost (d. per therm)	
		(a) load factor 65%	(b) load factor 45%
Continuous vertical retorts	Coal	13.89	18.04
CWG	Coke	12.23	13.45
Continuous reforming	LPG	9.51	10.33
Gas Council rich	Naphtha	6.69	7.27
Continuous reforming	Methane	9.04	9.52

Source: North Thames Gas.

commercial scale was demonstrated on 20 February 1959 when, on a cold foggy winter's day, a specially converted ship, *Methane Pioneer*, docked at Canvey Island. The ship had carried 2000 tons of Texan natural gas in liquid form – at minus 258°F – from Lake Charles in Louisiana to the special installations and storage tanks at Canvey constructed for the Gas Council by the Board. From Canvey the liquefied gas was regasified and pumped to Romford through a spur added to the existing Shell Haven and Coryton link, there to be transformed into town gas for the Board's grid. Further experimental voyages followed and by April 1960 the *Methane Pioneer* had landed six more cargoes of gas, equivalent to 6 million therms. This imaginative project naturally enough created a great deal of public interest and headlines such as 'Londoners to cook by Texas gas' appeared in the newspapers. However, a further five years' development was necessary before the Gas Council was ready to begin the importation of liquid methane on a full commercial scale.

The story of the liquid methane project, and the Board's involvement, already had a lengthy history when the *Methane Pioneer* first docked. It was in July 1954 that a chance meeting occurred between Gordon Roche, the Managing Director of the engineering contractors William Press, and W. Illiffe, from the International Bank for Reconstruction and Development. The meeting occurred on board the *Queen Elizabeth*, as the ship was bound for London. Illiffe was carrying a report of the Bank's appraisal of a project for shipping liquefied natural gas·which had been developed in the United States. The originators of this scheme were William Wood Prince, Chairman of the Union Stockyards in Chicago, who was interested in obtaining cheap fuel for refrigeration, and W. S. Morrison, who had developed a technique for shipping methane in liquefied form. In fact, the American project was never brought to fruition, since the threat of cheaper fuel was sufficient for Wood Prince's suppliers to lower their charges. None the less, the project seemed to have huge potential as a way of making the increasing supplies of natural gas – much of it simply being flared off at oil wells – available; hence the interest of the International Bank for Reconstruction and Development.

Roche was able to put Illiffe in contact with Michael Milne-Watson and also with Kenneth Hutchison, then Chairman of the South Eastern Board. Indeed, meetings were arranged over the ship's radio. Milne-Watson turned the scheme over to Burns and Leslie Clark and they reported that the project deserved following up. It speaks much for the vision of these engineers and also of Milne-Watson and Hutchison that they were prepared to consider the scheme at a time when few thought of a future for the gas industry in terms other than of coal carbonisation. It was especially important that both Hutchison, with his scientific background, and Milne-Watson, as Chairman of the biggest of the Boards and with his pre-eminent standing within the industry, should jointly have backed the project. As a result, the Gas Council and the Ministry of Fuel and Power gave their approval for a more detailed examination. Leslie Clark, then the Board's Development Engineer, paid two visits to the United States before the end of 1954 and, along with representatives from William Press, met Morrison and Wood Prince and began investigations into the feasibility of the scheme. It appeared that liquid methane could be landed at Canvey for about 7*d*. a therm, and the prospects for long-term supplies (thought at that stage to come from the Middle East) were good. In the light of these preliminary findings the Gas Council approved further and more detailed investigations.

The succeeding years saw the plans gradually brought to fruition. The steps involved were many and included the establishment in 1955 in the United States of a company, the Constock Liquid Methane Corporation, to handle the American side of the project. During the summer of 1955 the offer of an assured supply of gas from Venezuela had been obtained, and at the end of the year Sir Harold Smith, Chairman of the Gas Council, met Wood Prince and confirmed the interest of the Gas Council. He confirmed also that the North Thames Gas Board would act as agent for the Council in the development of the project.

By the end of 1957 the scheme was well under way. During the year a tanker, *Normati*, was purchased by the Constock Liquid Methane Corporation for conversion and the North Thames Gas Board, in the light of all the information gathered previously (including a visit to Russia by Leslie Clark and others to see an LNG plant in operation), felt able to give final authorisation, with the approval of the Gas Council and the Ministry of Power. Denis Rooke, Development Engineer at the South Eastern Gas Board, was seconded to the Gas Council to work with Leslie Clark on the technical problems involved and both men spent a great deal of time in the United States during 1958 checking on the trials and performance of the ship, now renamed *Methane Pioneer*. By January 1959 all was ready. A meeting of leading officials was held at Lake Charles, the participants including Milne-Watson, Hutchison, Burns and Wood Prince, and they were able to see and to examine the preparations which had been made to transform the fuel. And on 30 January the first cargo of liquid methane left Lake Charles, with Denis Rooke, representing the Gas Council, on board. In the meantime, the North Thames Gas Board had constructed two aluminium 1000-ton storage tanks and a gasification unit at Canvey to receive the methane, and the pipeline link to the Romford Works had been built.

The immediate aftermath of the arrival of the *Methane Pioneer* on

20 The *Methane Pioneer* arrives on a misty morning at Canvey Island after her historic first journey from Texas, 20 February 1959.

Friday, 20 February 1959 was not particularly auspicious. Against the wishes of the Board's Chief Engineer it was decided to delay unloading the cargo over the weekend, while the passengers and crew took a well-earned rest after a cramped and uncomfortable crossing. That Friday night, despite the strictest safety and security precautions, a major fire broke out in the storage terminal, which resulted in considerable damage and a delay of a week in unloading the precious cargo. The Board was fortunate to be able to keep publicity about the event to a minimum, because public fear about the dangers of shipping liquid methane, albeit unfounded, was one of the ghosts the project was supposed to lay. In any event, the damage was repaired, the methane transferred to the Canvey storage tanks and, at the end of the month, the Romford Works became the first in the country to receive and to reform methane gas for mixing with ordinary town gas.

From this time onwards the thoughts of the gas industry turned increasingly towards natural gas, for also in 1959, a vast natural gas field was discovered in Holland at Gröningen. The possibility of gas and oil under the North Sea, long suspected, now became a probability. A

21 The first connection on the ship-to-shore pipeline for the *Methane Pioneer*, February 1959. The connection is being made by Denis Rooke, now Chairman of the British Gas Corporation.

number of consortia were formed, one of which included the Gas
Council. The first seismic surveys were taken in 1962. In 1964 the
Continental Shelf Act vested in the Crown all the rights within the UK
sector of the North Sea and the Ministry of Power was enabled to grant
licences to explore for oil and gas in the area. The first licences for
exploration in the UK sector were granted in this year and drilling
commenced in December. On 21 September 1965 BP's drilling rig, *Sea
Gem*, made the first gas strike. Further major strikes followed in the
spring, among them the Gas Council – Amoco group from their *Mr
Louie* rig. This American rig, under the command of experienced Texan
drillers, made its first strike on 18 May 1966 and this find put the Gas
Council in a powerful bargaining position during subsequent negotiations over gas contracts. A list of the major discoveries is given in Table
4.5. By May 1967, sixteen wells out of a total of fifty or so drilled had
shown really significant quantities of natural gas, a phenomenal score
when judged by past drilling experience.

Table 4.5   North Sea gas discoveries, 1965–73

Field	Licensees	Date discovered	Production started
West Sole	BP	September 1965	March 1967
Leman Bank	Shell/Esso Amoco/British Gas Arpet, Mobil	April 1966	August 1968
Hewett	Arpet, Phillips	October 1966	July 1969
Indefatigable	Amoco/British Gas Shell/Esso	June 1966	October 1971
Viking	Conoco/BNDC	May 1968	July 1972
Pough	Amoco/British Gas	May 1968	October 1975
Forties	BP	October 1970	September 1977
Frigg (Norway)	Elf/Total	June 1971	September 1977
Frigg (UK)	Elf/Total	May 1972	September 1977
Pipec	Occidental	January 1973	November 1978

Sources: R. Cassidy, *Gas: Natural Energy* (London, Frederick Muller, 1979) p. 54,
and *Annual Reports*, Gas Council and British Gas Corporation.

The success of the *Methane Pioneer* experiment was firmly established
by 1960 and in March of that year the ship made her seventh and final
voyage to Canvey. The Gas Council now went ahead with plans for a
large-scale and more permanent scheme. The expected supplies of
Venezuelan gas did not materialise and it was decided in 1961 to take
supplies from a company set up in Algeria to exploit new-found gas and
oil reserves in the Sahara. The gas came from the Hassi Er R'Mel field
and through a 295-mile pipeline which was laid to the port of Arzew,
where a liquefaction plant and other installations were constructed. In

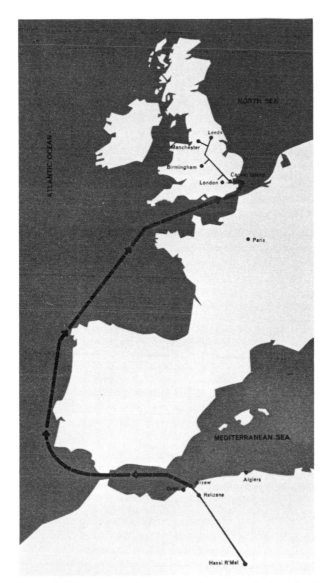

Figure 4.1   From October 1964 Algerian methane reached eight Area Boards through the specially laid 'methane grid', a 200-mile main and a further 150 miles of branch lines. But first the methane had to journey by a 295-mile pipeline from its source to the liquefaction plant at Port Arzew, there to be carried in liquid form by tanker to the Canvey Island methane terminal for regasification. The quantity so received amounted annually to about 10 per cent of Britain's total gas requirements.

May 1961 a British team, which included Sir Henry Jones (Chairman of the Gas Council), Milne-Watson and Leslie Clark, visited Hassi Er R'Mel and discussed the terms of an agreement with French and Algerian representatives. On 25 May Milne-Watson, as the leading figure in the original plan, was given the honour of initialling a note of agreement and in November 1961 the British Government gave its approval. So, in December 1961, the formal agreements were signed. The following year work was begun on the construction in Britain of two tankers specially designed for the Gas Council, each with a capacity of about 12 000 tons. The first, the *Methane Princess*, was launched in June 1963 and the second, the *Methane Progress*, a year later. The *Methane Princess* loaded her first cargo at Arzew on 7 October 1964 and the *Methane Progress* followed sixteen days later.

Meanwhile, the North Thames Gas Board, acting for the Gas Council, had designed and erected a large methane terminal at Canvey to receive the methane. This included a 750ft jetty carrying the insulated pipelines, which took the liquid methane to five large storage tanks, each of 4000 tons and storing the methane at minus 258°F (in liquid form occupying 1/600th of its volume as a gas). From Canvey, after regasification, the gas could be pumped to eight Area Boards through the entirely new high-pressure grid constructed by the Gas Council. Work had begun on this grid in 1962, the 200-mile 18-inch main running from Canvey to Leeds, with a further 150 miles to branches. For North Thames the delivery point was Bromley and the Board immediately took its full allocation of methane to the Romford reforming plant. The scale of the operation was vast. With a journey time of about five days, the two ships could each make about sixty round trips a year, bringing no less than 700 000 tons of liquefied methane. This represented about 354 million therms, not far short of the North Thames Gas Board's entire capacity in the early 1950s, and some 10 per cent of the nation's entire gas consumption in the early 1960s. Later, in 1966, the Gas Council drew up plans for special underground storage reservoirs for liquefied gas at Canvey. Four enormous tanks, each holding 21 000 tons of liquid methane, were constructed during the following two years.

The arrival of the *Methane Princess* on 12 October 1964 was thus a historic day not only for the Board – which had from the outset been linked with the scheme and had developed the Canvey terminal on North Thames territory for the Gas Council – but also for Britain's gas industry itself. It was sad for the Board that Michael Milne-Watson's tenure as Chairman did not quite extend to the culmination of this scheme, which he had been so instrumental in initiating; Milne-Watson had relinquished the Chairmanship in April of that year in order to take up an appointment with the nationalised steel industry.

Abundant supplies of high-quality gas at considerably lower costs made possible by the new oil processes and imported natural gas opened a new chapter for North Thames. After 1959, confidence slowly returned and a tone of optimism began to pervade the Annual Reports and other publications by the Board, and also the conference speeches made by the principal officers. From this time until the natural gas era at the end of the 1960s, each succeeding year brought mounting sales of gas appliances and growing activity in the marketing and commercial sections of operations.

Clearly the turnaround in fortunes was closely associated with the technological advances which made gas increasingly competitive with other fuels. Table 4.6 shows that domestic gas prices were held stable for long periods between 1959 and 1970, yet this was a time when prices for other fuels grew markedly. Between 1962 and the end of 1968 the average domestic electricity tariff rose by 45 per cent, prices of coal and coke by 33 per cent and fuel oil by a similar figure. Increases in the price of gas, amounting to some 20 per cent, were well below the average retail price index level, which grew at about 30 per cent. The impact of the new technology can be seen from the fact that, whereas the average cost of coal-gas to the Board (after deducting coke sales) was around 12*d.* to 15*d.* a therm in 1960, gas from oil-based processes cost about 7*d.* to 8*d.* a therm. And gas from methane, when it arrived in 1964, was available at about 8*d.* a therm.

Table 4.6   Domestic gas tariffs (credit quarterly), 1960–71

Date	(*d. per therm*)
1 Aug 1960	25.35 (+ 7*s.* primary charge)
1 Aug 1965	27.00 (+ 10*s.* 3*d.* standing charge)
1 April 1968	29.00[1] (+ 13*s.* standing charge)
1 Jan 1971	31.92[1] (+ 26*s.* standing charge)

[1]Natural gas consumers paid ½*d.* per therm less.
Source: North Thames Gas.

Between 1957 and 1968 it was necessary to increase the flat rate tariff only once, while in 1959 a very significant step could be undertaken with the introduction of a new promotional two-part tariff. This domestic and hot water tariff, as it was called (although it applied to all kinds of gas consumption), was specifically designed to help large domestic consumers and so to encourage sales of central heating boilers. After an initial standing charge (£3 a quarter), consumers paid only at the rate of 16*d.* a therm, so that a consumer using some 300 therms a year or more would pay less than hitherto. Comparison of costs between rival fuels is, of course, beset with difficulties, but in 1961 the North Thames Gas Board could claim that for a given amount of heat from a space heater, gas was cheaper than either electricity or coal. In the same year the independent Institution of Heating and Ventilating Engineers reported that gas central heating from an average-sized boiler (45000 BTU per hour) was cheaper than a comparable oil installation because of lower service and installation charges, although the actual running costs of gas were about 20 per cent a year higher.

A further significant tariff change was made in August 1960. For the first time the Board introduced a primary, or standing, charge, in addition to the flat rate for all customers. Under this tariff the flat rate was reduced slightly and a 7s. quarterly charge introduced. The importance of the revision was that North Thames could now develop a more rational tariff structure, based on the actual cost of supplying gas to consumers.

There were a number of other factors which helped North Thames's revival at about this period. One was the continued spread of smokeless zones in London. Another was help from the Chancellor, for purchase tax on many gas appliances was reduced substantially in April 1958: the rate on room heaters, refrigerators, washing machines and water-heaters fell from 60 per cent to 30 per cent, and the following year the rate was further lowered to 25 per cent. Hire-purchase terms were also eased considerably. From 1962 electricity tariffs were gradually rational-ised and revised, with a policy of higher peak-rate charges and more emphasis on cheaper off-peak rates. There was also a decisive shift away from the old-fashioned coal fire, which still dominated the domestic heating market in 1960. In ever-increasing numbers housewives de-serted the dirty and inconvenient fuel, and the growing numbers of flat dwellers found in the Board's central areas were especially likely to switch to gas or electricity. No doubt rising coal prices, coupled with uncertain quality and deliveries, hastened the change. During the arctic winter of 1962–63, the worst for two centuries, there were numerous coal shortages in the Board's territory. London's gas supplies, despite the severest of demands, never failed. North Thames broke all its previous records. Until now the largest output reached on a single day had been on 1 December 1952, when output stood at 330 m. cu ft (passing the 300 m. cu ft barrier for the first time). But on 21 January 1963, after a succession of new records, no less than 430.3 m. cu ft was supplied.

The expansion of the space heating load was gained largely at the expense of coal. In the early 1960s the Board estimated that some 70 per cent of its sales of space heaters was to replace coal fires and a further 10 per cent to replace oil heaters. The importance of this load in the expansion of the 1960s can scarcely be exaggerated, as Table 4.7 indicates. Year by year domestic sales outstripped industrial and commercial sales, so that the proportion sold to domestic markets,

22 Fulham Works during the 'arctic winter' of 1962–63. All previous output and delivery records were broken during the prolonged weeks of freezing temperatures.

which had declined during the 1950s, now rose steadily. In all, domestic sales rose from 53 per cent of the total in 1961–62 to 67 per cent in 1968–69. Credit customers accounted for a growing share of sales in these years, reflecting the success of the promotional two-part tariffs. In 1961–62 credit consumers had taken only 23 per cent of total sales, compared with 30 per cent sold to customers with coin meters. But in 1968–69 prepayment consumers accounted for only 22 per cent of sales, compared with just 45 per cent sold to credit customers. By contrast with domestic sales, industrial sales were at this time stagnant, for gas could not compete effectively with oil in this market. Nearly all the growing domestic load was for space heating, both central heating and individual space heaters. The cooking, refrigerator and separate water heating

Table 4.7   Appliance sales, 1954–71 (000s)

	1954–55	1959–60	1964–65	1970–71
Refrigerators	6.0	25.0	16.9	5.8
Cookers	149.2	138.5	113.6	102.1
Water-heaters	64.6	44.6	42.2	19.8
Central heating boilers	–	0.3	21.6	36.9
Warm air units	–	0.2	6.9	9.5
Space heaters	10.1	35.0	97.4	90.2

Source: North Thames Gas.

loads were stagnant and the significance of space heating to the Board can readily be appreciated. It will be recalled that in 1960 the average annual consumption per domestic consumer was about 115 therms. This was not far above the average annual consumption of a living-room gas fire (about 100 therms), so that the purchase of a new gas fire could well double a consumer's consumption. The growth of room heaters was substantial; sales of little more than 10 000 in 1957–58 leapt fourfold to around 42 000 in 1961–62 and the following year topped 73 000.

More striking still was the impact of central heating. Domestic central heating sales were almost entirely a product of the post-1959 era. In the year 1957–58 only 21 warm air units and 134 central heating boilers were sold. By 1962–63 some 2700 of the former and 9400 of the latter were sold. The average size boiler now consumed some 700 therms a year, and central heating sales therefore made a dramatic contribution to the growth of the domestic load. In 1963–64 the Board sold about 19 000 central heating units of all kinds (a 60 per cent increase on the previous year), 103 000 space heaters (a 41 per cent rise) and 108 000 cookers (an 8 per cent rise). The load from the central heating sales alone was greater than that for the space heaters and cookers combined, and by 1967–68, on the verge of the natural gas era, central heating was accounting for over three-quarters of all new business. Table 4.8 shows how growing domestic sales were concentrated among credit customers, and it illustrates, too, how dramatic was the change in the commercial fortunes of North Thames during the 1960s.

The leap in business could not have been achieved without a sufficient number of attractively priced and efficient appliances, or without corresponding effort from the Board's selling staff. These years saw a number of significant improvements in gas appliances, and the research expertise of Watson House proved invaluable in supporting the manufacturers. A big step was the development of convector gas fires. The first, the Port Royal, was introduced in 1954 by the firm Bratt Colbran. At that time the average thermal efficiency of the normal radiant gas fire was less than 50 per cent, but the new fire had an

Table 4.8   Growth in gas sales, 1950–71 (million therms)

	1950–51	1959 60	1963–64	1970–71
Domestic credit	82.5	83.2	124.5	374.8
Domestic prepayment	137.7	120.0	133.0	130.8
Total domestic	220.2	203.2	257.5	505.6
Industrial	68.1	78.9	76.2	107.0
Commercial	73.2	92.0	107.7	159.3
Public lighting	5.6	2.7	1.1	0.3
Total sales	367.1	376.8	442.5	772.2
Customers (000s)	1782	1897	1902	1923
Average domestic consumption (therms)	133	115	144	279
Average per credit customer (therms)	160	150	202	439
Average per prepayment customer (therms)	101	101	114	136

Source: North Thames Gas.

efficiency of 57 per cent. For the first time a gas fire (soon termed 'space heater' by the industry) could give adequate heat at reasonable cost in a living-room. The 'Gas Miser' heater, launched in 1956 by Cannon Industries, proved particularly popular, and by 1959 new models of convector heaters regularly achieved a thermal efficiency of 60 per cent to 64 per cent. The Crystalglow, in 1962, had an efficiency of 72 per cent. An outstanding model of the period was Flavel's elegant Debonair, with its then revolutionary mahogany frame. Between 1961, when the model was introduced, and early 1965, over half a million Debonairs were sold, and other manufacturers began to produce similar attractive designs. These various improvements helped the gas fire climb the social scale and came at just the moment when so many potential customers were turning from solid fuel for heating. In 1962 the Board estimated that four in five of the space heaters it sold went into living-rooms, compared with only one in two in 1960.

The growth of central heating was ultimately even more influential in its effect on loads. During the early 1960s, in the wake of the new domestic tariff, manufacturers increasingly turned their attention to domestic central heating needs. A feature of the period was the introduction of 'packages', with Board, manufacturers, and installers combining to offer a boiler, radiators, and installation for a standard fixed price. An example was the 'International Gas-Pak' with a boiler and five radiators, promoted in 1963 for £199.10s. The Board also promoted various low-interest loan schemes to encourage sales, and in 1962 introduced 'budget billing' to help householders spread payments throughout the year. Naturally, the growing number of heating appliances brought huge new peak demands in the cold winter months. In the winter of 1965–66 the Board surpassed a production level of 500 m. cu ft gas/day for the first time and the then record of 556.9 m. cu ft was sent out on 19 January. Two years later the 600 m. cu ft level was passed, 660.1 m. cu ft being produced on 11 January 1968.

Reflecting the Board's revived fortunes was an increasingly vigorous marketing effort. The Board's own Market Survey Department under Stirling Everard had noted in 1959 that new living styles were producing new heating needs. The growing number of working women meant houses were empty throughout the day. In the evening the need was for speed; speed to heat water, to heat living rooms, to produce a meal. The Gas Council's 'High Speed Gas' campaign, launched in 1962, caught this theme exactly and helped in the transformation of the industry's image which was already taking place as new technological developments captured the public imagination. The previous year, 1961, the North Thames Gas Board had also introduced a new style of advertising. These advertisements featured 'Dotty', a thoroughly modern young lady, 'dotty about gas'. The idea was created by the Board's advertising agents, W. S. Crawford Ltd, in order to bring a more up-to-date image to gas, and it marked the beginning of Mr Therm's slow decline.

The new era for gas was marked also by a new era for the Board's commercial organisation. The change was heralded in 1959 with the departure of S. G. Aberdein, who retired as Commercial Manager after sixteen years in that post with the Gas Light & Coke Company and with the Board. His career had started with the Brentford Gas Company as long ago as 1914 and he became a dominating figure on the commercial and marketing side of the Board's activities. His particular achievement was to organise and co-ordinate the sales and service side of the Divisions, and he controlled the Divisions in a manner which inspired awe and respect rather than affection. Aberdein's successor was T. V. Garrud, hitherto Controller of Services, who had started as one of the Gas Light & Coke Company's early apprentices. But more significant was the creation of the new post of Sales Manager, filled by J. A. Buckley. Buckley, another Gas Light man, already had a wide commercial experience, having been Divisional Manager of the Eastern Division for four years, and he was well equipped to carry the Board's sales organisation into the new era of expansion and aggressive marketing which followed. He succeeded Garrud as Commercial Manager in 1962, a year which saw A. I. D. Frith appointed to the new post of Sales Promotion Manager. Buckley and Frith were driving forces in the various promotional and sales campaigns which marked these years. In 1964 Buckley received the distinction of becoming the first full-

time 'executive' to be appointed by the Board. He left in 1966 on
becoming Deputy Chairman of the East Midlands Gas Board, and the
following year he became Chairman in succession to A. F. Hetherington, who went to the Gas Council as Deputy Chairman. The new
Commercial Manager was Paul Rhodes, who had been Chief Service
Manager from 1961. Later, both Buckley and Frith also joined the Gas
Council as part of the 1968 reorganisation.

Reading through the various issues of *News, Thames Gas* and other
publications by the Board at this time it is impossible not to capture
something of the excitement, which stood in such stark contrast to the
dismal 1950s. During 1962 the Commercial Department accepted a
target of doubling the domestic load in ten years, an average annual
increase of 7.2 per cent. At the time this seemed ambitious, but
expanding sales soon showed the target to be conservative. In the
event, domestic sales ran from 248 million therms in 1962–63 to 600
million therms ten years later, 40 per cent more than envisaged, and
Table 4.9 shows the year-by-year growth rates achieved in these
expansive years. New technology, mounting appliance sales, increasing
production records, sales promotions and advertising campaigns all
coincided and reinforced each other. Optimism was certainly the
keynote at the Board's first Sales and Service Conference held in 1962,
addressed by the Chairman, Deputy Chairman and Commercial
Manager. Selling through the Board's ninety or so showrooms was
stimulated by a programme of modernisation, and between 1961 and
1963 over thirty showrooms were modernised. At the same time a
programme of closing showrooms in declining shopping centres and
opening new ones in growing areas was begun. Co-operation with
authorised dealers, which had languished during the 1950s, was also
stepped up and many new authorised dealers were appointed. By the

Table 4.9   Growth in gas sales, 1961–71

Year	Percentage increase in sales
1960–61	3.0
1961–62	3.4
1962–63	9.4
1963–64	0.8
1964–65	7.7
1965–66	7.5
1966–67	5.1
1967–68	10.1
1968–69	9.6
1969–70	7.9
1970–71	10.1

Source: North Thames Gas.

23 This new showroom, opened in Victoria Street in 1964, was the first combined showroom and Heating Advisory Centre.

mid-1960s the authorised dealer network approached some 400 outlets, and they were accounting for business worth more than £2 million annually.

The competitiveness of gas heating at this time can be seen from Table 4.10. The cost calculations relate to the winter of 1963–64, and the table shows how relatively inexpensive gas heating with a convector fire had become, especially with the two-part tariff, by comparison with coal and electricity. With living-room heating some two-thirds more expensive by electricity (at the normal tariff) than by gas, it is small wonder that so many households in smokeless zones adopted gas heating.

Expansion was not without its problems, however. One problem was the pressure expanding sales put on other aspects of the Board's organisation, especially service of appliances, supplies of appliances and appliance parts, and customer accounts. The Board undertook numerous improvements, but the race between the growing volume of business and the necessary back-up facilities was an uneven one. During the conversion era after 1968 it was these crucial areas of customer service and accounts which were the most troubled and troublesome.

The Board was faced with several interconnected difficulties. The 1960s generally saw a rise in consumer awareness and growing scrutiny

Table 4.10 Relative costs of living-room heating by various methods, 1963–64

Fuel	Price per cwt. s. d.	Cost per therm (old pence)	Cost per useful therm (old pence)				
			Old type of open fire	Simple modern open fire (gas-ignited grate without convector)	Convector	Closed stove	Portable appliance
Coal (Gp. 1)	12.5	10.23	51.1	40.9	29.2	–	–
Coal (Gp. 3)	11.4	9.52	47.6	38.1	27.2	–	–
Coal (Gp. 5)	10.4	8.86	44.3	35.4	25.3	–	–
Gloco	13.6	11.56	–	31.3	25.7	–	–
Selected nuts	13.0	11.37	–	–	–	17.5	–
Cleanglow	16.0	13.45	53.8	36.4	29.9	20.7	–
Coalite	15.1	12.68	50.7	34.3	28.2	19.5	–
Warmco	14.10	12.47	49.9	33.7	27.7	19.2	–
Rexco	16.1	13.51	54.0	36.5	30.0	20.8	–
Sunbrite	12.0	10.50	–	–	–	16.2	–
Phurnacite	16.11	13.63	–	–	–	21.0	–
Gas (general two-part rate)[1]	–	19.44	–	–	29.0	–	21.6
Gas (standard rate)[1]	–	25.35	–	–	37.8	–	28.2
Electricity[1]	1.65d. per unit	48.36	–	–	48.4	–	48.4
Paraffin oil	2s. 3d. per gall.	17.64	–	–	–	–	19.6

[1] Excluding standing charge.
Source: North Thames Gas.

of the performance of nationalised industries. London, as always, had the largest and most concentrated, articulate and vocal group of customers in the country. Against this background, rising gas sales, especially to domestic consumers, brought their own problems. One was that the much greater variety and sophistication of appliances called for new, specialised skills from the fitting and maintenance forces. This was especially the case with central heating. And since the load was seasonal, demand for servicing too tended to be concentrated in the winter months. The steeply rising proportion of credit consumers meant increasing numbers of accounts handled by the billing offices. At the same time the growing use of the telephone put increasing pressure on these facilities.

One response taken by the Board was to set up new-style service centres with modern automatic telephone equipment, where the work of several outlying offices could be concentrated. The first of these was opened in July 1964 at Brentwood, and others followed at Kilburn, Hornsey, Hackney, and elsewhere. Seven of these Centralised Service Units, as they were called, were in operation by 1967. Each handled the service requirements of some 120 000 to 150 000 customers and each had a team of chargehand maintenance fitters specially trained at Watson House to look after central heating.

A further problem of expansion in the 1960s was that sales now threatened to outstrip the Board's available capacity and distribution network, notwithstanding continued investment in new plant and mains. Each year in this decade, as we have seen, domestic sales, with their heavy peak-load space heating requirements, grew faster than total sales. In some years the rate of increase was as high as 12 per cent or 13 per cent and this produced a peak-load increase of some 20 per cent to 25 per cent a year. Particularly acute was the growing inadequacy of storage and distribution facilities to store and pump sufficient gas at peak times. The new butane/air plants were a help, and another solution considered in 1965 was to raise the calorific value of town gas from 500 to 550, thereby raising the thermal capacity of a given volume of gas and so easing the pressure on capacity. In the same year a plan to link the North Thames and South Eastern grids was drawn up, to give mutual support at times of strain. But during the mid-1960s an even more attractive possibility was being considered – the use of 'neat' methane, with its high CV of about 1000.

5

The Canvey Experiment and the Beginnings of Conversion

In October 1965 the North Thames Gas Board, with the support of the Gas Council, took the decision to convert Canvey Island to natural gas. This was to be the first major conversion exercise in Britain and in the event it turned out to be the forerunner for the massive conversion programme of the entire country, which occupied the years until 1977.

In that same month, October 1965, British Petroleum made the first major strike of gas in the North Sea, discovering the West Sole Field, and in a very few months it became clear that the conversion of large areas of the country to natural gas was a commercial possibility.

As a result of the conjunction of these events, the Canvey project is often regarded as a pilot scheme by the Gas Council to gain experience for the country as a whole. In reality, however, the possibility of converting Canvey Island to natural gas had been under consideration by the North Thames Gas Board for some years, long before the prospect of North Sea gas had opened up and even before the arrival of the first commercial cargo of liquefied methane in October 1964. The initiative, it must be stressed, came entirely from the North Thames Gas Board itself and was based upon the economic circumstances of the Board. All the early planning stages envisaged the use of liquefied natural gas from Algeria and, indeed, when the conversion was completed in the summer of 1966 this was still a full year before the first North Sea gas came ashore at Easington.

The decision to convert Canvey to natural gas arose from the dilemma presented by the sudden growth of sales in the early 1960s, and was part and parcel of that series of initiatives undertaken by the Board's engineers to try to solve the dilemma of growing sales and growing peak loads against a background of limited capacity and storage and distribution facilities. An average expansion of 8 per cent annually and a peak-load increase of 14 per cent a year (in some areas where the central heating load was severe the peak-load increase was nearly 30 per cent annually) threatened the Board's ability to meet demand, as we have seen. A study undertaken in 1963 showed, alarmingly, that in only four or five years there was the prospect that the peak demand for gas would have doubled from the existing capacity to reach some 1000 m. cu ft gas/

24 Aerial view of Canvey Island methane terminal, 1965, built and operated for the gas industry by North Thames. The *Methane Princess* is discharging Algerian liquid methane.

day. R. S. Johnson informed the Chairmen's Meeting of the Gas Council in July 1964: 'If the anticipated increase in gas load materialises there will clearly be considerable problems in future years of manufacture, distribution and storage.' The cost of fully replacing the 10 000 miles of mains to meet the new demand would cost something in the order of £150 million, even if the existing shortages of labour and materials allowed the Board to contemplate this.

It was to consider these problems that Milne-Watson had convened a special subcommittee in 1963 to investigate the economics of future gas demand. This committee was attracted to the possibility of using 'neat' natural gas as a long-term solution. The great advantage of methane was that it had double the calorific value of town gas (about CV1000 compared with CV500). A given volume of methane thus had twice the thermal content of manufactured gas and the distributional capacity was accordingly doubled. Unfortunately, the properties of neat natural gas meant that it could not be consumed directly in appliances manufactured for town gas. Natural gas requires twice as much air as town gas to burn a given volume, otherwise a smoky and unstable flame is produced. This meant that any conversion programme would therefore involve modifying the burners of all existing appliances (unless consumers could be persuaded to buy new appliances) in order to use the new gas. The committee realised, of course, that conversion would be a complex matter, involving not only the physical procedure of converting customers' appliances but also the attendant technical, public relations, legal and many other problems. Accordingly it recommended an experimental conversion in an appropriate area, and Canvey was for many reasons the obvious candidate. The committee had also considered converting to gas of an intermediate calorific value (CV750), which had the attractions of possibly being usable in many existing appliances without further modification and of being easier to cope with in relation to the existing plant, should higher calorific gas be used over a wide proportion of the Board's area. But the obvious drawback was that an intermediate gas would not give the same savings in storage and distribution capacity and the committee was struck by the fact that in some American cities which had adopted this solution a later costly reconversion to gas of a higher calorific value had been necessary.

Committees and subcommittees rarely initiate completely new developments, of course: often they simply crystallise schemes already mooted and make recommendations on the basis of work already investigated. In the case of this 1963 committee the members were well aware that the conversion to natural gas had been undertaken, and was being undertaken, in several American and European cities. Moreover, Milne-Watson had considered using natural gas in this way for a long time. As early as 1961 he had asked Paul Rhodes to draft a plan for a pilot conversion of Canvey Island, an idea which at the time seemed visionary to the point of insanity. But Michael Milne-Watson had inherited his father's sixth sense of the direction the gas industry would take, and from 1963 the plan to convert Canvey Island took definite shape.

Canvey Island was an obvious and almost ideal place to experiment with methane. Natural gas would be on hand from the Gas Council's storage facilities at the terminals there. The distribution system within the island was relatively new, most of the 6600 customers being supplied by a high-pressure system with separate regulators outside each premises. Canvey Island lay wholly within the Board's area and it could easily be isolated from the rest of its distribution network. Moreover, there was little awkward industrial and commercial demand on the island, the great bulk of sales being to residential consumers. As a result of the decisions taken in 1963 the Board went ahead with a preliminary census of all the gas appliances in use on Canvey to get some idea of the total number, different models and ages of appliances. House-to-house calls were made throughout the island a:.. .:1e census was completed early in 1964. At the same time, co-operation was maintained with Watson House to work out the technical details of

converting so many appliances. It was realised, too, at an early stage
that public relations during conversion would be a crucial matter and it
was felt desirable to gain experience of this. All the technical problems of
conversion and the procedures to be adopted, as well as the various
legal issues involved, were all matters which needed thorough investi-
gation.

By April 1964 the Commercial Committee was able to receive an
important report from its subcommittee, which presented in detail the
case for converting all the appliances on Canvey Island to natural gas.
The preliminary census had discovered the existence of some 17 500
appliances and it was reckoned with the then existing state of
knowledge based on the work undertaken at Watson House that some
70 per cent of these could be converted and the rest would need
replacement. The report pointed out that the summer months, being a
slack period for heating demand and the time when gas fitters could be
spared from other areas, would be the best time for the conversion. It
was felt at this stage that the summer of 1965 would be ideal. The
necessary preparatory work would take at least six months and it was
expected that the total direct cost would be in the order of £15–£20 per
customer. Realising that the consumers of Canvey would be put to some
inconvenience, and fearing that natural gas would not perform very
satisfactorily in converted appliances, it was also felt that the Board
should reduce the price of gas as a special concession, and a reduction of
1*d.* a therm was suggested. The report discussed the practical problems
of conversion in some detail, setting out the important principle that the
bulk of conversion work for each household should be completed in one
day. Hence, the area should be split up into small units, and it was
thought for Canvey that a unit of about 300 houses and a work-force of
about 100 skilled fitters was appropriate.

The Board's own fitters rather than contractors were to be used 'in
order to establish a nucleus of staff trained in conversion work'. Clearly,
the Canvey scheme was always considered simply as a forerunner to a
wider development. The Board approved the scheme subject to a more
detailed idea of the costs involved and also considered that the Gas
Council should be involved. Although the project was thus conceived as
a North Thames exercise, carried out at North Thames's expense with
North Thames fitters in a North Thames area, it was none the less
thought appropriate to seek Gas Council approval, since it was fully
realised that the project had implications for the gas industry generally.
Moreover, the involvement of Watson House and the negotiations with
appliance manufacturers also made it advisable to work in conjunction
with the Gas Council. The Board's case to the Gas Council was
presented by the new Chairman, R. S. Johnson, who had taken over
from Michael Milne-Watson in April 1964.

Unexpectedly, however, the Gas Council was unenthusiastic about the scheme. At their meeting in August 1964 several members of the Commercial Policy Committee expressed strong reservations either about the desirability of using neat natural gas at all, or about the time schedule involved. The Council's Deputy Chairman, Sir Kenneth Hutchison, felt that there should be a preparatory period of some years, during which the majority of appliances incapable of burning methane could be phased out, as new appliances with appropriate burners were bought. Hutchison felt that the Canvey experiment would give a costly answer to a question which might never have to be raised, because it would be better to avoid converting any area at short notice. There was also a feeling in favour of possible conversion to an intermediate gas. As a result of this reception by the Gas Council, Johnson reluctantly agreed to suspend work on the Canvey scheme and for North Thames to examine instead the technical details of converting to intermediate gases which would work in conventional burners. This was the first time that the Council had determinedly opposed any major North Thames project and the episode might well have caused friction had Johnson not agreed to comply with the Council's suggestions.

This decision meant, of course, that an experiment at Canvey during 1965 was impracticable in view of the length of time needed to plan. During the ensuing months efforts were concentrated on investigating intermediate gases, but from experiments by Watson House it soon became clear that a gas suitable for existing burners would have to have a calorific value no higher than CV680 rather than 750. Given the load problem facing the North Thames Gas Board this was simply not sufficient. Moreover, gas consumption within the Board's area was continuing to rise all the time at ever-higher rates. The rate of growth was higher than foreseen in 1963 and was making a solution to the peak-load problem increasingly urgent. By September 1965 the Board was no nearer finding such a solution other than by conversion to natural gas. As a report in that month put it: 'Quite apart from the economics of the situation, there is the blunt fact that the type of thermal loads anticipated simply cannot be physically carried by the existing distribution system at a calorific value of 500, nor does it seem physically possible to relay larger mains in sufficient quantity in the time available.'

Accordingly, the Board decided once again on 17 September 1965, subject to consultation with the Gas Council, to go ahead with the Canvey experiment the following summer. The total direct cost was now estimated to be about £30 per customer, a total of some £180000. Together with additional costs incurred, such as the erection of buildings and training of workers, the final cost would be in the order of £250000. In informing the Chairman of the Gas Council, Sir Henry

Jones, of the Board's decision, the Deputy Chairman wrote: 'As far as this Board is concerned we believe this matter to be urgent, for with the present rate of load growth we feel that some relief on the distribution system by the use of higher CV gas will be essential. It is our intention that the methane supply to Canvey Island should be part of our quota from the Saharan scheme.' This time, with the prospect of North Sea gas opening up, the Gas Council made no objection. The Board began in earnest to put its plans for the conversion into operation. At a special meeting convened under the Commercial Manager, J. A. Buckley, in October the important decision was taken to go ahead with the project the following summer, beginning on 1 June, despite the lack of time. A special conversion team was set up under Paul Rhodes, the Chief Service Manager, and initial steps were put into operation immediately. Even at this early stage it was noted that 'Public Relations would play a vital part in the whole project and a preliminary plan should be formulated immediately. This sphere was of great interest to the Gas Council from a national point of view and the whole plan must be co-ordinated with them.' The earlier plan to lower the price of gas by 1d. a therm was continued and great pains were taken to keep the Consultative Council, the Canvey Urban District Council and other appropriate bodies informed about the Board's plans once these could be made public, which they were in December.

During the autumn months the various stages in the overall plans were developed. Contact was made at once with the appliance manufacturers to prepare conversion sets; a site for the Conversion Unit next to the Methane Terminal was agreed upon for stores, workshops, canteen and offices; and such matters as training of fitters and the operational details of conversion were also planned. In November, Paul Rhodes and Jimmy Greene, who had been appointed as Methane Conversion Officer, visited some thirty leading appliance manufacturers. Visits were also made by the Board's principal officers to West Germany and France in order to get firsthand experience of the conversion work undertaken there. Close liaison was, of course, maintained with Watson House and in January 1966 two Liaison Officers were appointed by Watson House to work with North Thames on the technical aspects of the Canvey conversion. Experiments on suitable conversion sets were conducted both at Watson House and at the Board's Stove Works at Harwood Terrace.

The general procedures adopted at Canvey became very largely a blueprint for national conversion. Canvey therefore occupies an important place in the history of conversion and the Board's experience was published in a major paper, 'Conversion at Canvey', which was delivered by Paul Rhodes to the Institution of Gas Engineers in November 1966 and which was awarded the Institution's Gold Medal.

In planning the Canvey project the conversion team decided to use the Board's own fitters rather than bring in outside contractors, just as the original plan had envisaged. The island was divided into 24 sectors, each containing about 350 houses, for which a large fitting force of some 250 men was assembled. The fitters came mainly from the Essex Division, although they were brought in from the adjacent Eastern and Northern Divisions, too, and they were all given a two-day training course in the theory and practice of conversion at Stratford or at Canvey. The procedure adopted was for the complete force to commence operations in a given sector at 8.00 a.m. on 'C Day'. The fitters were then divided into teams of ten, with a chargehand and a supervisor, and these teams remained together for the entire operation as it unfolded sector by sector in order to preserve continuity and to build up a sense of team spirit. The great bulk of conversions in a sector would take place on the first day, and a priority was to give householders some means of cooking by midday (often the hot-plate burners could be converted by this time, but not the grill or oven). Most appliances would be converted on the spot but more difficult cases would be taken to the special workshop at the Canvey Base Unit. Two days were then left for completing conversion and 'cleaning up', so that the fitting force could convert two sectors a week. This three-day cycle was deliberately employed to allow the fitters plenty of time for what was inevitably a novel and untried job, but by the second month of conversion the Board was able to operate a two-day cycle (three sectors a week). The few commercial and industrial installations on Canvey Island were handled separately by the Board's Industrial Division.

Prior to actual conversion, technical work of valving had to be undertaken, so that each sector could be isolated from town gas on 'C Day' and the existing town gas then burned off before the natural gas was let in. Many gas meters, especially prepayment meters, were unsuitable for natural gas, with its higher calorific value. These meters had to be altered or, in many cases, exchanged. All meters had to be fitted with governors, so that the new gas would flow at the appropriate operating pressure. Often, too, filters were fitted as a precaution against dust being discharged from the mains into the atmosphere. Contact with consumers was made by the special survey team, consisting of a Survey Manager and fifteen representatives. The house-to-house survey was a vital element in the plan. Not only did it produce the definitive list of appliances from which orders for conversion sets and estimates of work-load for the fitting force could be made, but it was also an opportunity for the 'selling out' of old appliances through attractive offers which were made to induce consumers to buy appliances already constructed to burn natural gas. North Thames agreed that on top of normal discounts there should be added the average conversion cost of the appliance. The resulting sales amounted to over 1600 appliances, more than 1000 of them gas cookers.

The survey was conducted between January and March 1966 and it revealed more than 30 000 domestic appliances to be converted, as Table 5.1 shows. Table 5.2 also illustrates the antiquity of many of these appliances and, in fact, the Unit's workshops had to carry out *ad hoc* conversions on over 6000 appliances (one-third of the total), rather than on the 1500 or so originally estimated.

Table 5.1   Appliances at Canvey

	Preliminary survey, 1964	Final survey, 1966
Meters	6600	7885
Cookers	6126	6959
Water-heaters	3750	4505
Refrigerators	1513	1927
Fires	1042	2696
Portable heaters	485	717
Radiators	179	392
Central heating boilers	143	545
Solid fuel grates	1088	911
Wash boilers	1270	1203
Washing machines	144	133
Boiling rings	346	446
Drying units	201	239
Pokers	425	597
Pistols	548	581
Miscellaneous	785	760
	24645	30496

Source: R. P. Rhodes, *Conversion at Canvey* (Institution of Gas Engineers, Communication 730, 1966).

Table 5.2   Age categories of appliances at Canvey, 1966 (%)

Appliance	Under 5 years	5–10 years	10–15 years	Over 15 years
Cookers[1]	30	17	12	22
Room heaters	48	14	3	35
Sink water-heaters	14	40	1	45
Bath and multipoint water-heaters	42	25	21	12
Washing machines and wash boilers	34	22	7	37
Refrigerators	31	42	24	3

[1]In addition, 'London' cookers of all models accounted for 19%.
Source: R. P. Rhodes, *Conversion at Canvey*.

Bearing in mind the pioneering nature of the project, the Canvey conversion was a smooth and successful operation from start to finish and it bore the fruits of the careful and painstaking work conducted beforehand. The complex and demanding timetable drawn up in advance for the Canvey operation, requiring meticulous co-ordination among many departments, is shown in Table 5.3. The first domestic conversion started as planned on 1 June (although the island's holiday camp had been converted by the Industrial Division the week before). The last sector was converted on 5 August. The final cost of about £32 per householder was strikingly close to the original estimates and the experiment provided much valuable experience for later conversion programmes.

Unfortunately, though perhaps inevitably, various problems arose during conversion, some of which proved intractable with the state of technical knowledge at the time. The rate of post-conversion 'call-back' to deal with complaints was exceptionally high. Indeed, there were as many complaints as there were numbers of conversions during the three months following the finish of the conversion. Many of the problems arose, the Board admitted, due to inadequate work by the fitting force. Shortly after conversion finished a *Which?* survey found that no fewer than 40 per cent of its sample had reported gas leaks in their houses (although a high proportion of these arose from over-odorisation of the gas). About one-third of consumers had experienced delays in the completion of conversion (usually due to the late or even non-arrival of conversion sets ordered by the Board from manufacturers) and a further half were satisfied with the performance of the gas itself.

There can be no doubt that this last statistic exaggerated the dissatisfaction felt by consumers. In many cases the problem was simply the different characteristics of natural gas – its colour, it shape and its heating properties – which took a little getting used to. But there remained some real problems. There were a number of 'hard-core' cases, mostly of obsolete appliances, which proved impossible to convert satisfactorily. At the end of conversion these numbered some 3 per cent of the total. A further difficulty was with existing automatic ignition systems, which often failed to work with methane. Housewives had particular problems with cooker hot-plates and the Board's solution of supplying a battery-powered hand-igniter was hardly satisfactory. Moreover, natural gas burned more noisily in central heating boilers and room heaters than did town gas. There were other technical problems, too, the solutions to which could only be developed through the concentrated research efforts of Boards, manufacturers and the Gas Council. Even A. A. Hall, the Essex Divisional Manager, in whose area Canvey was situated, estimated in November that 'the number of

Table 5.3   Canvey Project timetable

Publicity	Distribution	Fitters	Manufacturers
1.11.65 Drafts to Commercial Manager for Chairman	20.10.65 Sectional plan	1.1.66 Divisions advised number required	15.10.65 Letters from Commercial Manager
	1.11.65 Commence insertion of valves		
Public Relations Officer, Press Officer and Divisional Manager, Essex Division		22.1.66 20 minibuses delivered	Nov. Visits by Chief Service Manager
	31.3.66 Completion		
	1.6.66 First section commenced	1.2.66 Fitter to training 1.4.66	1.1.66 Orders despatched
15.11.65 Statement to Gas Council	31.7.66 Last section completed	2.4.66 Foreman to and 15.4.66 Chargehand special training	1.2.66 Follow up
2.12.65 Gas Council meeting			Feb. Supplementary orders
3.12.65 Meeting with Canvey Council		22.5.66 Final briefing	30.4.66 All parts received
6.12.65 Press release		1.6.66 to Conversion 30.7.66	
10.12.65 Letters to consumers		1.8.66 Rear party consolidation	
15.5.66 Final letters to consumers			
'C Day' Postcard to – 2 consumers			

Source: North Thames Gas.

Sales	Buildings	Administration	Industrial and HQ Divisions
3.12.65 Notice to Showrooms (restricted appliance list)	18.10.65 7 Buildings agreed	15.10.65 2 Clerks recruited	Oct. and Nov. Survey of all industrial and commerical premises
1.1.66 20 Representatives recruited	19.10.65 Advice to Staff Controller	19.10.65 Further Map Section Survey commenced (180 roads) 2 men	15.12.65 Recommendation for conversion of appliances – liaise with manufacturers
2.1.66 Briefing	7.11.65 Internal plan of buildings to Chief Engineer	31.10.65 List of appliances for each manufacturer completed	
15.1.66 Commence sales canvass	7.11.65 Telephones and workshop equipment required	1.12.65 Map Section Survey completed	1.1.66 Parts ordered
15.4.66 Sales canvass completed	15.1.66 Buildings completed	6.12.65 Details on existing survey form completed	1.2.66 Follow up
	1.2.66 Canteen completed	31.12.65 Master control record completed	1.6.66 Conversion by Industrial Workshops
		15.1.66 Recruit 1 Senior and 2 Sales Clerks	
		1.2.66 Recruit Service Office, Stores, Warehouse and Workshop staff	

25 Canvey Island Conversion Unit, June 1966. Behind can be seen the insulated holders for liquefied methane and the methane reception terminal. The spherical gasholder in the foreground was erected after the war by the Gas Light & Coke Company.

consumers who are far from satisfied at present must be over 2,000, i.e. about 30% of the Island'.

Nevertheless, the positive sides of the project, which by its nature was experimental and designed to bring problems to light, far outweighed the negative. A complex and demanding task had been carried out with efficiency and precision and all subsequent conversion programmes undertaken by Boards throughout the country owed a great deal to the pioneering work undertaken at Canvey Island by the North Thames Conversion Unit. Relations with the Urban District Council remained excellent throughout. The Clerk of the Council wrote to Mr Johnson that 'the very close consultation afforded us has gone a long way in removing any problems which might otherwise have arisen, and we are satisfied that by and large the conversion has been a major success ... we would especially like to record the courtesy and help always afforded us by your Divisional Manager, Mr A. A. Hall, and by Mr Jimmy Greene. We have no doubt that the enthusiasm of these officers and their close colleagues has meant much in ensuring the success of the scheme.' Mr Johnson also received a standing invitation to visit the Council's Sewage Disposal Works whenever he liked.

A rather muted highlight of the Canvey project was the official opening ceremony on 19 July. Muted because the occasion coincided with the announcement by the Government of a price freeze and other emergency measures to cope with one of the nation's recurrent economic crises. This was the time chosen for full details of the scheme to be made known and given to the press, but the Canvey experiment could not compete for news headlines with the national emergency. A great many representatives of the national and local press were invited, including such obvious candidates as the *Scottish Plumber's Journal* and *True Romances*. The ceremony was jointly hosted by North Thames and the Gas Council, a fact which showed an increasing involvement and enthusiasm for the Canvey project on the part of the central organisation.

The months of May and June 1966 had, indeed, seen a significant change in the Gas Council's attitude towards the Canvey conversion. In the early stages of the scheme the Gas Council had been decidedly lukewarm in their attitude. Indeed, the Board's proposal to call the new gas at Canvey 'Supergas' had been turned down by the Council on the grounds that the Canvey experiment might prove a failure and the gas turn out to be anything but super. 'It might be that some of the inhabitants will invent a name for it themselves, whether we like it or not', wrote the Deputy Chairman, Sir Kenneth Hutchison. But the North Sea discoveries changed the whole picture. A national conversion scheme was now on the cards and the happy coincidence of the North Thames Gas Board's pilot project at Canvey was naturally welcomed by the Council. In May 1966 the Gas Council set up a working party to examine the prospects for a national conversion. Plans for a national methane grid were drawn up and the Council asked each Board to prepare plans for a full-scale programme and encouraged representatives to visit Canvey. Accordingly, Jimmy Greene accompanied a number of visitors from other Boards to see the closing stages of conversion on 1 August.

The Canvey ceremony of 19 July took place in the wake of massive publicity about the natural gas discoveries which were being made at that time in the North Sea. Indeed, within six months of the discovery of the West Sole Field in September 1965 sufficient supplies of gas had been discovered to make national conversion a viable prospect. On 21 June 1966, at the commissioning of the North Sea drilling rig *The Orion*, Sir Henry Jones, the Gas Council Chairman, held out a glittering prospect for Britain's gas supplies: 'As one North Sea strike is followed by another, I do not think history, or at any rate industrial history, can ever have been made at such a pace ... We have already made the big decision – town gas is to become natural gas, and the necessary appliance conversion programme will begin as soon as practicable.' A few days later Sir Kenneth Hutchison predicted that gas prices might fall by half with the arrival of North Sea supplies. It was in this atmosphere of excitement and almost euphoria that the Canvey experiment became not simply a North Thames solution to its distribution problems but the opening curtain on what Sir Henry Jones thought 'might turn out to be the most important development in this country since the Industrial Revolution'. Not all were enthusiastic, however. Lord Robens, Chairman of the National Coal Board, remarked at the time, 'it would take about 70,000 man-years to convert the 12 million households connected to gas. There simply aren't enough men with spanners available'.

From this time onwards the Gas Council played an ever-increasing role in the overall direction of Britain's gas industry. For one consequence of the arrival of natural gas, both imported from the Sahara and from the North Sea, was the far-reaching reorganisation of the gas industry's own structure which took place at this time. There was now a need for a centralised purchaser of natural gas and also for a national distribution system. A new Gas Act in 1965 made some fundamental changes to the purely federal system which had existed since 1949. The Gas Council was strengthened and was given the duty of promoting and assisting the co-ordinated development of efficient and economical gas supplies in Great Britain. The Gas Council was empowered to manufacture gas or acquire it from elsewhere, either at home or abroad, and supply it in bulk to any Area Board. As part of the Council's reorganisation the Minister was given power to appoint three additional members (increased to five in 1968). By 1968 it was clear from ministerial pronouncements that still further changes would be introduced. The discovery and exploitation of North Sea natural gas had completely transformed the industry's situation and made necessary the institution of strong central authority to organise and distribute the gas through a national grid.

Over the next year or two, government thinking gradually took shape, and by 1970 it was clear that a massive reorganisation was envisaged, comparable with the changes established in 1949. On 5 August 1971, Sir John Eden, Minister for Industry, announced the Government's plans for setting up a new Gas Corporation in place of the Gas Council. He said, in introducing the changes, that 'over the last twenty years the Area Boards have made a great contribution to the development of the gas industry. I should like to pay tribute to all who have served in them, especially for the way in which they have co-operated with the Gas Council in planning and executing the change to natural gas. But we now must look to the future and devise a structure which will meet the needs of the industry in the years ahead. Given the nature of the technological advances which are being made I am sure that the creation of a single statutory authority will enable the industry to make the most of its opportunities while serving the interests of its customers.'

To implement the changes, the Conservative Government introduced its new Gas Bill into the House of Commons in 1971, and this became the Gas Act of 1972. Under the Act the gas industry was reorganised, with each Area Board losing its autonomy and becoming a Region of the newly formed British Gas Corporation. On Vesting Day, 1 January 1973, all the assets of the various Boards were vested in the new Corporation which was given statutory obligations 'to develop and maintain an efficient co-ordinated and economical system of gas supply for Great Britain and to satisfy, so far as it is economical to do so, all reasonable demands for gas in Great Britain.'

The Chairman of the new Corporation was Arthur Hetherington, who had joined the Gas Light and Coke Company in 1935, had at one time been Divisional Manager of Central Division, and had become Chairman of the Gas Council at the beginning of 1972 in succession to Sir Henry Jones. Hetherington's place as Deputy Chairman of the Council was taken by Denis Rooke, who subsequently became Deputy Chairman of the new Gas Corporation.

The setting up of the Gas Corporation gave a considerable impetus to centralisation, which steadily increased over the years as general policy guidelines, research, national targets, and various measures of standardisation were introduced. However, the Corporation decided to retain the existing area organisations for their operations, and the supply of gas, servicing of appliances, domestic sales, installations, and accounts remained decentralised. None the less, the extent of centralisation was considerable. The regional Chairmen were to be appointed by the Corporation and subject to the overall directions of the Corporation, which formulated national policy, while large industrial contracts were negotiated by the Corporation. The 1972 Gas Act also abolished the Area Consultative Councils, replacing them with a new National Gas Consumers' Council and twelve Regional Consumers' Councils.

As we have seen, each Area Board had been requested by the Gas Council in July 1966 to prepare plans for full-scale natural gas conversion within its own territory. As a first step in developing its own long-term programme a preliminary scheme was mapped out for North Thames by a small team comprising the Commercial Manager, Chief Engineer and Chief Distribution Engineer during July and August. In formulating the plan 'the overriding factor to be taken into account ... is that a conversion rate of over 175,000 customers a year must be achieved if the Board is to avoid a large programme of construction of gas-making plants, which otherwise would be essential if the Board is to meet the estimated increases in demand for gas as outlined in the present Capital Development Programme.' At this juncture a start on full conversion was envisaged the following year, 1967, with two Conversion Units 'based on the Canvey model' set up. These Units would, for distributional reasons, operate on the eastern and western sides of the Board's territory, around Basildon and Amersham. The gas would be available for the Basildon Region from Canvey and 65 000 conversions was the suggested target for the first year. For Amersham, where 12 000 conversions were planned, gas would come from the Slough–Reading branch of the Gas Council's planned methane grid. During 1968, by which time North Sea gas was expected, three more Units would be brought into operation in the eastern and western areas, converting 221 000 customers; the five Units would then converge on London at the rate of 450 000 conversions annually, completing the programme at the end of 1972 or the beginning of 1973. The Units would be manned by the Board's own fitters and supervising staff. The preliminary plan also recommended the immediate establishment of a centrally located Conversion Division to handle the multiplicity of problems and to co-ordinate the many aspects of conversion which would arise in a full-scale programme.

In drawing up this plan there were still many unknowns, and in the event it was greatly modified. Two points are worth emphasising. One is the importance of the Canvey model. Procedures and techniques of sectorising, pre-conversion work, survey, the length of the conversion cycle (2–3 days), the organisation of the Unit and the fitters' teams, and public relations arrangements were all taken from the Canvey model, modified in the light of experience gained there. The other point is the continued emphasis on the need for conversion because of demands on the Board's capacity. Although both the Gas Council and the Ministry of Power were anxious for Boards to plan conversion programmes as quickly as possible, in the case of North Thames internal pressures were dictating this course in any case. Estimates made in 1967 indicated that, while the total cost of conversion for North Thames might be some £80 million, new plant and distribution costs to meet anticipated loads if natural gas was not used 'neat' could amount to £250 million.

The new Conversion Division, equivalent in status to the existing Divisions, was established in October at Imperial House, Fulham, in convenient proximity to Watson House, the Industrial Division's laboratories, and to the Distribution Planning Centre. The new Divisional Manager was N. L. Henson, drafted from the North Western Division, and he was responsible to the Commercial Manager, Paul Rhodes, who therefore became the leading figure in the Board's conversion plans.

The following months saw the original skeleton scheme gradually take shape. By the beginning of 1967 locations for the first Units had been decided upon: on North Thames land at Basildon, and at the defunct Beaconsfield Film Studios, where the Board was fortunate enough to acquire a lease. The Basildon Unit made use of the entire Canvey buildings, offices, workshop, stores, and canteen, which were dismantled and erected at Archers Fields, alongside the Basildon District offices. Sectorising the areas (into sizes of approximately 600 consumers for the Basildon Unit and 250 for Amersham) and valving of sectors was quickly put in hand, as was the necessary pre-conversion work of exchanging prepayment meters and fitting filters and governors for the new gas. So, in February 1967, a six-year conversion programme was put to the Board for approval, which proposed a start at the two Units in July 1967, to be completed in Central London early in 1973. The Board accepted the plan, agreeing also to apply to all new natural gas consumers the small price concession given already to Canvey. In the same month, February, the Minister of Power, Richard Marsh, made the public statement that the Government was giving 'the highest priority' to the development of North Sea gas, adding that 'the national interest demands that we should exploit the gas as quickly and efficiently as possible'.

However, almost at once the Board's conversion programme received the first of its many setbacks. Even before the end of February it became clear that the leading appliance manufacturers could not develop and produce the necessary conversion sets in time. Such development included the submission of prototypes to Watson House, testing to exacting standards, and, after approval, commercial production. The Radiation Group of companies, for example, which were to supply about one-third of the conversion sets, could not guarantee any supplies at all until December 1967. Even then, as Table 5.4 shows, these covered only about three-quarters of the Board's orders, and left over 1 million appliances without firm prospects for sets at all.

Under these circumstances there could be no question of a prompt start and Rhodes informed the Management Committee in April 1967 that 'despite the earnest endeavours both at Board and national level' conversion could not begin until 1968. This would involve 'a massive rethink' in order to make up for the lost time. Certainly, additional Units would now be needed, and the Conversion Division had come to the conclusion that help from outside contractors should be sought. The first two Units would, as planned, use the Board's own fitters but further Units would be operated by contractors under the Board's management and supervision. The contractors' teams were to be trained by the contractors themselves, but their instructors received training at the Board's centres in Fulham and Stratford.

The 'rethink' resulted in a Revised Outline Plan, presented by the

Table 5.4   Conversion schedule of Radiation Group (000s)

Category	Cookers	Fires	Water-heaters	Total	Date supplies expected
A	2800	1400	1700	5900	Dec. 1967
B	600	300	50	950	Feb. 1968
C	130	50	380	560	April 1968
D	–	–	112	112	–
E	75	270	150	495	–
F	450	5	2	457	–
Total	4055	2025	2394	8474	

Notes: A Sets designed and submitted to Watson House by 30 June 1967.
   B Sets designed and submitted to Watson House by 30 September 1967.
   C Sets designed and submitted to Watson House by 31 December 1967.
   D Sets which will give an unacceptable level of performance.
   E Appliances where Watson House is still working on suitable sets.
   F Obsolete (mostly over 15 years), with no sets available or programmed.
Source: North Thames Gas.

Conversion Division to the Board in July 1967. The scheme now envisaged three Units working in 1968 (two on the western side, one on the eastern), two more operating in 1969, and the five then working through ten fixed areas until Central London was cleared by the end of 1973 (this critical area being started early in 1972). The rate of conversions under the new schedule was less than originally hoped for but still above the 'critical' targets set by the Management Services Department. The programme now expected 92 000 conversions from the two western Units in 1968 and 61 000 from Basildon in the east. It was estimated that after a 'running-in' period the Units could each convert at a maximum rate of about 2000 consumers (6000 appliances) a week. From now on, distinguishing numbers were given to each Unit. The ten fixed areas were numbered 2 to 11 (Canvey Island being termed Area 1) and the Unit working in an area would be given the number of that area. Thus, Area 2 was served from Basildon, so this Unit became Conversion Unit 2 (Basildon) and so on. The conversion team finishing one area would move to another and take on the number of that area. Under the July Plan it was thought the first 'turn-in' would occur in the Chalfont St Peter area, undertaken by CU3 (Beaconsfield) in mid-March. This timetable involved a start of survey on 2 October in order for the necessary preparations to be made. The plan noted that 'it has become abundantly clear that the corner-stone of preparation rests in agreement at this early stage on the provision of Unit sites' and a preliminary list of sites, in addition to Basildon and Beaconsfield, was drawn up. The search for appropriate sites was not easy. Ideally, the site should be on the Board's own property and provide two or three acres for the necessary buildings, parking and loading space. The location of the site should also cut down the length of operational journeys as far as possible. On the basis of these criteria the July report listed possible sites and alternatives for all areas except Central London, since it was recognised that the peculiar problems posed here made it advisable to delay detailed planning for a while. Later, in July 1970, revisions led to the abandoning of plans for Units at Kensal Green (Unit 10) and Poplar (Unit 11). These areas were now added to existing Units and the Inner London Unit at Nine Elms became CU11.

During August 1967 the Gas Council gave its blessing to the Board's programme, including the plan to reduce the natural gas tariff (by ½d. a therm) and to declare the calorific value of the new gas at CV1000. By September the Board was ready to inform the North Thames Gas Consultative Council of its plans, prior to a public announcement on 28 September. As Henson reported to the Board, 'going public' was 'a source of considerable satisfaction to all of us in the Division, as we now feel we are "under way"'.

What was under way, was, of course, part of a national effort, a truly epic event. Most Boards were planning to start conversion in the spring of 1968, at about the same time as North Thames, and in addition to Canvey there were a few other pilot schemes (the most important being the conversion of Burton-on-Trent by the West Midlands Gas Board in 1967). 'Perhaps the greatest peacetime operation in this nation's history' is how Sir Denis Rooke described conversion, while George Cooper was little less dramatic: 'One of the most complex and controversial operations of its kind in history, both in the practical and in the political sense.'

Before continuing the North Thames story we should look briefly at the national scene. First and foremost the advent of natural gas revolutionised Britain's energy supplies, allowing total gas sales to more than treble in the decade following 1967–68, while industrial sales rose sixfold. Table 5.5 gives an idea of the pace at which new North Sea discoveries were made in the mid-1960s, while the first gas arrived at the new Easington terminal in 1967.

Natural gas also meant the end of manufactured gas, both coal-based and oil-based. With these changes came a complete reorganisation of Britain's gas industry. As we have seen, the need for a central controlling authority to distribute natural gas led to a progressively greater role for the Gas Council. Early in 1966 a committee chaired by Arthur Hetherington (a former Gas Light & Coke Company man, who had been Divisional Manager of the Central Division until 1955), then Chairman of the East Midlands Gas Board, had recommended some form of permanent organisation to co-ordinate the conversion programmes drawn up by the Area Boards; at the end of the year a Conversion

Table 5.5   Major natural gas discoveries

	Field discovered	Production started
1965	West Sole[1]	1967
1966	Leman Bank	1968
	Hewett	1969
	Indefatigable	1971
1968	Rough	1975
	Viking	1972
1970	Forties	1977
1971	Frigg (Norway)	1977
	Brent	1982
1972	Frigg (UK)	1977
1973	Piper	1978
1974	Morecambe Bay	1985

[1]First North Sea strike, September 17.
Sources: British Gas Council Annual Reports; British Gas Corporation Annual Reports.

Executive was accordingly established, with W. D. Ellis, formerly of Watson House and until 1963 Henson's predecessor as Divisional Manager of the North Western Division, as Conversion Manager. During 1967 further steps were taken to strengthen the Gas Council and early in 1968 three new functional divisions were created, with James Buckley, as Member for Marketing, being particularly involved with the conversion programmes. These changes were, of course, part and parcel of the strengthening of the Gas Council, which led eventually to the demise of the Boards in 1973.

Table 5.6 shows something of the scale of the conversion operation planned by the Boards and carried out by them and the Gas Corporation. The total cost was in the order of £577 million, less than the forecast of £400 million made by Sir Henry Jones in 1966 if we make allowance for inflation. In addition, some £450 million worth of obsolete plant had to be written off. The total programme involved the laying of a 1300-mile high-pressure grid and further massive investment in port and harbour facilities, compressor stations, and so on. The Boards and Regions had to deal directly with some 13 million consumers, 35 million appliances, 8000 different models, and a bewildering variety of industrial and commercial equipment.

Although each Board drew up its own conversion programme and developed its own internal organisation, the Gas Council's role was of increasing significance in co-ordinating the whole exercise. Research into the testing of appliances and conversion sets was carried out very largely at Watson House, and the Gas Council negotiated the terms for the supplies of conversion sets with manufacturers. Agreement here

Table 5.6   National conversion programme, 1966–78 (000s consumers converted)

Year (ended 31 March)	Domestic	Commercial	Industrial
1967	7.8	0.1	0.0
1968	42.2	0.6	0.3
1969	400.5	15.2	2.5
1970	1050.5	36.8	5.0
1971	1972.3	52.6	7.9
1972	2322.1	69.3	10.5
1973	2036.7	56.8	8.0
1974	2049.7	51.8	7.2
1975	1611.4	54.4	7.6
1976	1087.0	37.4	6.6
1977	319.2	8.9	1.4
1978	95.4	2.3	0.3
Total	12994.8	386.2	57.3

Source: C. Elliott, *The History of Natural Gas Conversion in Great Britain* (1980) p. 110.

was reached in 1968 for the manufacturers (where they were still in business) to provide conversion sets for all current and non-current (under fifteen years old) appliances. For large numbers of obsolete appliances more than fifteen years old Watson House would develop prototypes to be produced commercially. Otherwise, *ad hoc* conversions would be undertaken by the conversion teams, or replacements (usually from reconditioned traded-in appliances) provided.

North Thames's role in this gigantic operation was distinctive, for it included the most critical and difficult programme of all – the conversion of London. North Thames not only had more domestic consumers to convert than any other Board, but also had more industrial and commercial customers too (Gas Council statistics, based on different classifications, are misleading in this respect). Apart from Scotland, the Board's programme was the most costly per consumer converted and also ran the longest. In all, North Thames converted 1 908 000 premises (industrial, domestic and commercial) and 5 164 256 appliances. Rather more than 7.5 million communications, letters, cards and leaflets were sent to customers, and in Central London alone over 35 000 substandard appliances were found and rectified.

Having announced its 1968 programme the previous September, North Thames had yet again to revise its plans. This time, delays in completing the Gas Council's methane grid made it necessary to reduce drastically the conversion levels in the South Western Division and to compensate by increases in the Essex Division. This meant establishing a further (contractor-based) Unit at Brentwood, to commence in

26 Conversion brought an increased demand for domestic meters. Meter production was concentrated at Harwood Terrace by 1968 and the new Meter Proving Bay, opened that year, was part of the development of the Meter Section there. This picture shows the moving conveyor carrying meters for testing.

September 1968. For this Unit the Board acquired a three-year lease on the large 'Beautility' factory, which not only provided accommodation for the Unit but also solved the storage and warehousing problems for all the conversion sets and materials for the eastern areas.

The revisions meant that the first 'C Day' now occurred in April at Corringham in Essex. Earlier that month a big plant at Fords in Dagenham had been satisfactorily converted by the contractors, Seaflame Industrial, in a single weekend. But the real starting point of the Board's programme was Monday, 29 April 1968 when the first fitting force from CU2 (Basildon) arrived at Corringham, a significant date in the Board's history. CU3 (Beaconsfield) was second in the field on 15 July. On 3 September CU6 (Brentford) began operations and this was the Board's first contractor-based Unit, operated by William Press and Sons Ltd. This firm had a long association with the Board, already had conversion experience in Holland, and maintained excellent relations with North Thames throughout conversions. Press eventually under-

27 The first 'C Day', 29 April 1968. No. 5 Conversion Team from the Basildon Conversion Unit begins the Board's programme at Corringham, Essex.

took the critical conversion of Central London, and it was a happy coincidence that in 1969 Michael Milne-Watson became Chairman of the firm (the same year that he received a knighthood), and his signature once more appeared on North Thames contracts.

To detail the spread of conversion, Unit by Unit, sector by sector, would be both tedious and repetitive. It is unnecessary also to chronicle the innumerable detailed changes which were made to the programme from time to time. Table 5.7 shows something of the scale, progress and timing of the operation. It was a mammoth, rolling process, planned to an exacting timetable. Naturally, there were particular highlights and problems at the various stages of conversion as it moved inexorably from east and west towards London. The variety of appliances, especially the commercial ones, brought a continual challenge to the fitters' ingenuity, and Jimmy Greene built up an international reputation for his technical expertise with unusual conversion problems. An 1884 farm milk heater resisted all attempts and the programme turned up many other appliances dating from before the First World War. An early test was at the Slough Trading Estate where 200 industrial customers used some 2 million therms annually. Conversion here was successfully carried out by Seaflame in July 1969. The following year saw the

Table 5.7 Progress of conversion

Unit	Operated by	Location	Start	Finish	Conversions
1 (Canvey)	Board	Canvey Island	23 May 1966	6 August 1966	7885
2 (Basildon)	Board	Archers Fields, Basildon	29 April 1968	22 October 1970	141301
3 (Beaconsfield)	Board	Beaconsfield Film Studios	15 July 1968	1 April 1971	137186
4 (Kew Bridge)	Seaflame	Brentford Holder Station	29 May 1969	5 October 1971	146901
5 (South Harrow)	William Press	South Harrow Holder Station	3 September 1969	7 December 1972	224862
6 (Woodford)	Seaflame	Woodford Holder Station	2 February 1970	31 January 1973	197998
7 (Mill Hill)	Board/Press	Bittacy Road, Mill Hill	2 November 1970	17 September 1973	165433
8 (Brentwood)	William Press	Kavanaghs Road, Brentwood	4 September 1968	25 July 1972	223917
9 (Kew Bridge)	Seaflame	Brentford Holder Station	6 October 1971	3 October 1973	236841
10 (Hornsey)	Ellis/Wave	Clarendon Road, Hornsey	14 April 1971	12 February 1974	177026
11 (Nine Elms)	William Press	Nine Elms Station	3 September 1973	23 August 1976	246443
Total					1907793

Source: North Thames Gas.

conversion of Southend Pier and Windsor Castle, at the two extremes of the Board's territory. The latter was completed successfully in September, but only after the Deputy Governor there had arranged two special meetings for household staff prior to the Board's 26 fitters being let loose on 89 cookers and some 300 additional appliances. The Deputy Governor later reported that the Board had done 'an extremely fine job'. In this month the total number of conversions reached 500 000 and in December 1971 the Board became the first to pass the 1 million mark – half-way, though with Central London still to come. The following year saw the eastern and western halves meeting, when the operations of CU10 (Hornsey) linked up with CU6 (Woodford) at Lea Bridge Marshes.

Public relations and communication with customers were, of course, of the utmost importance. A particular problem arose in those areas of the Board's territory where there were high concentrations of non-English-speaking immigrants. In Southall, for example, notices were inserted in Indian and Pakistani language newspapers, and conversion cards were printed in Urdu, Bengali, Punjabi and Gujarati. Board officials also held meetings with local community leaders and made special visits to schools to talk to the children, who were often the interpreters for immigrant families.

A broad picture of the ten-year programme for North Thames Gas would have to highlight the overall success of the operation. Year by year the Units moved through their sectors efficiently and smoothly and the Board was especially pleased with the performance of its three major contractors. Industrial and commercial work was undertaken separately in all areas except that of CU11, which covered Central London. Contractors were used for this work – Seaflame Industrial covering the western areas and H.G.S. Industrial the eastern – under the general supervision of the Board's Industrial Division. These specialised conversions were carried out by the contractors with the minimum of disruption and with remarkably few problems.

This overall picture may seem surprising in view of the many widespread and well-publicised complaints, which, although they affected all Boards, were especially strong in the case of North Thames. We should, however, put these complaints in perspective. North Thames's customers were not only numerically the largest of any Board, they were often the most articulate and the ones with the easiest access to the media (often it was a case of the media having access to them). The Board rightly stressed the gains in safety and efficiency which came from each appliance being individually checked and serviced free of charge during the process of conversion, but to the average customer there was little obvious benefit in the change. If an appliance worked as well afterwards as it did before that was hardly a gain. If it did not, there was justifiable cause for complaint. And all consumers had to suffer the

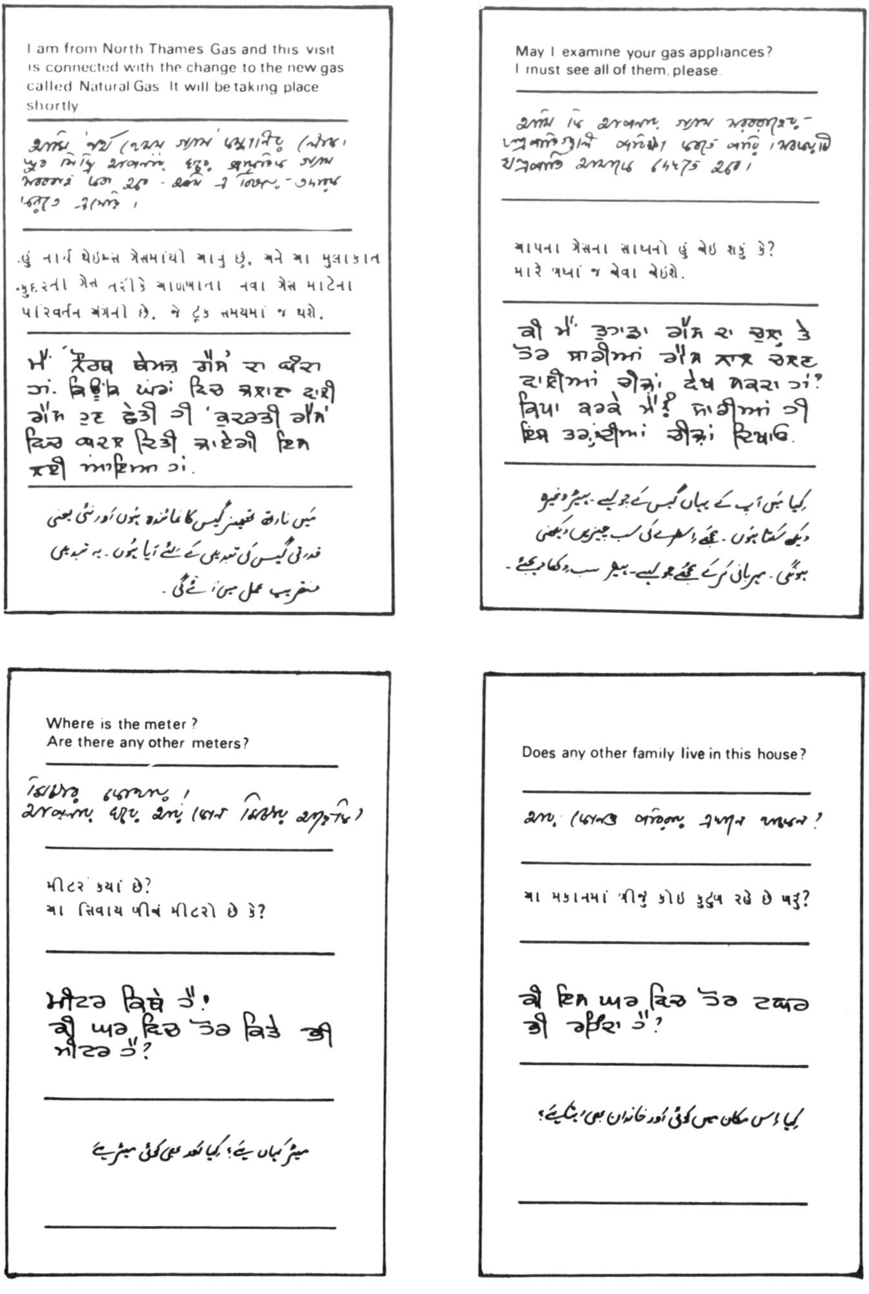

Figure 5.1 Cards specially printed in Urdu, Bengali, Punjabi and Gujarati to help conversion staff and their customers in areas with a high proportion of Asian immigrants, 1970.

actual inconvenience of the work being carried out. It is difficult not to sympathise with the housewife who in 1969 wrote to a national daily: 'It seems quite wrong that, after two weeks' training, ex-bus conductors, postmen and so forth can walk in and take one's cooker to bits.'

We should also try to distinguish between the technical process of conversion carried out by the Conversion Units, and the burdens placed by conversion on the normal customer service provided by the Divisions and the Accounting Centres. Both gave rise to complaint, but it was pressure on the latter which became the Board's major problem. Now there can be no doubt that conversion did place an enormous additional burden on the Divisions and on Customer Accounts, but there were strains in any event coming from growing business and sophistication of appliances, as we have seen. It is quite impossible to disentangle the two. Natural gas itself brought expanding sales, and the 1973 oil crisis gave another unexpected boost with the quadrupling of oil prices.

Against this background we can look at three of the principal events of the conversion programme: the two periods of particular crisis when the entire programme had to be halted, and the epic achievement of converting Central London.

The first serious check arose in the autumn of 1968. At the Basildon Unit, which had reached its maximum conversion rate of 2000 a week in August, the call-back rate had reached an ominous 33 per cent in September. 'Call-back' was an eight-week period during which the Conversion Units themselves dealt with complaints before their being handed over to the Divisions. I was unfortunate that, despite the Canvey experience, for some models there was still no technical solution. Particularly acute was noise in gas fires and central heating appliances, and problems with ignition for cookers and water-heaters. Another problem was the failure of some manufacturers to deliver conversion sets, meaning that a much higher level of *ad hoc* conversions had to be undertaken than anticipated. Since the average time for an *ad hoc* operation was eight hours for each appliance, instead of only one hour if a conversion set was available, a huge backlog of work quickly began to build up. There were also cases of faulty work by fitters, still at this early stage, of course, constantly encountering new models and problems. There was also an alarming rise in reported escapes, the number at Basildon rising to a rate of 1400 a week in place of the pre-conversion average of 150.

Each of the three operating Units was in mounting difficulties and Paul Rhodes reluctantly decided on 13 November to recommend a drastic slowing-down of conversion. The rate would drop to one-third of its former level and work would stop on 16 December for an extensive Christmas break. Thereafter, the programme would run at half rate until April, when a combination of warmer weather, improved supplies, and a better trained labour force would enable the rate once more to be stepped up. But before the Board could consider the Commercial Manager's proposals North Thames was assailed from all quarters. It was assailed by the press, the Consultative Council, the Gas Council, local authorities, and even by the Ministry of Power. For example, the Maidenhead Borough Council, complaining of delays of several days in carrying out conversions and the frequent inability then to complete the task 'owing to the lack of proper inspection prior to the commencement of conversion', urged the Board, through the Consultative Council, to call an immediate halt to conversion. The Editor of the *Maidenhead Advertiser* told the Consultative Council: 'Apart from the natural annoyance of people being left without heat, hot water and cooking facilities for days, there is an all-round frustration at not being able to get in touch with anyone who can give the answer.' And on the morning of 21 November the North Thames Gas Consultative Council, without waiting for the arrival of R. S. Johnson, who was due for lunch, overwhelmingly passed the resolution 'that this Council condemns the Board for pursuing the policy of conversion without the necessary components to do it within 24 hours and that conversion should stop until they are up to date with conversion'. The Chairman decided that he had little alternative but to call a halt, and this he did from 6 December. The date for restarting would be given later on the personal authority of the Chairman and in the mean time various steps would be taken to improve the conversion operations. One such step was better public relations, for the Board fully accepted the widespread complaints that the public had not been informed adequately about the process and effects of conversion. On the technical side of the operations the Board accepted the need for improved facilities during and after conversion, so that complaints could be dealt with without delay, and the Board also re-examined its stocking and ordering policies in an attempt to avoid running out of conversion sets, which had happened with depressing regularity.

During the following two months a range of improvements was introduced. The Controller of Supplies was made directly responsible for ordering and distributing conversion sets and it was decided to set up a large main store for the sets at Products Works, Beckton. In future, the Conversion Committee would authorise conversion of individual sectors week by week in the light of up-to-date information on the state of call-back and supplies of parts and labour. New conversion letters and information leaflets for the public were prepared and a public relations officer was to be attached to each Unit. The call-back period was extended to twelve weeks to relieve pressure on Divisional resources, while Mobile Report Centres, open until 7 p.m., were now to be situated in each sector for two weeks after conversion.

These new arrangements and the steady clearance of the backlog of work enabled the Board to recommence conversion once more early in February 1968. The rate of conversion, though, was reduced. The modified programme now progressed satisfactorily, and each of the remaining Units began operations on schedule. When CU6 (Woodford) commenced on 2 February 1970 six Units were operating for the first time and during the second quarter of 1971 the Board reached its peak conversion rate of about 10 000 a week. Overall, the average rate of striking between January 1970 and December 1972 was almost 9000 a week, far more than achieved by any other Board; thereafter, the rate dropped to 6000 in the second half of 1973, about 4000 in 1974 and 2000 in 1975.

Undoubtedly the most worrying feature of the 1968 crisis was the strain put by conversion on the Divisional service organisation. By 1970 the problems were mounting once more, and in the following year the disruptions caused by internal reorganisation introduced under the new Chairman, George Cooper (dealt with in Chapter 7), and increasing difficulties with customer accounts brought another, and far more serious, period of crisis.

A particular trouble spot was the conversion being carried on by CU7 (Mill Hill), which was responsible for converting some of the most exacting customers in the North Western Division. It was unfortunate that this Unit, for reasons connected with the original rescheduling of the conversion programme, mixed Board and contractor labour together. Approximately two-thirds were from the Board and most of the remainder from William Press. Differences in working conditions, bonuses, overtime, and even the colour of the overalls made for constant disputes and ill feeling and there was no doubt that the Board's labour was less efficient than that of William Press. Indeed, it became a policy of the Board in its negotiations with the unions to permit the transfer of as few of its own fitters and conversion assistants as possible to the new Nine Elms Unit planned for the conversion of Central London and, in fact, this latter Unit was eventually completely contractor-operated. A study in February 1972 estimated that CU7 (Mill Hill) was converting only 13.1 appliances per man/week compared with 18.9 at CU6 (Woodford), and concluded that the Board's own 111 fitters at Mill Hill were achieving even less than 13.1. As a result, the direct costs per conversion were also the highest at Mill Hill, as Board data for the six months ending 30 September 1971 show (see Table 5.8).

The year 1972 was a critical one. By this time conversion had reached the heavily populated North London suburbs and although pressure was felt throughout the Board's area, it was in the North Western Division, with its articulate consumers and high level of central heating,

Table 5.8   Conversion costs by Unit, April–September
1971

Conversion Unit	Cost (£s per conversion)
CU7 Mill Hill	18.48
CU5 South Harrow	15.99
CU10 Hornsey	14.11
CU4 Kew Bridge	13.95
CU8 Brentwood	13.59
CU6 Woodford	13.17

Source: North Thames Gas.

that the strains were most acute. In March, criticism of North Thames began to mount in local press and radio, and the Board, under pressure from the Gas Council, considered slowing the rate of conversion once more. Unwisely, it was decided to continue at the planned level. The difficulties only increased. As mentioned already, the blame could only partly be laid on the doorstep of conversion. What conversion did was to overload an already strained organisation. These pressures will be discussed subsequently when we look at the internal problems of the Board's organisation, but the size of the problem can be seen in the mounting figures of complaints received by the Board. In July 1972 Head Office had received some 2133 complaints by letter, telephone or personal call, itself an abnormally high figure and more than double the corresponding figure for the previous year. In November 6999 were received. Complaints to the North Thames Gas Consultative Council were also running at three times the previous level. Many individual cases were distressing. One poor housewife had been without the use of her oven cooker since conversion on 8 August 1972 and it was still out of action on Christmas Day, despite 'repeated appeals'. Another family was left without gas or water heating after conversion on 18 October until 20 December. The backlog of conversion delays longer than one month awaiting appliance parts rose from about 4000 in October to 7000 in December, and the average call-back rate rose sharply from 13 per cent in September to 17 per cent in November.

The majority of complaints were related directly or indirectly to conversion. Many were taken up by Geoffrey Finsberg, Conservative MP for Hampstead. Sadly, North Thames had not made a good job of conversion either at Mr Finsberg's home (broken appointments to fix a filter governor) or at the home of his parents. By December he had submitted a large number of cases of broken appointments, bad workmanship and so on. The *Evening Standard* ran a series of critical articles during December, with front-page headlines on two consecutive days, and *Gas World* carried an article which A. J. Vinegrad, Head of

Public Relations, considered so 'unpleasant and critical' that he feared it would have 'a demoralising effect on the Board's employees'. However, the Board's Executive Committee did not adopt Vinegrad's suggestion that the Board's own purchases of *Gas World* should be reduced from 187 to two.

On 27 November 1972 Peter Emery, Parliamentary Under-Secretary of State for Industry, visited the Essex Divisional Headquarters at Southend and his discussions with the Chairman of North Thames included the accounts and service problems that were facing the Board. On 23 November the annual meeting between the Consultative Council and the Chairman and chief officers of the Board was held and the Board 'were called upon to answer a formidable number of searching questions on the Board's performance, mostly relating to customer service'. Worse still, Mr Finsberg put down a critical Adjournment Motion in the House of Commons, which was debated on Friday 22 December. Perhaps fortunately for the Board, there were too few MPs present at this pre-Christmas gathering for a vote to be held; indeed, the attendance consisted virtually of only the Deputy Speaker, Mr Finsberg himself, and Mr Emery. None the less, Finsberg had some scathing comments to make about the Board's performance, accusing it of ignoring letters, breaking appointments, supplying the wrong equipment to fitters, and being inaccessible to human contact, especially by telephone. He detailed a number of case histories and called for vigorous steps to be taken to improve performance.

Once again, there was no alternative but to stop the entire conversion programme. Again, time was necessary to clear up the backlog of work and sort out better procedures. In November it had become clear that the entire schedule would have to be modified, and conversion was halted on 11 December, in the expectation of restarting at a reduced rate early in January. In his report to the Board on 15 December the Chairman pinpointed the trouble at the North Western Division, where most of the conversion was then taking place. This Division was not alone, however. Problems were mounting everywhere and the Western Division, too, was receiving an alarming number of complaints.

This, sadly, was the situation which the North Thames Gas Board handed over to the British Gas Corporation on 1 January 1973. Henceforth North Thames was a Region of the Corporation, and the Board ceased, though to the public North Thames has remained 'the Gas Board'. It was hardly an auspicious moment. But it is worth remembering that by this time the Board had completed three-quarters of its programme: some 1 400 000 customers had been converted, involving conversion of nearly 4 million appliances. This was far more than any other Board, and it had been carried out during the difficult period of reorganisation.

Naturally, great efforts were now made to improve the situation, not only for conversion but for the servicing and accounting organisations too. One decision was to extend the call-back period even more, now to be from twelve to sixteen weeks; telephone hours were also extended and a new 24-hour emergency link to the Kensington Control Room was arranged. However, the backlog of work proved too great for conversion to restart in January. Not until early February did North Thames feel that three of its Units could begin operations once again, although even now CU7 (Mill Hill) and CU10 (Hornsey) were still not felt to be ready. But hardly had work restarted when a variety of industrial disputes caused yet another lengthy cessation and not until April 1973 could the programme get under way once again.

Although conversion progressed more smoothly after April, the problems were by no means over. In the autumn of 1973 serious labour shortages in some of the contractors' units appeared and there were continual difficulties with customer service. In an effort to boost morale the chief officers from headquarters visited Kilburn and South Harrow, and at Kilburn found 'a low state of morale and lack of confidence in the Region's policy'.

During the summer of 1973 the Region, as we must now call it, found itself in the public gaze to a greater extent than ever before. The full force was felt of that ever-present danger – the unhappy coincidence of technical difficulty in conversion, administrative inefficiency in dealing with it, and the likelihood of arousing the ire of a public figure able to make his views known to a wide audience. On 16 August the saga of Mrs Levin's geyser, told in *The Times* by her son, Bernard, in his weekly column, became a national event. Due to what was, according to Paul Rhodes, the Deputy Chairman, in a follow-up letter to *The Times*, 'obviously incompetence', a catalogue of unanswered complaints, visits by fitters without the requisite parts, broken appointments and other misdemeanours was delivered with the author's characteristic wit and force. Even North Thames's immediate and effective response brought ridicule and criticism in a subsequent article: not only had an unnecessarily large army of gas officials arrived, including one whose sole task seemed to be to apologise, but the very promptness displayed the unequal treatment given to a 'celebrity', on the one hand, and to plain 'Mrs Levin', on the other.

The significance of the episode was not so much the public airing given to a particular grievance, nor the somewhat vivid criticisms of North Thames Gas ('the organisation seems to be putrescent from top to bottom, its officials leaving letters unanswered, phone calls ignored, and customers offered nothing but false assurances of action'). The real lesson was the responsiveness of the chord struck. Bernard Levin himself claimed that no single subject in his columns had ever brought such an avalanche of lettters from readers and that *The Times* Business News had told him that the subject on which they regularly received the largest correspondence was the 'North Thames Gas Board and its incompetence'. Paul Rhodes received a shoal of replies to his request, in a letter to *The Times*, that dissatisfied customers should write to him personally.

Discomforting though the episode was, it occurred at a time when North Thames was already pushing ahead vigorously with plans to rectify its well-known shortcomings. Certainly, though, it made Chief Office even more sensitive about its dealings with influential public figures, especially since the conversion of Central London was imminent. From this time regular 'VIP' lists were drawn up for the Inner London sectors and conversion teams warned accordingly. Needless to say, damage done to North Thames's public reputation was substantial and many of the chief officers felt that the attacks had been unfair not only in language and content, but also in singling out North Thames at a time when every Board was encountering major conversion problems. There was, therefore, some quiet internal satisfaction at Staines when, in September 1977, Bernard Levin attempted once more to arraign North Thames for incompetence. This time he found himself on the receiving end of a hard-hitting reply from the Chairman, John Gadd, which successfully showed the partial nature and even the stark untruth of many of Mr Levin's unchecked assertions. This particular matter dropped quietly.

Bad news gets publicity, but throughout the conversion operation there was also a steady stream of letters from satisfied – and relieved – consumers. Many of these letters mentioned the unfair publicity they thought the Board was getting, and they arrived from consumers of all kinds, including housewives, hoteliers, businessmen, ambassadors, television stars and even vicars, who might be expected to have some expertise in conversion matters. One of the latter wrote: 'If only we could meet with such kindness every day, how much better the world would be to live in.' A countess reported on 'the marvellous way the conversion operation was carried out in my part of Marylebone High Street today ... my particular technician fitter was highly efficient, courteous, very tidy and someone who can only enhance the name of the Gas Board, and friends on the street have told me their fitters were the same and that the whole operation had the efficiency of a "D Day" planning.'

The long and unexpected four-month break in the conversion programme which had taken place after December 1972 had provided time for much of the backlog of complaints and other outstanding work to be cleared up. But one of its important results was a further and final major modification to the conversion schedule. Above all, this modifica-

tion meant the slowing-down and replanning of the conversion of
Central London. It is to the special problems of converting Central
London, in so many ways the crux not only of the Board's but also of
the entire national programme, that we will now turn.

6

The Conversion of Central London

The task of converting London might well have daunted even St Augustine. Central London was both the critical area for North Thames and the linchpin of the national effort. Many, some even within the industry, felt that such an undertaking was impracticable. For almost every conversion problem was magnified in the capital. The operation affected a wide section of opinion-formers and influential individuals, including nearly every Member of Parliament. It involved such institutions as Buckingham Palace, foreign embassies, Fleet Street, the Bank of England, Westminster Abbey and Parliament itself. Public attention was inevitable. The density of London's population and the existence of so many underground mains and pipes of all kinds made sectorising and valving a particularly intricate technical operation. The numbers of flats and bed-sitters in certain areas, such as Kensington and Earls Court, often made access on 'C Day' a nightmare, while the itinerant nature of much of London's population made the information gathered by the survey representatives quickly out of date. Moreover, pre-survey of appliances discovered an unusually high proportion of potentially dangerous (PD) installations. Most arose from inadequate ventilation and each case had to be checked and dealt with. Again, London had the nation's greatest concentration of 'commercial' consumers and the special needs of restaurants, hospitals, shops, and so on had all to be met and satisfied on a scale unmatched elsewhere. Traffic congestion was another problem and the closest possible co-operation had to be maintained with the Metropolitan Police to help with parking North Thames vehicles at Report Centres, and also to deal with access to premises.

Planning for the conversion of London was, therefore, very sensibly undertaken by North Thames at an early stage, even though actual conversion would take place at the end of the programme. A special Conversion Planning Group for inner London was set up in 1969 and it held its first meeting on 10 November, under the chairmanship of F. A. Collins, Assistant Divisional Manager of the Conversion Division. The membership of the committee included representatives from the Central Division, since it was realised that many of the burdens of service and customer relations would fall particularly upon this Division. The terms of reference were very general, covering 'identifying the main problems of Central Area Conversion' and drawing up a timetable for operations. Although the Units at Kew Bridge and Hornsey were to undertake some work in Central London – CU9 (Kew Bridge) converting the Earls Court and Kensington areas – the vast bulk, including the sensitive Westminster and City areas, would fall on the inner London Unit (CU11). A priority was, therefore, to find an appropriate site, and in July 1970 Nine Elms was decided upon. Nine Elms had a number of advantages. The site was large enough to accommodate all the necessary staff and buildings and was central to both the easterly and the westerly directions that conversion was to take as it moved towards Beckton and Southall from Central London at the end of conversion. Work on the site started in the summer of 1971 and the final cost of establishing the Unit was to be about £250 000. An advanced survey of appliances was also undertaken during 1970 and 1971 in order to get a clearer picture of the numbers involved and especially to attempt a 'sell-out' of appliances and to clear up PD installations, which would otherwise seriously delay actual conversion. The survey was completed in May 1972, and was based on every commercial and industrial premises within the Central

28 CU11: the conversion unit at Nine Elms in 1973, from where the bulk of the conversion of Central London was undertaken.

London area and upon two thirds of the domestic appliances. It revealed that some 550 000 major domestic appliances, 75 000 commercial and 10 500 industrial appliances would have to be converted. No less than one in four of the domestic appliances were found to be PD, usually through lack of adequate ventilation.

At the time of these initial planning stages, conversion of inner London was due to begin in April 1973 and run until the end of 1974. The Conversion Committee estimated that the successful contractor would need about a year to get ready and, accordingly, draft contracts were prepared for tender in the autumn of 1971. Only two contracting firms were invited to tender, since only William Press and Seaflame were thought to have the necessary facilities and expertise to carry out the arduous contract. The Conversion Committee noted that, 'Our two main contractors have proved their capability over the past two years, and are now well established and integrated with our organisation.' The successful tender was submitted by Press, who were awarded the contract in May 1972. Unlike the contracts for all the other Units, this contract included commercial and industrial work as well as purely domestic. The successful tender, for almost £3 million, worked out at about £3.20 per appliance against the average at that time of £3.80.

However, the winter crisis of 1972–73 meant a considerable slowing-down in the planned rate of London's conversion. The schedule had originally envisaged a peak of some 5500 to 6000 conversions a week by the winter of 1973–74, with a corresponding heavy workload placed on the resources of the Central Division. However, the experiences of the North Western Division made the Board fearful of this schedule, especially in view of the concentration of sundry notables found in the Central Area. The Conversion Committee was well aware that 'because of the nature of Central London and the type of customer whom we have to deal with there, conversion, and, of course, general service work, too, are inevitably even more in the public eye than elsewhere'. Other factors worrying the Board at this time were the greater service loads, springing from new Government safety regulations in the aftermath of the Morton Report (see page 137), and also 'increasing pressure from various sources towards customer protection'. Unfortunately, also, the administration of customer service in the Central Division had not shown hoped-for improvements. At a confidential meeting on 1 December 1972, chaired by George Cooper, it was therefore decided to slow down considerably the planned London schedule. In particular, CU11 would operate at only half rate, making 2000 conversions a week instead of 4000. CU9 would continue at its scheduled 1500 a week, though double valving would permit this rate to be halved also if necessary.

Informing the Chairman of the Gas Council of this decision on 4

29 Sir Michael Milne-Watson, Chairman of William Press and Son Ltd, and George Cooper sign the contract for the conversion of Central London in the Kensington Board Room, 1974. This, the nation's largest single natural gas conversion contract, was awarded to Press in May 1972 but subsequent delays led to considerable revisions.

December, Cooper wrote: 'I have come to the conclusion that it would be unrealistic to expect the Central Region's [i.e. Central Division's] Service Department to cope with the situation ... I believe the Central Region itself is not strong enough to deal with 6,000 conversions a week anyhow. This is in spite of it having been reorganised for almost a year now.'

The result of these changes, with weekly totals dropping from an average of about 5500 conversions per week to 3500 or less, was to extend the period for converting Central London by almost two years. The conversion of London was now estimated to finish in April 1976 and the additional cost of the longer conversion period, delayed closure of town gas plants, additional feedstocks, and so on, amounted to no less than £4 million. The industrial troubles early in 1973 added even further delays of several months both to the start and to the finish of the London programme, since CU7 could not now meet its schedule to bring natural gas to the sector which would supply CU11.

A number of steps were taken to remove pressure from the Central Division in advance of actual conversion. In February, a team from the new British Gas Corporation spent two weeks studying the Central London work zones. Among the arrangements decided was that call-back would be kept at sixteen weeks (double the national policy of eight weeks) and telephones at the Conversion Unit would be kept open until 7 p.m. The Conversion Department was made directly responsible for clearing all PD installations, rather than impose this burden on the resources of the Division, and in May 1973 the Region (as it now was), appointed Fred Collins, the Conversion Manager, as Conversion and Service Co-ordinator, based at Vincent Street and responsible for the day-to-day co-ordination of the customer service aspect of the entire conversion operation in London. In succession to Collins, Jimmy Greene, formerly Manager, Central London Conversion, was appointed Conversion Manager. A Management Services team also retrained staff on customer service at Vincent Street in the spring and early summer of 1973. Another precaution was to prepare special VIP lists, which included 'those who by position or influence can form opinion in a large number of people'.

By May 1973, with the industrial troubles over, the Management Committee felt able to give a firm date for the start of CU11: 20 August 1973 – although this was subsequently delayed until 3 September, on which day the Unit began its 'running in' programme at Kentish Town. CU11 was not due to start converting in the Central Area until the spring of 1974, but both CU9 (Kew Bridge) and CU10 (Hornsey) would commence on the western and north-western fringes of the Central Area in June 1973. Between July and October 1973 areas covering Fulham, Marylebone, Paddington, Bayswater and North Kensington were scheduled for conversion.

An operation so complex and demanding as the conversion of London naturally brought its problems. A new element was the intervention of the Department of the Environment, which insisted on firm dates for the conversion of major buildings, such as 10 Downing Street, Buckingham Palace and the Tower of London. But to the relief of all at North Thames no great crisis occurred as the Units worked through their sectors. There were a number of reasons for this satisfactory progress. Improved procedures and the technical advances in the conversion sets supplied by the manufacturers, together with the low conversion rate and excellent work by the contractors, all helped. Another contributory factor was the longer period during which modern appliances had been available, so that very gradually the proportion of 'difficult' appliances remaining to be converted dropped. The peculiar problems arising in London led to some special arrangements not taken in other areas. One, at the request of the police, was to have all vehicles in position by 7.30 a.m. in order to ease traffic flows. Additionally, conversion sets were delivered to customers on 'C Day' itself rather than a few days previously, because the risk of theft and the problems of access to the innumerable flats and bedsitters made the normal arrangements impracticable.

Despite the succession of warning letters and visits by survey representatives, access to premises was, in fact, to prove a particular headache. Problems were especially acute in such areas as Kensington and Earls Court, where the conversion teams sometimes encountered 'squatters'. The three-day working week during the national emergency in the winter of 1973–74 (which did not directly affect conversion) meant a big rise in the number of 'no admits', especially to commercial and industrial premises. The Region's policy was to visit all premises on 'C Day', even if not officially recorded as having a gas supply. At times North Thames was forcing entry to as many as forty premises a week. These entries were always made in close consultation with the Metropolitan Police but, in fact, North Thames had no legal right of any description to force entry in this way. To the relief and surprise of the chief officers, not a single householder ever took legal action against North Thames Gas. The costs borne by North Thames of replacing broken doorframes and glass must have been quite considerable. But considerable, too, was the potential threat to the entire conversion programme from the large number of premises where the conversion teams could not gain access.

To give one example of the disruption which could be caused by access difficulties, we may take Sector 032, where 'C Day' was on 1 April 1974. This sector covered Connaught Street and part of Bayswater Road. In one large block of flats there were no fewer than 106 'no admits' when the fitters first called in the morning. Perhaps the inhabitants had decided the appointment card was an April Fool joke. Even by 5 p.m. entry had still not been gained to fifty flats, and it proved impossible to supply any natural gas to customers until nearly midnight, by which time several flats had had to be broken into. In this same sector a single 'no admit' in each of two mansion blocks similarly caused all customers to be deprived of gas throughout the day. As a result of this and a number of similar cases even greater efforts were made by the Public Relations Department to bring home to customers the importance of admittance. This was, indeed, a busy time for Derek Dutton, Head of Public Relations from 1974, and for his department. Public Relations had, of course, been one of the key departments in the conversion exercise from the beginning, and during the first two years of conversion had organised no less than 1000 public meetings of various kinds. With the conversion of Central London the department's role became even more critical and even more difficult. The diffuse and variegated pattern of London's inhabitants did not make for easy communications, while the original excitement and novelty that had attracted customers initially to the publicity campaigns were fading fast. During the London programme North Thames made particular efforts to ensure good relations with civic dignitaries. Special presentations in advance of conversion were made both for the City of Westminster, in July 1974, and for the City of London, in June 1976. And for the individual sectors the VIP lists were both extensive and comprehensive. A single sector in the Victoria area, for example, produced two embassies, two MPs, three princes, one princess, and eight other titled individuals.

A particular problem in London arose from the great number and variety of commercial appliances found in the area. Since so many customers needed their equipment during working hours, this meant at times almost continual night working. Between July 1975 and March 1976 CU11 was converting appliances at the rate of about 900 a week in the City and Westminster areas, and Table 6.1 gives an idea of the number of different commercial establishments eventually converted.

Table 6.1   Commercial establishments converted by CU11

Offices	3839
Restaurants	1497
Shops and stores	1405
Municipal buildings and embassies	815
Public houses	809
Cafés and snack bars	693
Hotels	357
Colleges and universities	283
Schools	262
Churches	219
Launderettes	135
Hospitals	103
Police, fire and ambulance	93
Main-line stations and termini	17

Source: North Thames Gas.

Conversion from the various Units proceeded sector by sector on the planned schedule. By November 1973 CU10 (Hornsey) had completed its Central London programme; the following autumn CU9 (Kew Bridge) wound up with the conversion of Watson House, having completed the Earls Court area in June and July. This left only CU11 to complete its programme, moving through Westminster, the City and East London towards Beckton. From 1 April 1974 conversion headquarters had moved to Nine Elms from Fulham, reflecting the scaling down of operations.

The conversion of Central London was difficult and time consuming, but it was also varied and interesting. Most conversions, whether in the

30 'C Day' at Buckingham Palace, 11 August 1975. From left to right, Jack Grey, Manager of Commercial Sales (Conversion Section), Jimmy Greene, Conversion Manager, George Cooper, Chairman, and Syd Mealey, Customer Service Director.

homes of the rich and famous or in humble flats and bed-sitters, were all in a day's work for the conversion teams. But sometimes the unexpected happened. One conversion team was held in an East European trade centre for two hours while its credentials were checked with North Thames Gas. On another occasion the conversion team had to wait its turn in a queue at one of the more dubious of Soho's 'clubs'. The conversion of Buckingham Palace on 11 August 1975 was naturally a highlight, and fortunately this passed without mishap. Conversion here was conducted in the presence of George Cooper, Jimmy Greene, the Conversion Manager, and Syd Mealey, Customer Service Director, although not in the presence of the Queen. For this delicate operation, North Thames brought thirty-three of its most experienced fitters, and during the course of a single day they converted nearly 200 appliances, including *ad hoc* conversion of gas lamps outside the palace. The only difficulties were encountered with two rather antiquated ('archaic' was George Cooper's description) kitchen appliances, which the Queen's chef, despite urging to the contrary, refused to exchange for more modern equipment.

In mid January the conversion programme had reached Fleet Street itself, a prospect naturally viewed with some trepidation at Chief Office. In the event the conversion of Fleet Street was untroubled and scarcely noted in the national press, a mark of the success and efficiency which the conversion team had established by this period. By the middle of February the Unit had reached the Guildhall, the Tower of London and the heart of the City, and at the beginning of April a relieved George Cooper could write to Fred Collins, the Conversion Co-ordinator: 'I wanted everyone in Conversion to know how pleased I have been with the way the City of London Conversion has gone. You know that there have been many eminent people who categorically stated that it could never be done. Well, it has been completed and very successfully, too, and I am particularly grateful to you and Jimmy Greene and all the staff in Conversion for the tremendous effort that has gone into the job.'

With the City finished, the weekly Central Area Conversion Co-ordination Committee meetings were disbanded, the seventy-fourth and final meeting congratulating the contractors, William Press, for their 'excellent effort'.

The finish of conversion in August 1976 brought mixed feelings at North Thames. The programme had dominated activities for a decade, and, despite the crises and traumas, a very strong sense of team-work and comradeship had built up in the Conversion Division. The end of conversion brought the dismantlement of the conversion team and the disappearance of some familiar faces, among them Fred Collins and Jimmy Greene. Both had joined the Gas Light & Coke Company in the same year, 1935, and both had played an integral part in North Thames's entire conversion exercise from its inception at Canvey some ten years before. The end of conversion brought also the end of manufactured gas, and hence the close of a chapter that had started with F. A. Winsor in 1812. The final switch-off was made at the Romford Works at 1 p.m. on Thursday, 26 August at a special ceremony attended by Robert Evans, the Deputy Chairman. Romford was then the last operational gasworks in England and Wales and gas had been manufactured there continuously since 1892. By this stage enough town gas had been stored to last until the very final sector was converted on Monday 29 August, appropriately at Beckton, where the last houses were mostly occupied by North Thames gas workers.

7

Organisational Change and the Time of Troubles

Throughout its first two decades the internal organisation of North Thames Gas remained fundamentally unaltered (see Figure 7.1). Commercial activities continued to be concentrated in the territorial Divisions, under the overall control of the Commercial Manager. A separate Headquarters Division handled such matters as new housing, public services, lighting, and industrial sales. Production and distribution lay within the orbit of the Chief Engineer, while the Controller of Services looked after transport, meters, and showrooms. The Controller of Supplies was responsible for the purchase and storage of appliances and materials; and the Controller of By-Products controlled the processing and marketing of the materials produced by the two Products Works at Beckton and Southall. There were separate Coal and Coke Managers, who looked after purchases and sales of these materials. Meanwhile, at Chief Office were grouped the Secretarial, Legal, Public Relations, Personnel, Finance, Management Services, and Medical sections, housed in various buildings around Kensington and Fulham.

Some changes took place in internal organisation, of course, especially during the 1960s. Shortly after becoming Chairman in 1964, R. S. Johnson set up a small Management Committee which could consider the overall strategy of the separate departmental functional committees. The new Management Committee held its first meeting on 16 July. Commercial organisation was streamlined in 1965, when the Mid-Essex and East Essex Divisions were amalgamated into a single Essex Division upon the retirement of A. R. Shirley, the Mid-Essex Divisional Manager. The following year, with the retirement of the North Divisional Manager, W. J. Butler, this Division was absorbed into the enlarged North Western and Eastern Divisions. In 1963 a new Industrial Division was formed to try (but not very successfully) to develop this side of the Board's business. The arrival of conversion also necessarily brought a number of organisational changes, including the formation of the new Conversion Division. Changes in production technology led to the amalgamation in 1967 of the Coal and Coke Departments and some reorganisation among gas-making stations. By 1970, since coal carbon-

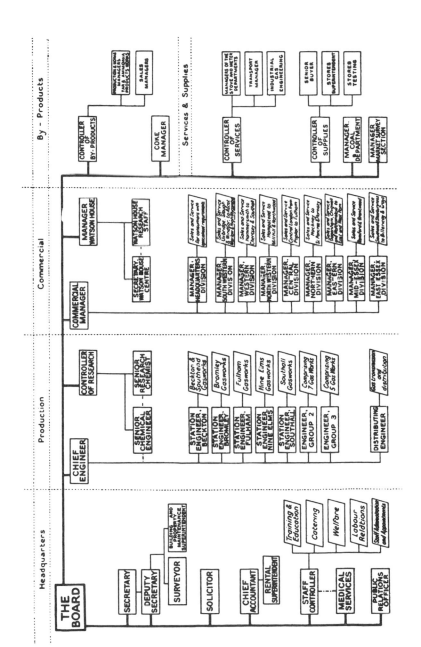

Figure 7.1 North Thames Gas Board organisational chart, 1960

isation had ceased, the manufacture of by-products at the Products Works finished also. The responsibilities of the Chief Engineer were then divided between a Director of Engineering and a Chief Distribution Engineer. In 1969 the Management Services Department was split into a Productivity Services Section and a Corporate Planning Section, while the growing Computer Sections were placed within the Chief Accountant's Department. In 1969 also, the Chairman introduced a policy of appointing a Director at the head of each main function. In 1969, E. J. Edwards became Director of Engineering and the following year Paul Rhodes became the Director of Marketing and R. G. Bloom (Chief Accountant) became Director of Finance. In 1971, an Executive Committee, meeting weekly, replaced the separate functional committees, which had operated hitherto. None the less, for all these changes the broad structure remained that which had been inherited from the Gas Light & Coke Company. Essentially, the decentralised and functional organisation evolved under Edgar Sylvester still remained.

The Gas Light's heritage and the organisational structure of North Thames combined to make the role of the Chairman critical. The Chairman had always been the figure-head, administrator, policy-maker and executive. Indeed, under a strong Chairman reluctant to delegate, such as Michael Milne-Watson, the position of Deputy Chairman could be rather anonymous; Jim Burns certainly found the role boring after his years as Chief Engineer.

Each of Board's four Chairmen, differing widely in approach and background, has made distinctive contributions to North Thames. Michael Milne-Watson, despite his inexperience and only thirty-seven years of age, had been an obvious choice to succeed Sylvester as Governor of the Gas Light & Coke Company. It was a wise decision of the Minster of Fuel and Power to keep him at the helm in 1949, and from then until 1964 he continued in many ways the traditions of his father. Outstanding among his qualities were charm and courtesy, and under his leadership North Thames maintained its rather close-knit and almost paternalistic character inherited from Gas Light days. By temperament he was autocratic and not given to divulging information without good reason. It was characteristic that he did not permit the circulation of Board minutes, these being read by the Secretary from a lectern at each monthly meeting. But whereas Sir David had looked outwards, to amalgamations and to national organisations, Michael was essentially inward-looking. He was a little disdainful both of the Gas Council and of ministerial involvement. Indeed, his evidence and report to the first Select Committee on Nationalised Industries in 1961 was easily the most opaque and uninformative of all the Area Boards. He was always genuinely involved in the social and welfare aspects of the Board's activities and rarely missed the numerous presentations for employees of forty years' service or the sports days. It was, indeed, the warmth and feeling of pride in the organisation engendered at the pre-war Annual Gatherings which had originally decided him, at the age of twenty-three, to join the Gas Light & Coke Company in 1933 (on probation, in the welfare section, at a salary of £200 a year); certainly, his father never suggested he do so.

When Michael Milne-Watson resigned from the Board in 1964 to become Deputy Chairman and later Chairman of the State steel firm, Richard Thomas and Baldwin, a Milne-Watson had held high office in Company and Board for six decades. There were many who felt that his departure meant the end of an era. The legacies he left were numerous, but what stands out was his vision and enterprise in backing such schemes as the liquid methane project and the Canvey conversion. These schemes raised eyebrows both inside and outside the Board but, as a colleague put it, 'you don't argue with Milne-Watson', and he proved right in both instances. In 1961, Milne-Watson was made a Companion of the Institution of Gas Engineers – a rare distinction for a

31 Meeting of the Board at 30 Kensington Church Street, March 1966. From left to right are J. S. Barnes, Secretary; J. A. Buckley; F. L. Levy; Lord Collison; L. J. Clark; R. S. Johnson; G. Dillon; E. Bayliss; and the Earl of Halsbury. Behind the Chairman is a portrait of F. A. Winsor, founder of the Gas Light & Coke Company in 1812.

*Photograph reproduced from Thames Gas magazine

non-engineer but wholly appropriate in view of his interest, foresight and encouragement in the field of technical change.

Milne-Watson's successor in May 1964 was Richard Stringer Johnson, Chairman of the East Midlands Gas Board since 1956. But Johnson was no stranger at North Thames. He was a former Gas Light man, starting in 1935 and later becoming Solicitor and Controller of Services. He had left the Board on nationalisation, his position as Solicitor being taken by J. S. Barnes, who in turn became Secretary to the Board in 1965. Familiarity of practice born of such continuity was a characteristic feature of North Thames in those years. Quiet and meticulous, Johnson laid great stress on improving communications within the Board and in maintaining good relations with the Gas Council. He was more ready to delegate than his predecessor and under him the role of Deputy Chairman and other principal posts were enhanced. Johnson it was who first brought full-time executive officers on to the Board (which mirrored a trend occurring in the nationalised industries and also in other gas Boards) and, as we have seen, at the end of his Chairmanship he introduced a policy of appointing officers at director level for each of the principal functions. His chairmanship was an eventful one, for it coincided with the great central-heating boom, the opening of new reforming plants and the phasing out of carbonisation, the Canvey conversion and the full conversion programme, fears about gas safety, and the beginnings of the great pressures on customer services. Inevitably, in the light of later problems, Johnson has been blamed for not making more fundamental changes to the Board's organisational structure in order to prepare better for the strains of conversion. It is certainly true he was not a man for rapid action or impetuous decisions. Indeed, many colleagues were often exasperated by the hours he would spend in committees and other meetings drafting letters and attending to details. He was, of course, a lawyer and lawyers are cautious about such matters. On the other hand, it was impossible to foresee just how great the problems at North Thames would become. Moreover, Johnson's health was not good and on several occasions illness caused his absence for prolonged periods.

It was during Johnson's chairmanship that the biggest and most widely publicised gas disaster in the Board's history occurred. On 16 May 1968 an explosion occurred at Ronan Point, a tower block at Canning Town in East London. The explosion caused the partial collapse of the building and the death of five people. On the day following the explosion both the Chairman and the Deputy Chairman visited the scene, and a public inquiry was at once set up by the Government. The subsequent report, published in August the following year, confirmed that the explosion was due to a gas fault. However, the Board's workmen were exonerated from any blame, and the direct cause was found to have been a gas leak from a fractured nut, broken when an unauthorised individual had tampered with it while making a connection.

Further public alarm about gas safety followed soon after. This time there were fears about the safety of natural gas and the problem arose during the winter of 1969–70. These fears were caused partly by the publicity given to a number of gas explosions and partly by the generally unfavourable press coverage of conversion at the time. It must be recalled that early conversion operations, not only in the North Thames area but everywhere, resulted in a massive increase in reported gas escapes. Often, as we have seen, these were not serious and in some cases were caused simply by over-odorisation. But the climate of public opinion was hostile and the issue became something of a political one. There was considerable feeling within the gas industry that attacks in Parliament and in the press were unfair; in August 1970, for example, a note from the Gas Council Public Relations Adviser recalled that 'every single employee of the gas industry was, during the course of last winter's mass media-generated hysteria about conversion, subjected to both criticism and questions about the safety of the industry'. A House of Commons debate was held in February and the Government decided to hold an independent public inquiry into the safety of natural gas. The inquiry was conducted by a distinguished Professor of Chemical Engineering from Manchester University, Professor Frank Morton and it commenced in March 1970 and reported the following August. The Paymaster General, Harold Lever, in setting up the inquiry, said that he 'would rather have an unnecessary independent public inquiry than unnecessary anxiety and an unnecessary unjustified feeling that anyone wishes to whitewash the industry'. Professor Morton and his team visited North Thames in April and had meetings with R. S. Johnson – in his last month as Chairman – Paul Rhodes, and other senior officers. In the event, the inquiry fully supported the Gas Council's claims about the inherent safety of natural gas and the adequacy of the safety precautions undertaken during conversion. Indeed, the report pointed out quite rightly that the testing and checking of customers' appliances would add considerably to safety and, since natural gas was, in fact, non-toxic, the number of accidental poisonings (and, of course, deliberate suicides) would eventually disappear. In general the report found that the number of accidental deaths attributed to gas had fallen steadily throughout the 1960s, being 7.1 per cent of all such deaths in 1963 and only 1.8 per cent in 1969. Gas, moreover, was safer than any other of the major fuels in terms of fatalities caused by fires; in the five years following 1963 gas had been responsible for 141 fire fatalities, electricity 513, solid fuel 500 and oil 247.

During the period of Johnson's chairmanship the Gas Council became increasingly concerned about certain aspects of North Thames's performance. Setting criteria by which to judge the economic perform-ance of a nationalised undertaking is far from easy. In the case of the gas industry the position of individual Regions since 1972 has been additionally clouded since, for reasons that would be unconvincing even if they were clear, the Gas Corporation has not published separate Regional balances. For earlier years, though, we do have profit and loss figures, and year-to-year fluctuations in the financial performance over the years 1949 to 1972 are shown in Table 7.1. Yet comparisons here with other Boards can be misleading. For one thing, there was no standardisation of accounting methods. Commenting to the Select Committee on Nationalised Industries in 1961 on figures which showed North Thames to have the lowest administrative costs of any Board, Milne-Watson said that 'in my humble opinion, those figures are

Table 7.1　North Thames Gas, revenue account,
1949–72

Year	Net surplus/deficit (£000s)
1949–50[1]	556
1950–51	314
1951–52	106
1952–53	708
1953–54	556
1954–55	−155
1955–56	−322
1956–57	370
1957–58	1 486
1958–59	−53
1959–60	62
1960–61	637
1961–62	490
1962–63	480
1963–64	980
1964–65	1 220
1965–66	1 660
1966–67	80
1967–68	−3 350
1968–69	3 000
1969–70	2 430
1970–71	180 000
1971–72	309 000
1972–73[2]	−5 495

[1] 11 months
[2] 9 months ending 31 December 1972. This excludes the winter quarter, when revenue is normally greatest.
Source: North Thames Gas.

absolutely useless. I don't think we are any better or worse than the other Boards. There is a tremendous latitude in organisational accounting.' Additionally, characteristics of supply and demand varied enormously between Boards. North Thames had the great advantage at the outset of a compact area and a well-developed organisation, based on the facilities and the structure of the Gas Light & Coke Company. But it had to pay more for its coal than any other Board, and had a high interest burden to carry because of the allocation of British Gas Stock assigned to North Thames. North Thames had to make virtually all of its gas and did not have the cheap supplies of coke-oven gas available elsewhere. In 1960, for example, the Welsh Board manufactured only 20 per cent of gas it distributed. Other costs in London too, were higher than elsewhere: the cost of land and property, the cost of wages and salaries, the cost of mains-laying and servicing in congested streets, and so on. The large domestic load was expensive, both in terms of mains service and maintenance and in terms of the necessarily high peak-load capacity which was involved.

Looking at the annual fluctuations in the Board's accounts we should remember that these were influenced considerably by forces outside the Board's control: factors like coal prices, nationally negotiated wages and salaries, changes in purchase-tax and hire-purchase regulations, price freezes and other government economic regulations, and many others. Even the weather could affect results significantly. Mild winters meant low sales, but the Board nevertheless had to provide stand-by capacity to guard against exceptional conditions (usually aiming to cater for expected demand from a 'one in fifty' winter). During the 'shockingly good' winter of 1960–61, to use Milne-Watson's phrase, no more than 351 m. cu ft gas/day was sent out on one day, against a total capacity of 440 m. cu ft gas/day.

In view of the constant pressure on costs exerted by rising coal prices and the highly competitive market conditions, the Board's achievements during the first decade or so after nationalisation were considerable. The general duty of meeting normal costs with revenue was accomplished successfully (except during the mid-1950s, when rising coal prices produced a deficit) and the reserve fund was built up steadily. The accumulated surplus of revenue over costs was over £4.4 million during the first decade, considerably more than that achieved by any of the other Boards. Moreover, North Thames was able to finance a high proportion of capital investment out of its own resources. The self-financing ratio averaged about 65 per cent in the 1950s and rose to around 80 per cent between 1960 and 1965.

However, during the 1960s pressure mounted. For one thing, the financial targets set by the Government changed. The 1961 White Paper on the Financial Obligations of the Nationalised Industries paved the way by encouraging the industry to adopt a more commercial outlook. For the five-year period beginning 1962–63, subsequently extended until 1968–69, the Board was required to earn an average gross return (including depreciation, interest and surplus) of 9.5 per cent on net assets. These new financial obligations increased the role of the Gas Council and in 1961 a Select Committee paid particular attention to the relations between the Council and the Boards. This was the first tentative step on the long road towards centralisation, later accelerated by the Gas Act of 1965. For the quinquennium from 1970–71 the financial target set by the Ministry was increased to 7 per cent net of depreciation (an increase of some 3 per cent on the old basis).

The new target figures for the first few years were just about achieved, but 1967 produced a crisis and the Board experienced the worst deficit in its history. In June of that year the war in the Middle East resulted in the closure of the Suez Canal and a large increase in oil prices (by now the principal feedstock used by the Board in producing gas). Oil prices rose by no less than 50 per cent. For three months, also, supplies of liquid natural gas from Algeria ceased. The results of the Middle East crisis cost North Thames an estimated £3 million in all. Application by the Board for a price increase of 8 per cent was referred in October to the Prices and Incomes Board on the basis of a decision taken the previous month that charges by nationalised industries should be so dealt with. No increase was permitted until the following April. Devaluation of the pound in the autumn of 1967 further raised the cost of imported oil. R. S. Johnson, speaking at the Annual Conference for Joint Consultative Committee Delegates in December, declared that: 'The Board's economic position at the present time is worse than it has ever been ... we are going deeper and deeper into the red every day'; and the Board had by now exhausted its reserves.

All the time new plants were adding to the Board's debt, and interest charges (interest rates themselves were on the increase) mounted. In the two years ending March 1969, North Thames had invested more than £40 million on new capital projects. In the first year of the Board's operations interest charges had been under £2 million. For the last nine months of 1972 alone they amounted to nearly £12 million. The self-financing ratio dropped sharply and borrowing grew steadily, as Tables 7.2 and 7.3 show.

A direct consequence of the 1967 crisis was a drastic pruning of the Board's investment projects and a general economy drive to cut costs and improve efficiency. By the end of February 1968 the Board's revenue account was showing a deficit of £4.3 million (of which £2.5 million was directly attributable to the Middle East crisis) and the Chairman of the Gas Council, noting that North Thames was one of the five Boards expected to record a deficit for the financial year 1968–69, emphasised to

Table 7.2 Interest charges and self-financing ratio, 1965–71

	1965–66	1966–67	1967–68	1968–69	1969–70	1970–71
Interest per therm (p)	0.93	0.99	1.08	1.23	1.32	1.49
Self-financing ratio (%)	94	33	33	36	48	31

Source: North Thames Gas.

Table 7.3 Cumulative advances from Ministry of Power and Gas Council (up to 31 March)

1958	£11.3 million
1961	£18.3 million
1969	£84.1 million
1971	£131.0 million

Source: North Thames Gas.

the Chairman 'the importance of making every possible saving on revenue account'. We may note here the growing role of the Council in gas industry affairs, and increasing Council concern with the state of affairs at North Thames in these years. The economy measures which the Board felt obliged to make were doubly unfortunate in view of the pressure at the time on facilities and the additional pressures which were soon to descend during the conversion programme. Yet again, in 1970, the Board was obliged to wait for a year while its next proposed price increase (in the wake of substantial wage and salary rises) was once more referred to the Prices and Incomes Board.

Many of the problems facing North Thames in the 1960s confronted other Boards also, but North Thames's comparative performance was disappointing. In nearly every year the return on the Board's assets was lower than the average for the industry as a whole and North Thames's average results failed to reach the targets set by the Ministry.

The high reputation of the Board began to suffer in these years. The problem was not simply one of aggregate finances. Customer service complaints began to grow, yet increasing expenditure in this area seemed unmatched by corresponding improvements. There was a feeling outside the Board that North Thames was too 'inbred' and too unwilling to change and reorganise itself. The retirement of Johnson as Chairman in May 1970 therefore brought an opportunity for change. In selecting a new Chairman the Ministry looked outside the Board for the first time and brought in George Cooper, Deputy Chairman of the West

Midlands Gas Board, with a more or less explicit brief to reorganise the North Thames Gas Board.

Cooper was fifty-four years of age at the time of his appointment, and already had substantial experience in the gas industry. However, he was not a Londoner (he was born and brought up in Wolverhampton), had built his career in the midlands, always retained a suspicion of metropolitan ways, and felt a lack of sympathy with his new environment. By profession George Cooper was an accountant, and his early career had been in local government in the midlands. He joined the West Midlands Gas Board in 1950, was Chief Accountant (1965) and Director of Finance (1967) and, at the beginning of 1968, Deputy Chairman.

There is no doubt that Cooper's chairmanship proved a troubled time for the Board. Perhaps this was inevitable in view of the many and deep-seated problems, and Cooper experienced all the difficulties of a newcomer in a hostile environment. He brought to his task determination and courage, together with friendliness and an often disarming candour. He was certainly not afraid to lead from the front and throughout his chairmanship was always ready to take responsibility for the Board's failings. But he himself never felt at home at North Thames and never felt that the Board's officers gave him full co-operation and support, and in their turn many of them resented bitterly the changes he introduced. Nevertheless, many of his reforms were necessary and, in the longer term, effective; and, in addition, he provided North Thames at long last with a new Chief Office building.

To understand the background to the Board's 'Time of Troubles' which occurred during Cooper's chairmanship we should return to the expansive era of the 1960s. The revival of sales which had started around 1960 reached new heights with the arrival of natural gas. Based on the Government's decision to press ahead with North Sea development as quickly as possible, projections of future supplies of natural gas made by the Gas Council in 1967 showed that supplies of some 4000 m. cu ft gas/day would be available by 1975, four times the consumption of manufactured gas in 1965. Considerable emphasis was therefore placed on selling the new gas. This meant developing existing loads, but it meant also seeking out new areas of growth, especially among industrial consumers. All the Area Boards were expected to play their part in expanding sales of gas to all classes of consumers at this time.

At North Thames the main domestic load builders – central heating boilers and space heaters – were promoted vigorously. In 1968, for example, a variety of new central-heating packages were launched in joint promotional campaigns with the South Eastern and Eastern Gas Boards, and for the first time the selling of central heating was extended to the Board's authorised dealers. In the following year the Gas Council and all twelve Boards co-operated in the major 'Guaranteed Warmth' campaign and North Thames launched its new 'Gold Star' tariff to consumers using natural gas (extended later to those on town gas). Mobile caravans displaying central heating toured the Board's areas. By 1976, space heating of all kinds accounted for about 75 per cent of all domestic sales by the Board, a far cry from the position two decades earlier when cooking had been dominant and space heating little developed. The overall achievements were impressive. From 384 million therms sold in 1958–59, sales reached 538 million in 1966–67, 772 million in 1970–71, 1281 million in 1974–75 and 1960 million by 1985–86. Most of the domestic sales were concentrated among credit customers, who continued to form an increasing proportion of the total throughout the period.

With the arrival of natural gas, the gas industry was also able to offer attractive rates to industrial consumers and for the first time there was a really significant expansion on this side of North Thames's business. Expansion here was concentrated largely in the space of just a few years from 1969 until about 1973. From around 70 million therms in the late 1960s, sales jumped to 107 million in 1970–71, to over 200 million therms in 1971–72 and to 361 million by 1974–75. Included in this growth were some very large contracts indeed. Some were on the 'interruptible' basis introduced by the Gas Council in 1969, whereby the consumer might be required to use stand-by gas during periods of peak demand. Indeed, some 90 per cent of the total growth of industrial consumption in the years between 1969 and 1975 was accounted for by interruptible contracts. One such was the three-year contract signed with Tunnel Cement Ltd in 1971. This contract was the largest to be concluded by any Area Board and amounted to 75 million therms annually, which was more than the total level of North Thames's annual industrial sales during the 1960s. The average price agreed was 4.45 new pence per therm. This compared with an average selling price for industrial contracts of nearly 6 pence the year before, and by 1973 gas prices charged by North Thames to industry were well below half their average 1969 levels. Another contract in 1969 sold over 30 million therms a year to the Slough Industrial Power Station and in 1972 a similar volume of gas was sold to the Tate & Lyle Sugar Refinery at Silvertown. These industrial contracts were highly attractive to the gas industry. Industrial demand had a low space-heating content and therefore tended to take even quantities throughout the year. From about the middle of the 1970s, however, the period of rapid expansion came to an end as the recession, higher prices, the slower growth in supplies, and the steady movement of industries away from the London area combined to depress sales.

From 1969 also, substantial inroads into commercial heating markets began to be made. At that time gas held only about 7 per cent of this market compared with 70 per cent for oil and 23 per cent for solid fuel. Among major new commercial contracts were several large hotels, including the Dorchester with an annual consumption of 1 million therms, which changed from oil in the summer of 1971. In 1970, St Paul's Cathedral had changed from solid fuel to gas, and in the same year some 500 local authority schools in the Board's area made a similar switch.

We have seen already how the sales boom of the 1960s strained the service and accounting sides of the Board's operations, and various measures were taken to improve operations. In 1964 new Centralised Service Units were set up, and from 1967 some of these were transformed into new units – Centralised Sales, Service and Accounting Units – where all customer enquiries and requests could be directed to a central location serving 120 000 or so customers. Various other measures were taken to raise efficiency. One was to pre-assemble cookers and other appliances in order to ease the fitters' tasks (incidentally thereby reducing the losses through chipped enamel from about 25 per cent to 2 per cent), a measure started in 1962. In 1965 arrangements were made for the manufacturers themselves to pre-assemble cookers.

In the offices, computers and other types of machinery were increasingly installed. The Board had begun to investigate the possible use of computers as early as 1955 but little was achieved beyond the introduction of some electronic calculators. Indeed, at first the use of computers was not envisaged beyond that of an aid to the accounting departments, and it was not until the 1970s that their applications in such areas as distribution, sales, and transport were fully appreciated. Early in 1966, however, a new installation known as GINA (Gas Industry Network Analyser) was introduced to assist engineers with gas-load problems. At the beginning of 1959 the Chief Accountant, L. W. Smith, announced a programme to introduce computers for credit customer accounts and for weekly wage sheets. In 1960 the Cost Office, located at Vincent Street, Westminster, was renamed the Mechanised Accounting Office and experimental electronic equipment was instal- led. Even then it was estimated that the complete mechanisation might take five years to complete. From 1964 there was a growing use of Banda machines to record sales and installations and in the following year the decision was made to computerise the accounts of all North Thames's 750 000 credit customers. Accordingly, an ICL 1904 computer was installed in the Accounting Department at the Carnwath Road offices in October 1966. This was to operate the new CAESAR system (Customer Accounting Enquiry System with Automatic Retrieval), North Thames being the first Board to introduce this. But even now progress was only slow and hesitant. Many teething troubles were encountered in the transfer of accounts, which were unbelievably complicated. Indeed, at the time there were no fewer than 100 separate procedures before bills were compiled under the old system. Yet by 1970 only about 45 000 accounts had been computerised and in other fields also the adoption of computer facilities was tardy. Thereafter the pace quickened and by early 1971 the accounts of some 230 000 credit customers were accessible on visual display units at the Fulham Customer Accounts office. In 1968 the Board's payroll was put on a 1904 computer and the following year an ICL 1905 computer was installed.

The mounting volume of complaints and attendant publicity brought conversion to a halt in the winters of 1968 and 1972, as explained in Chapter 6. But conversion merely exacerbated the growing problem, it did not create it. For example, of the complaints received by the Consultative Council during the nine months ending 31 December 1972, those concerned with conversion numbered 1825; but 2222 related to sales and service, while no fewer than 3241 concerned disputed gas accounts.

The steady deterioration can be seen in a variety of ways. Table 7.4 shows the complaints received by the Consultative Council. These totals were only a small fraction of total complaints, the majority, of course, being dealt with directly by District Offices. There was also, as we have seen, an alarming increase in complaints to Head Office ('Chairman's Complaints'), shown in Table 7.5. Representations of this

Table 7.4 Complaints to Consultative Council, 1967–73

	1967–68	*1968–69*	*1969*	*1970–71*	*1971–72*	*1972–73*
Service (inc. central heating)	182	366	479	1220	901	2151
Disputed accounts	116	177	256	363	577	2978
Conversion	–	93	742	1236	1162	1643
Others	40	61	253	697	665	1733
Total	338	697	1730	3516	3305	8505

Source: *Annual Reports*, the North Thames Gas Board Consultative Council and the North Thames Region Gas Consumers' Council.

Table 7.5 Complaints received at Chief Office, 1971–72

	Total complaints	*Complaints per 100 000 customers*
November 1971	4501	24.81
July 1972	2133	11.76
September 1972	4676	25.78
November 1972	6999	38.59

Source: North Thames Gas.

nature have to be treated with a great deal of caution, since to some extent such factors as the national publicity given to North Thames's affairs and the growing use of the telephone produced a rising trend anyway. Nevertheless, a tenfold rise in complaints in the four years up to 1970–71 and then a more than twofold increase by 1972–73 was obviously a sign that something was deeply wrong, and nothing like these volumes of complaints were encountered by other Boards. The writer of a letter to *The Times* in November 1972 thought that nothing short of Prime Ministerial intervention could improve matters, asking 'Could the malfunctioning of Mr Heath's gas cooker be contrived, causing him to request service from the North Thames Gas Board?'

Table 7.4 shows the increasing pressures brought by conversion, while service complaints grew even faster after 1969–70 (these were, of course, related to conversion in many cases). Most dramatic was the number of disputed gas accounts, which jumped to nearly 3000 in 1972–73. Problems encountered by the Customer Accounts Department were many. Some stemmed from administrative changes. In 1962 it was decided to centralise the accounts for credit customers, instead of operating a locally-based system. From 1962 the accounts for western area customers were gradually transferred to Fulham, where a new building was opened at Carnwath Road to accommodate Watson House as well as several North Thames departments. In the eastern areas, centralisation of accounts was at Ilford. However, during 1970 a new office was acquired at Middlesex House, Alperton, and the following year the Fulham accounts were transferred there. As a result of this move, which took place at a time when the work-load was intense and growing, the Board lost no less than 150 experienced staff. At the same time both eastern and western areas were in great difficulties with computerisation, as they changed from one system (the ICL 1004) to another (the ICL 1904). The latter system was superior, but the process of transferring hundreds of thousands of accounts with insufficient and inexperienced staff was daunting. When Kenneth Pickthall joined the Board from the Gas Council as Head of Customer Accounting in October 1972 he found that at Ilford 'The billing records were in a deplorable state ... and the long hard haul to bring it up to date resulted in more and more disputes and a very large backlog of unanswered correspondence. Follow-up of outstanding accounts had come to a standstill.' Disputed accounts and other matters which were handled by District Offices were affected adversely by reorganisation. For example, the Western and North Western Divisions, which were still without central headquarters in 1972, were 'struggling to operate systems designed for a centralised administration, while the work is carried out at a number of decentralised local offices'. There were then over 30 000 unanswered letters and 50 000 disputed accounts. One of

Pickthall's first decisions was to halt the transfer to the new computer system. This gave a breathing space in which to improve the staffing position and to modify the 1904 system, which had been running into trouble. At the same time a crash programme to clear the backlog of work was undertaken. For two months the staff were called upon to give up much of their leisure time and to work long into the evenings and throughout Saturdays and Sundays. During the cessation of conversion, the Accounting Department 'borrowed' both survey representatives and sales representatives to help them out. As a result of these emergency measures the situation improved, although throughout the conversion period Customer Accounting continued to experience an unsatisfactorily high level of complaints and disputed bills. The pressures which built up on Customer Accounting during 1972 are illustrated for various critical operations in Tables 7.6, 7.7 and 7.8, and the problems affected nearly all areas throughout North Thames.

Table 7.6   Outstanding disputes received at Billing Centres and dealt with at District Offices (000s)

	Essex	Eastern	Central	Divisions: North Western	Western	Total
January 1972	3.3	4.7	6.9	15.9	13.8	44.6
February 1972	3.9	4.9	5.9	14.7	13.2	42.6
March 1972	3.9	3.8	6.4	14.2	13.7	42.0
April 1972	4.4	3.8	6.3	12.8	13.3	40.6
May 1972	4.9	4.3	6.5	12.2	12.2	40.1
June 1972	5.8	3.7	7.1	12.3	12.6	41.5
July 1972	6.7	3.8	7.8	13.2	13.2	44.7
August 1972	7.2	3.6	8.2	13.1	14.9	47.0
September 1972	8.7	3.9	8.3	14.5	15.5	50.9
October 1972	9.3	3.8	12.1	13.8	15.7	54.7
November 1972	8.3	4.1	11.0	13.1	16.2	52.7
December 1972	8.2	4.9	11.3	12.2	16.2	52.8
January 1973	8.9	4.1	10.5	11.9	15.0	50.4

Source: North Thames Gas.

Table 7.7   Outstanding correspondence at Billing Centres (000s)

	Ilford	Alperton	Total
3 Jan. 1972	22.5	31.7	54.2
4 April 1972	19.2	26.8	46.0
2 October 1972	5.5	25.1	30.6
1 January 1973	2.2	8.2	10.4

Source: North Thames Gas.

Table 7.8   Average delay between meter reading and despatch of
account (*days*)

	Ilford	*Alperton*
January 1971	43.2	25.5
July 1971	66.0	33.1
October 1971	40.4	37.6
January 1972	24.3	31.9
June 1972	17.5	22.8
December 1972	14.3	22.1

Source: North Thames Gas.

Bad publicity over conversion, the constant stream of complaints at the Board's showrooms, the loaning of sales representatives to Accounts and the impact of the strike in the first quarter of 1973 combined to hit appliance sales. Declines were felt nationally but were especially severe for North Thames. In the summer of 1973, appliance sales were described by Paul Rhodes as 'catastrophic' and reached their lowest levels since the war.

It was the Board's misfortune that so many problems should coincide at this period. Minutes of a confidential meeting on 1 December 1972 held at Kensington Church Street to discuss slowing the conversion programme summed up the misery: 'The Chairman reviewed the present situation with regard to conversion and customer service and referred to the increasing pressure from various sources towards customer protection; the interest of the Ministry in our operations; the appointment of a Director-General for Fair Trading; the position of Baroness Macleod as the Chairman of the Industry's Consumers' Council, and the present difficult time we are having with regard to customer complaints at both Chief Office and local level, and mentioned that the progress on the Central Division with regard to the administration of customer service was less rapid than had been expected.'

It was in these difficult and highly inauspicious circumstances that the Board handed over its responsibilities to the new British Gas Corporation on 1 January 1973: customer complaints, internal dissatisfaction, conversion halted, a huge deficit (over £5 million in the red during the first nine months of the financial year, although it was true that the revenue from the winter quarter was yet to come), the Adjournment Debate, and labour troubles looming.

For George Cooper, reappointed as first Chairman of the Region, for Paul Rhodes, appointed as Deputy Chairman, and for the other chief officers (who all remained in their former posts) the problems could not vanish with the old Board. Many of the reasons for the sad state of affairs, not a few of them lying outside the Board's control, have been discussed already, but one long-term difficulty needs emphasis if we are to understand the problems of North Thames in these troubled times. Throughout the first two decades of the Board's existence there was an almost constant drain of North Thames's most able officers to posts elsewhere. It is worth reflecting that under the Gas Light & Coke Company there were virtually no 'outside' jobs of comparable stature to those within the Company, but after nationalisation there were chairmanships, deputy chairmanships and other top management posts available for able executives in other regions, as well as posts with the Gas Council and its successor. The list of North Thames's losses is immense, although it would be invidious to attempt to document it. An analogous drain occurred with the conversion programme, for some of the Board's most able men in the Divisions were drafted to the Conversion Division and this considerably diluted talent 'on the district'.

The basic difficulty was that the Board's organisational structure proved inadequate to cope with the demands made upon it. The loads fell unevenly within the Board's area and it was the large and unwieldy North Western and Western Divisions that fared worst. In retrospect it was perhaps unwise to have enlarged the area and responsibility of the North Western Division in 1966 when, as we have seen, the old Northern Division was absorbed into adjacent Divisions. Table 7.9 shows the size of the various Divisions in 1970; especially striking in view of the added burdens to Customer Accounting was the number of credit customers handled by the North Western Division. One of George Cooper's first acts as Chairman of North Thames was to commission in 1970 a management consultants' study into some of the Board's customer service problems. The subsequent report showed clearly that the organisation at district level was sometimes inefficient and incapable of handling the work-loads.

The problems at district level really boiled down to three, although there were supporting elements. The first was simply the question of office procedures – the processing and filing of customer requests, notification of appliance sales and so on. The Banda revenue document, noting an appliance sale, might be located at any one of ten places in the course of processing; the normal service ticket was handled by eight different sections if the job was completed without a hitch, and by up to fifteen if there were any complaints. Moreover, there was no control copy of the service ticket so that no record of updating was kept with the latest information. The flow of all this documentation meant vulnerability to delays (especially at times of staff illness or shortage), with consequent arrears. It is no wonder that these problems on the clerical side made themselves felt in terms of fitters arriving to do a job without

Table 7.9   Customers by Divisions, 31 March 1970

Division	Domestic credit	Domestic prepayment
South Western	85965	77132
Western	142191	132397
North Western	233702	229024
Central	91745	151580
Eastern	150083	263259
Essex	121471	137639
Total	825157	991031

Source: North Thames Gas.

knowledge of any earlier call or of what had been diagnosed and no wonder that customers suffered so much from delays.

The second problem at district level arose from the sheer volume of work, especially during conversion. Take, for example, the North London area served by the Finchley Office. Conversion started here, at the rate of 1500 conversions per week, in June 1970. The total number of service tickets issued rose by 22 per cent in 1970 compared with 1969 and the number of revenue tickets by 24 per cent, conversion exacerbating this increase because of 'sell out'. Even worse, the number of priority and emergency tickets rose by 56 per cent. At the Ilford Centralised Unit, where conversion also started in 1970, reaching a rate of 1500 a week in June, rises were even more dramatic: revenues rising 57 per cent, service tickets 42 per cent and emergency tickets by 94 per cent. The numbers involved were considerable. In June 1970 there had been 1282 priority calls at Ilford and in October there were 4041. In June, 4993 service tickets had been issued and in October, 17128. In the same period revenues had risen from 4898 to 8097. Seasonal factors were only partly responsible, for the annual trend was sharply upwards. Priority calls were a special problem because if the normal emergency crew of fitters could not handle the business the fitting staff of the district were given the work, and these jobs had to be attended to even if the fitters already had appointments elsewhere. The very unevenness of the work made for considerable anomalies. Thus, in one District, feeling the full force of conversion, the fitters might be overstretched, the telephone bank jammed, and documentation piling up. An adjacent District might have excess capacity and underwork.

The third basic problem was the lack of clear lines of responsibility among senior staff, and no clear lines of responsibility between Divisional headquarters and Chief Office. This made for delays in taking appropriate action and even ignorance about what was happening at District level.

There were other sources of strain. One was a very high turnover of

Total domestic	Industrial	Commercial	Total
163097	1151	4944	169192
274588	1752	11444	287788
462726	2476	20922	486124
243325	7130	35385	285840
413342	3261	13281	429884
259110	995	6250	266355
1816188	16765	92226	1925183

staff. Offices throughout the Board's entire territory were affected by this but the problem was especially acute in London, where annual turnover rates in the early 1970s were as high as 50 per cent. This necessarily meant almost continuous under-staffing and a high proportion of untrained or inexperienced labour at the most crucial periods of conversion and rising sales. An additional problem after 1968, as we have mentioned, was the constant drain on the Districts' better staff into various parts of the conversion programme. Moreover, the procedures for recruiting or replacing staff were often lengthy and cumbersome; the average time taken to fill a junior post at London area offices was nine weeks, while a more senior post might take nine months.

Throughout the Districts and Divisions there was also a strikingly high proportion of middle-aged managers, many of them with the rather inbred attitudes stretching back to Gas Light & Coke Company days. At Finchley, for example, the average age of management was over fifty years in 1970 (nearly one-third of total employees there were over fifty) and the average length of their service with the Board and its predecessor was thirty-three years.

Conversion was a particular problem because it loaded calls on the office right from the date of the pre-conversion survey. Pressures were felt throughout the offices. To take Finchley again, following the start of conversion the number of telephone calls rose by 36 per cent. The conversion operation also caused the discovery of a great many potentially dangerous appliances, which were all the responsibility of the District office at this time. Thus, at Finchley in 1969 there were registered only 212 PDs; by 1970 there were 13547. Although about four-fifths of these concerned only ventilation, each had to be processed clerically by the Finchley unit and the remainder required more detailed processing and fixing.

There were no easy solutions to the problems, some of which lay outside the Board's control, while others were embedded within the organisational structure. It was this organisational structure that George

Cooper started to reform during 1971. The result was an intensely unhappy period at North Thames, which can only be understood if we recall how every problem seemed to converge at the same time: bad publicity, customer dissatisfaction, cessation of conversion, abolition of the Board, centralisation and reorganisation. The latter was determined upon in the autumn of 1970, although from the start of George Cooper's chairmanship in May it had been a question of *when* rather than *whether* to reorganise. An article in *Thames Gas* in 1971 put the point clearly: 'Among North Thames employees there was a general expectation that when our new Chairman was appointed, re-organisation would follow... most people would have been surprised had there been no changes.'

Cooper's proposals were approved by the Board in January 1971 and were announced immediately. Paul Rhodes, Marketing Director, now became Chief Executive, charged with the job of co-ordinating and implementing the reorganisation. In the words of the Annual Report, reorganisation was 'designed to strengthen the functional character of the organisational structure leading to better integration and greater efficiency'. At that stage it was expected that reorganisation would take rather more than one year to complete.

George Cooper was convinced that North Thames faced a fundamental problem from which all other difficulties flowed; this problem was an organisation based on territory rather than function. Divisional managers were too powerful and autonomous; they could frustrate central policy and resist efforts at standardisation and uniformity. Also too powerful were the engineers, whose roles should be downgraded in the new era of natural gas. The answer was to be a two-fold centralisation, at Divisional level and at headquarters, with lines of responsibility ending firmly at the latter.

We have seen that the role of engineers had indeed been a strong one. The Gas Light & Coke tradition continued throughout the first two decades of nationalisation. As a result, some areas of the Board's activities had received less attention than they deserved while the more immediate (and more glamorous) questions of developing new plants and importing natural gas were attended to. The problem of the divisional manager and territorial structure was also a real one, though Cooper's contention that managers were too autonomous was probably mistaken; divisional managers were not obstructive and the divisional structure was not completely inflexible. In fact, the organisation welded together by Aberdein was in many respects highly centralised, with divisional managers only too conscious of Chief Office, and, if anything, loath to undertake initiatives. The problem with the Board's structure, which unhappily Cooper's reorganisation did little to change, was that some of the Divisions were simply too big for the organisatio-

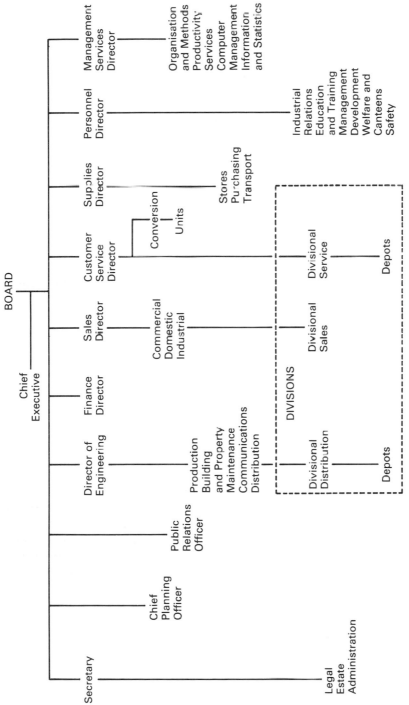

Figure 7.2 Reorganisation 1971. The simplified chart shows the major changes envisaged and the principal departments affected. The term 'Divisions' was soon changed to 'Areas'.

nal structure and office methods used; the North Western Division, for example, was itself the size of one of the smaller Area Boards, with the added complexities arising from the high standards of service required and the often difficult labour situation from which to supply it.

In planning reorganisation, Cooper was greatly influenced by changes already introduced at the Southern and, more particularly, the West Midlands Boards by C. H. Leach. As Deputy Chairman at the West Midlands, Cooper had worked alongside Leach during the reorganisation there in the 1960s. Cooper seems to have thought he had a ready-made blueprint for reorganising North Thames without fully realising the many differences and difficulties which would face him. These sprang, above all, from the entrenched traditions of the Gas Light & Coke Company and from the totally unforeseen problems brought by conversion.

The key point of Cooper's reorganisation was centralisation on functional lines. This involved four major steps. First, the old semi-autonomous divisional structure on which marketing and customer service had hitherto been based was to be phased out. The Divisions, now to be called Areas, were brought within a centralised framework where five functional directors at headquarters of Sales, Service, Supplies, Management Services, and Personnel, all had overall responsibility for their respective functions. All accounts activities, including customer accounting, and meter reading and collection were to be brought under the responsibility of the Finance Director. Hitherto Sales and Service had been combined into one marketing department, but were now to be separated. Second, within each Area there was to be centralisation, with Area offices becoming responsible (subject to the central directorate) for the five major functions hitherto carried out locally. These were at Staines, Willesden, Westminster, Ilford, and Southend. And, third, other steps for centralisation were to take place as soon as possible. Thus Customer Accounting was to be centralised at Alperton, at Middlesex House, and the Supplies and Transport Department was to centralise at a 10-acre site at Bromley-by-Bow. And, finally, the need (and hunt) for a central Chief Office now became vital, to take the place of the scattered and inefficient locations inherited at nationalisation.

So, as part of the reorganisation, the traditional roles of the divisional managers, with their polyglot responsibilities and large areas of autonomy, were to disappear, as were the old Regional offices and the Centralised Service Units. As part of the general reshuffle the territorial Divisions were to be reduced from six to five, and in April 1971 the former South Western and Western Divisions were merged into a single Western Division (Area).

No aspect of Cooper's reorganisation went smoothly, and unforeseen delays dogged nearly every aspect of the changes. The planned central stores complex at Bromley-by-Bow suffered various postponements and early teething problems, while strenuous efforts to find a new Chief Office proved unavailing. The rearrangements of jobs and responsibilities at headquarters and the consequent introduction of many 'outsiders' to top jobs also caused anxiety and bewilderment. Throughout the enterprise the deep traditions of loyalty and security which had characterised North Thames, and which had roots far back into the days of the Gas Light & Coke Company, disappeared overnight. Problems and ill-feeling were at their worst 'on the district', where the changes involved the greatest numbers of workers, especially those dealing directly with consumers.

Far from the original time horizon of twelve months, reorganisation was still incomplete after five years. Centralisation was finished first in the Essex and Central Areas, where the Board was fortunate enough to have planned new Divisional Headquarters. The moves here were started in November 1971. Essex centralisation at Southend was completed in January 1972 with the transfer of staff from the Basildon, Brentwood, Canvey Island, Grays, and Romford offices. Central Area headquarters was at Vincent Street, Westminster, where a new four-storey office block was completed in 1971. This replaced the hutted accommodation that had formerly housed Central and Headquarters Divisional staff until their move to College House, Kensington. In Central Area work from the Battersea, Edgware Road, Goswell Road, Rathbone Street, Stepney, Walham Green, and Westminster was progressively transferred to Vincent Street, and the process was completed in March 1972. Also in 1972, a large office building in Ilford was modified for the Eastern Area, while work commenced on new buildings at The Causeway, Staines, and at Pound Lane, Willesden. During 1974, centralisation of the North Western Area was completed with the move to Pound Lane, while the following year transfer of work in the Western Area was at last completed at Staines. Staines was soon to become a major centre for gas employment, for, by coincidence, North Thames found a new site there for its Chief Office the year following, and by 1978 there were some 1500 employees of North Thames Gas working at Staines.

How can we assess Cooper's drastic reorganisation? In principle, it cannot be emphasised strongly enough, reorganisation had much to commend it. The existing structure was clearly inadequate. The separate Divisions of varying sizes and traditions led to lack of standardisation and territorial jealousy. The arrival of natural gas and the needs of conversion made some organisational changes essential, and there was general agreement in the Gas Council that reorganisation could be delayed no longer. Nevertheless, the actual execution of reorganisation left much to be desired. Several points deserve emphasis. For the first time a significant number of men were brought into top positions outside North Thames. This was revolutionary, and to many it was unwelcome.

Also, the changes were pushed through in most unpropitious circumstances. To the strains of conversion was added a general climate of uncertainty caused by the knowledge from 1970 that there were to be changes within the national organisation of the gas industry. It will be recalled that in August 1971 the Government announced its plans for setting up the new Gas Corporation, and in an atmosphere of great uncertainty there were rumours of far-reaching changes, including that appliance sales and showrooms might be hived off to private enterprise. Cooper immediately consulted with Sir Kenneth Hutchison, Arthur Hetherington, and other Gas Council leaders, and received confirmation of his own opinion that reorganisation was considered 'essential', and that 'it would be fatal to try and stop now'. Indeed, the trade union representatives of gas staff and senior officers tried to persuade the Board to halt reorganisation until the establishment of the British Gas Corporation, but, in the face of some acrimonious exchanges, the Chairman stuck firmly to his timetable. The unions also made representations directly to the Gas Council, but Arthur Hetherington, Chairman designate to the proposed Gas Corporation, confirmed the need to press ahead with North Thames's reorganisation.

It was inevitable that major reforms involving changes in status, work responsibilities, new chiefs, and new locations, would bring disturbance, but aspects of reorganisation were mishandled. George Cooper himself later admitted that he attempted too much too quickly – 'ruthless', was the Board Secretary's term. There was a lack of information and communication, with the result that many employees were simply unaware how the changes would affect them, what jobs they would do, and where. Part of the problem here was that the Board itself had not settled the details of reorganisation when the broad outlines were announced. Only subsequently was the information available to be imparted. Cooper's plan envisaged setting up the new central structure, for example the new Sales Directorate and area managers, and then leaving them, in consultation with the Board, to make the attendant changes. This left uncertainty. For the office workers it left unsettled vital issues such as locations and conditions of work. Even the sites of the new area headquarters were not all announced at the outset. And for management it left countless matters such as job gradings and rates of pay to be negotiated with the unions, which made a mockery of the early tight time schedule. This time schedule was itself a problem, for George Cooper was anxious to push forward with

reorganisation as quickly as possible and it was announced at the outset
that in all Divisions where adequate accommodation was possible the
new organisation with its new procedures and systems must become
operational by the end of 1971.

In the event, reorganisation not only took much longer than expected
but was achieved with considerable acrimony and disruption also.
Negotiations with unions on new work procedures and locations were
lengthy and there were also delays in completing some of the new
Divisional headquarters where centralisation was to take place. Under
an agreement with the unions, all jobs created and retitled under the
reorganisation had to be advertised. This led to some bitterness, as
reorganisation 'created' hundreds of jobs in each major department.
Some employees found themselves applying for 'their' jobs, only to find
themselves passed over. Indeed, on several occasions employees took
the Board (unsuccessfully) to the Industrial Relations Tribunal.

Reorganisation was not the only source of labour discontent at this
time. Further disruption came early in 1973, with the gas industry's first
major strike since 1889. The root of the trouble was the rejection by gas
workers of a British Gas Corporation wage offer, in line with Phase Two
of the Conservative Government's anti-inflation policy. From the end of
January North Thames was hit by various forms of unofficial action,
including strikes and working to rule, which affected service to
customers as well as gas production and distribution. On 14 February
the dispute took a more serious turn when the General and Municipal
Workers' Union (the largest manual union at North Thames) and the
Transport and General Workers' Union declared an official work-to-rule
and withdrawal of overtime. Customers throughout the Region still on
manufactured gas were affected by reduced pressure, especially in
Central London where over 600 000 people were affected. It proved
impossible to undertake normal service work and only emergencies,
such as gas leaks, could be covered. The use of available labour for
emergency work only meant that more than 1000 consumers whose
appliances were in the process of being serviced had to have gas
supplies to these appliances cut off. Worse came on 28 February, when
strike action stopped output at Beckton and Southall. Serious pressure
reductions were now necessary throughout North Thames and, in
addition, over 700 large industrial and commercial consumers of gas,
including hotels, factories, schools and colleges, were cut off. For a time
the cutting off of supplies to large numbers of domestic consumers was
also a real possibility and at the height of the strike there were some
600 000 pressure reductions and hourly checks on supplies to hospitals.
The situation remained critical until the end of March, when a ballot
among union members accepted a new British Gas Corporation offer.

As we have seen, by 1975 the bulk of Cooper's reorganisation, with

32 End of an era at Beckton, 16 April 1969. *Sir David II* brings the last coal cargo to the works there on the vessel's final voyage in the Board's service. Launched in 1954, the collier carried nearly 2.75 million tons of coal from north-east ports to the Board's works.

the major exception of a new Chief Office, had been completed. Reorganisation was intended to put an end to the old Divisional structure, but the posts of Divisional Manager were allowed to be phased out as the incumbents retired. Eventually, in September 1975, the old titles finally disappeared with the retirement of A. A. Hall from Essex, and J. Smith from Eastern.

Reorganisation, of course, brought a great many of such breaks with past traditions, but this was only part of a process which had been going on for some time. In many ways the very successes of the 1960s and 1970s marked the start of a new era and the end of an old. Each year in the 1960s brought some new landmark, as coal carbonisation declined, gas stations closed, and by-products were phased out. During the natural gas era the oil gasification and reforming plants too were added to the list of closures, so that by 1976 North Thames no longer produced

33 Apprentices at the newly-opened Training Centre at Uxbridge, April 1969.

any town gas. Side by side went a decline in the number of employees, especially operatives at gas-making stations. Beckton, for example, had once employed 4500; by the late 1970s only around 100 remained. Early in 1967 gas-making in the horizontal retors at Beckton finished after ninety-five years' continuous output, and in April 1969 the collier *Sir David II* unloaded its final cargo at Beckton, where coal carbonisation now ceased after a century. The end of coal carbonisation also meant the shutting down of the Products Works. In 1968 the works at Southall was closed, while in September 1969 the last supplies of tar were processed at Beckton, so bringing to an end an operation which extended back more than ninety years. These two years saw also the end of gas-making at Lea Bridge, Bow Common, and Uxbridge.

Another nostalgic moment occurred on 23 January 1970 when the Board's last collier brought its final cargo of 2400 tons of coal to the Nine Elms Works. The *Falconer Birks* had joined the Board's fleet in 1953, which then numbered twenty-four vessels. By 1965 the number had dwindled to twelve, while at the end of 1967 only six remained. This last journey in 1970 brought to a close a period during which coal had been shipped to London's gasworks every year since 1814. In 1912 the Gas Light & Coke Company had begun to build its own fleet, and by 1970 over 92 million tons of coal had been brought to the Company's and North Thames's Works in its own vessels. In all, sixty-two colliers had been in service, and twenty-two had been sunk by enemy action in the two world wars. In March 1970 coal carbonisation at North Thames finally ceased altogether, when remaining plants at Bromley, Kensal Green, and Nine Elms were closed down. The oldest of these works, Kensal Green, had originally belonged to the old Western (Cannel) Gas Light Company and had manufactured coal-gas continually since 1845.

This same year, 1970, also saw the sale of the last of the Board's locomotives at Beckton. In its time the eighty miles of track had been intensively used for some 40 locomotives and 740 wagons carrying coal and coke throughout the works. Beckton railway station had ceased as a passenger station at the outbreak of the Second World War, though it was still used for goods traffic until 1958.

The year 1969–70 saw a fall in the installed capacity for town gas for the first time since the Second World War, to 779.4 m. cu ft gas/day compared with 938 m. cu ft gas/day the previous year, and all capacity was now oil reforming or natural gas reforming. Table 7.10 shows how capacity was then divided among the Board's remaining seven manufacturing stations.

Among the many breaks with the past in these years of accelerated change was the gradual phasing out of the 'Mr Therm' symbol at North Thames from 1971 after forty years of service (he had disappeared already from Gas Council national advertising in the early 1960s).

Table 7.10   North Thames Gas capacity, 1 November 1970[1] (m. cu ft gas/day) at oil gasification and gas reforming plants

	Continuous	*Cyclic*	*Total*
Beckton	115.0	28.0	143.0
Bromley	105.0	–	105.0
Fulham	75.0	6.0	81.0
Romford	108.0	58.4	166.4
Southall	140.0	–	140.0
Slough	72.0	–	72.0
Staines	50.0	–	50.0
Total	665.0	92.4	757.4

[1]In addition, up to 791 m. cu ft gas/day natural gas available.
Source: North Thames Gas.

Another break came with the retirement of E. H. Dodimead in December 1970 from his position as Editor of *Thames Gas Magazine*, a post he had held since 1954 (although he had worked on the magazine and its predecessor since 1947). Under his editorship the magazine won six awards in the National House Journal competition. After his departure North Thames introduced a new, larger format for the magazine, which by then could trace its history back sixty years to the first *Co-Partner's Magazine* in January 1911. And on 12 May 1970 Edwin Bayliss, the longest-serving member of the Board and the longest-serving chairman on any of the Consultative Committees, retired. He was succeeded by Christopher Higgins, who later became the first chairman of the new North Thames Gas Consumers' Council, set up under the Gas Act of 1972.

By around 1976 gradually but perceptibly the somewhat tarnished image of North Thames began to shine once again, though not until the early 1980s could improvement be said to be substantial. As conversion pressures eased, then disappeared, and as the benefits of reorganisation began to be felt, signs of greater efficiency and smoother running of operations became increasingly apparent. Great pains were taken to improve customer relations. In 1975, a working party consisting of Derek Dutton, Head of Public Relations; Trevor Johnson, Marketing Manager; and Alan Webster, Customer Service Manager, formulated a major internal campaign: 'Care for the Customer', for the Executive Committee. Launched in May the following year, the campaign made a significant impact throughout the Region in subsequent years, and was continued in one form or another until privatisation in 1986.

Customer complaints began to show significant declines, especially in the key areas of accounts and service (though the trend was to be temporarily reversed in the early 1980s). In both sectors, complaints to

34 Typical advertisements, c. 1960, reproduced from the Board's *News* magazine of January 1961. Note the new 'Dotty' advertisement (no. 2), which rapidly became a major feature of North Thames's campaigns.

the Consumers' Council were in 1975 only around half the levels reached in 1972, and complaints made directly to North Thames showed a similar downward trend. There were signs too of greater efficiency. In November 1974, for example, the delay between meter-reading and despatch of accounts was down to one week, compared with a month in November 1972, while in 1974 Essex Area won the first national Gold Flame award for 'most improved' customer service over a twelve-month period.

If by 1976 the worst was over, North Thames in 1976 could hardly be said to be an efficient Region, nor were prospects encouraging. Reorganisation had been dogged by difficulties, not least of them the pressures of conversion. But underlying many of the Region's problems was the failure of one of the four key points of Cooper's programme, the acquisition of a new central headquarters. The long quest for such a headquarters, which will be explored in Chapter 8, met with no success until 1976. The ultimate acquisition of the new Chief Office at Staines was, in fact, one of Cooper's last major achievements as Chairman, before he announced his retirement at the end of the 1976 and was succeeded by John Gadd the following April.

When George Cooper left North Thames Gas in 1977 the undertaking was vastly different from that which he had found on his arrival seven years previously. Cooper's appointment had been made by the Government, reflecting the autonomy then enjoyed by the Boards under the terms of nationalisation in 1949. His successor was appointed by the Gas Corporation, reflecting the new role of the Regions within the new organisation for British Gas. In 1970 most of North Thames's gas had been made by the Board; seven years later the entire supply was natural gas. Conversion, reorganisation (internal and industry-wide), and the enhanced role of gas as an energy industry had transformed North Thames in just a few years.

Nothing could emphasise more the extent of North Thames's transformation than the move of its headquarters from Kensington to Staines. Bit by bit the trappings and legacies of the Gas Light & Coke Company were being shed. The main activity of earlier years, making gas, had gone. So had its organisational structure. And now, breaking a tradition of 165 years, so had its location in the heart of London. The establishment of a new chief office at Staines marked a new era for North Thames Gas, now reorganised, reshaped and revived, and better prepared to serve its customers under the new regime of the British Gas Corporation and natural gas.

8

A Headquarters at Last

The 'Chief Office saga' straddled the entire period of the North Thames Gas Board's existence. The search for a Chief Office occupies a significant place in North Thames's history not only because the existence of scattered departments produced so many problems of co-ordination and organisation and not only because the search itself involved so much time and effort, but also because it shows the financial and planning constraints which even a major nationalised industry, notwithstanding the urgency and justification of its case, could suffer.

In 1937 the Gas Light & Coke Company demolished its Chief Office in Horseferry Road, preparatory to building a new office on that site. But war intervened and in 1940 the Government requisitioned the site for its own building, incorporating some of the Company's new works. As a temporary expedient, the Gas Light & Coke Company moved its Chief Office to 30 Kensington Church Street, where there was a showroom and District Office. There it was to remain for forty years. Despite leasing some nearby property, several major departments, including that of the Chief Engineer and Joint Chief Accountants, had to be housed elsewhere.

By 1947, with nationalisation pending, the Company tried to regularise the position. In May, the Ministry of Works was asked to return enough space in Horseferry Road for a showroom, a District Office and certain other accommodation, and to 'make available' sufficient office accommodation near Kensington Church Street for the dispersed major departments. Three months later a rather curt reply from the Ministry stated simply that the entire Horseferry Road site was required for Government offices and that the Ministry could not provide alternative accommodation. Despite further meetings and correspondence, nothing more was achieved by the Company before nationalisation.

After nationalisation the new North Thames Gas Board once more took up the matter and asked yet again for office accommodation in Horseferry Road, setting out in detail the Board's needs for an adequate Head Office. But Milne-Watson was told that the Cabinet decision to acquire the site was 'final'. However, in a letter of August 1949, R. Kelf-Cohen, Under-Secretary at the Ministry of Fuel and Power, wrote that 'the Ministry of Works will be pleased to give assistance to your Board in finding accommodation for your headquarters offices and, if it would be of help, the Minister will be prepared to do everything possible to impress upon the Ministry of Works the difficulties under which your Board are labouring in present conditions'.

Despite the great inconvenience caused by splitting the headquarters departments into six separate buldings in Kensington, Fulham and Westminster, the urgent problems facing the new Board and the general economic conditions in the country precluded further thoughts about a new headquarters for some time. By 1954, however, the issue was revived once more and once again the thoughts of the Board turned towards Horseferry Road. A small site was acquired in that area and in October of that year the Board appointed a firm of architects to make preliminary drawings and a good deal of work went into making accommodation plans, estimating costings and so on. But in July 1956 the Ministry of Fuel and Power told the Board that the national economic difficulties – caused by the Suez Canal crisis – meant that they were unable to sanction any capital expenditure, and the agreements with the architects and consultants had to be cancelled. During the following two years the Board considered the possibility of the site being developed by a property development company and leased back to the Board, but nothing came of these plans.

Meanwhile, during the 1950s North Thames bought up several properties in Fulham in the Michael Road area, between King's Road and the Fulham gasworks. The object was to build for the Gas Council new and larger laboratories and to house the Watson House Centre. But, in fact, the opening of a new building in Carnwath Road took care of this, leaving only a need to provide proper laboratory facilities for the London Research Station, for which there was more than enough space at Michael Road. Therefore, in February 1960 the Board considered developing a new Chief Office in conjunction with new premises for the London Research Station at Michael Road. The next step was to enter into lengthy and difficult planning negotiations with the London County Council (LCC), but in March 1961 the Board heard that the LCC was prepared to make a favourable recommendation to the Council's Planning Committee. As a result, in May of that year the Board's architect started to draw up outline plans for the Chief Office and London Research Station, and these plans were made in consultation with the LCC (which was led by a Mr Sames, the Area Planning Officer). The details were fully agreed and in September 1962 an outline planning application was sent to the Council. After further delay, planning consent was finally granted in July 1963 for the London Research Station laboratories, but planning consent for the Chief Office was granted only subject to approval by the Ministry of Housing and Local Government (because the development was contrary to current zoning of the area under the London Development Plan).

However, for reasons not apparent, but perhaps because it suspected the Ministry of Housing would look unfavourably on the Michael Road scheme, the Board had decided to look once more at the Horseferry Road site in December 1962. The Board's architect and Mr Sames were informed accordingly. The Board now tried to obtain planning consent for a Chief Office at Horseferry Road, but this was not to be forthcoming.

In 1964, with the arrival of the new Chairman, R. S. Johnson, fresh thought was given to the Chief Office project as a whole. Milne-Watson had always been lukewarm towards any move outside Central London and never saw the 'Chief Office problem' as a particularly pressing one in any case. The new Chairman asked the Assistant Secretary to prepare a report on modern techniques of office management. Developments in the gas industry were leading to the conception that a headquarters building would not only be an administrative centre but also a centre for operational control, which would be provided with the most up-to-date techniques, including computerisation. The principle became established that the Board was only likely to get the building it wanted if it erected one on its own site, and in July a review of eight works sites was undertaken. None, however, was deemed suitable. In July 1964 three further possible sites owned by the Board were considered and assessed. A seemingly possible site at the Acton sports ground foundered because of local planning difficulties. At this stage (November 1965) Mr Sames, now Borough Architect and Planning Officer of the London Borough of Hammersmith, informed the Board about the Borough's plans to redevelop Hammersmith Broadway and invited North Thames to participate in the redevelopment by erecting a Chief Office on a site on Hammersmith Road.

The Board was immediately attracted to the proposal. The site was excellently located for transport, there seemed to be no planning difficulties and the local authority was supporting the proposal and promised that a site would be made available quickly. There seemed space available for the size of Chief Office which the Board had in mind. In consequence, the Board approved the proposal in December 1966, and in February 1967 appointed an architect to draw up plans, which were prepared accordingly. In July a building of some 250 000 sq ft was accepted by Hammersmith as well as the need for car parking space for about 500 cars. Approaches to the Ministry of Power also met with a favourable response, and in January 1968 the Board made a formal application for an Office Development Permit (ODP) to the Board of Trade. However, only after 'arduous negotiations, in which we were vigorously supported by the Ministry of Power' was the ODP obtained in March 1969. The Board of Trade had asked North Thames to consider locating out of London – even outside the Board's territory – and asked it to look at Basildon, Southend, Stevenage, and Aylesbury. All this was very distressing to North Thames. The Board felt that the Government was under a moral obligation to help it in this matter in view of the requisitioning of Horseferry Road and the letter from Kelf-Cohen in 1949. But, in the meantime, negotiations with Hammersmith were causing concern. Despite early assurances, the Borough was tardy in producing a site. Only in September 1968 was the Board at last offered a definite site for which vacant possession was offered for late 1971 or early 1972. Yet Hammersmith Council now raised difficulties about the size of the accommodation it could offer and also began to raise difficulties about car parking provisions. Accordingly, when it became necessary to renew the ODP after a year had elapsed, North Thames reluctantly accepted a modified building of 170 000 sq ft and agreed to house the Accounts Department with the computer elsewhere. The renewed ODP was obtained in February 1970 and in the same month a further meeting was held with Hammersmith Council to discuss financial terms, so that a profitability statement could be calculated. Out of the blue the Council announced that it had already let part of North Thames's site to another body. An alternative was offered, but it was not so desirable and was set alongside a projected elevated road. The Board spoke bitterly of the 'breach of faith, which was perpetrated with no prior word of warning'.

The bombshell effectively killed the Hammersmith scheme, but the need for a headquarters remained pressing. With the arrival of the new Chairman, George Cooper, in 1970 the search for a new Chief Office gathered pace. The need became even more important as Cooper's reorganisation plans unfolded. The situation was absurd. North Thames was the only major Board without a central headquarters and the various headquarters departments continued to be housed in eleven separate buildings in Kensington, Westminster, Fulham, Alperton, and Ilford. The Chairman, Deputy and the Secretariat were at Kensington; the Engineering Departments at Monck Street, Westminster; Finance and the Computer Section at Fulham; and Customer Accounting at Alperton and Ilford. Cooper decided that the matter was urgent, and further that it was necessary to have a building large enough to house all the major departments and therefore to revert to the plans for a building of the original size. Once again the Board undertook a review of its own sites. The economic situation continued to be difficult. Vigorous restrictions on office buldings meant that there was no available property on the market, and visits to the appropriate borough authorities produced no sites worth serious consideration. A possible private development in Hanger Lane proved impracticable and the Board decided it would have no alternative but to build an office for itself on one of its own sites. As a result of a detailed review of possible alternatives, the holder station at Cannon Lane, Pinner emerged as the favourite location. Here was a large site of thirteen acres owned by the Board, yet only two acres were required for gas storage. Accordingly, in July 1970 the Board decided to go ahead with plans for a Chief Office on this site. The Chairman himself suggested that the Design Group for Industry should be retained as consultants to help with the early planning stages of the project, the necessary approaches were made for a new ODP, and negotiations were started with the local planning authority and with the Greater London Council (GLC).

It should have been clear almost from the outset that the scheme to develop the Pinner site would meet with immense difficulties. No doubt the Board felt some measure of desperation, faced with the collapse of the Hammersmith scheme, the restrictions on new office building in London, and the ever-increasing need for a Head Office as reorganisation took shape. At the same time the developments of computerisation and new office techniques made it even more urgent to have a single headquarters building. Nevertheless, as early as July 1970 at a meeting with planning representatives from both Harrow Council and the GLC the Board was told of great problems with the scheme. The Board knew that GLC planning approval was essential, since the scheme departed from the London Development Plan, so that Harrow's support alone was not sufficient. The GLC representative told Cooper that in his view the GLC would probably block the scheme because it proposed office development in a residential area. In particular, the GLC felt that there would be considerable traffic and parking problems generated by the new office. The Board was asked by the GLC yet again to look for a site elsewhere, perhaps in northeast London or in the Barking or Ilford areas, and was told also that if there were objections to the scheme from local interests 'there would probably have to be a Public Inquiry'.

Ignoring these danger signals, and probably influenced by some private encouragement from Harrow Borough, which was anxious for more office development, the Board went ahead. An ODP was applied for and obtained in October 1970, planning consultants were appointed and plans and accommodation schedules were drawn up. Now began a four-year saga of interminable meetings, promises, new plans and delays. It would be tedious to detail all the frustrations and toings and froings which took place over these four years. The final collapse of the Pinner project at the close of 1974 was later described by George Cooper as his greatest disappointment during his years as Chairman. The project failed because, despite all attempts at persuasion and despite numerous concessions and pressure at the highest levels, the necessary planning permit could not be obtained. It was unfortunate for the Board that it fought for its new headquarters at a time when both the

GLC and the Government were taking a rather hostile view towards office development in London. The newly created Department of the Environment (DoE) in 1971 was symptomatic of increasing concern with environmental matters and the Board found itself caught in a web of complex planning procedures, which ultimately proved impenetrable.

At first neither the Board nor its own planning consultants (from the first the Board appointed three firms to co-ordinate plans and designs and to deal with such problems as traffic and environmental disturbance) contemplated failure. Detailed plans for the headquarters building were ready by the spring of 1971 and it was optimistically assumed that speedy planning consent could result in a new office being ready some time in 1974. But despite support from the Harrow planning authorities, which gave approval in August 1971, the GLC remained implacably opposed. Repeating its earlier advice, the GLC now formally suggested to North Thames that it should look at either Ilford Railway Station or the Romford coal yard for its new headquarters building but the Board could not summon up much enthusiasm for either of these sites. The Board was somehow led to believe that the GLC would approve the Pinner project if various concessions were made, not realising that far more fundamental objections underlay those which were raised at the time. Concessions included release of other office sites in London, agreeing to open recreational facilities in Pinner to local residents, and agreeing to provide residential accommodation on the Pinner site. But despite these concessions the GLC remained hostile. It now raised the problem of traffic congestion and suggested that the expected increase in traffic would mean the construction of a new access road at the site. Accordingly, in March 1972 the GLC directed Harrow Borough to refuse planning consent.

The Board still pressed ahead. It now submitted a modified plan, trying to meet as many of the planning authority's objections as possible. A 'low silhouette' scheme was submitted and after further lengthy negotiations not only with the GLC but also with Harrow (which was now concerned about the construction of a new road on open space) and Hillingdon Borough (whose area the projected new road also touched) and after a further refusal of planning consent in February 1973, followed by still further concessions, the GLC finally gave consent to a modified proposal in June 1973.

Planning procedures now meant that the scheme had to be passed to the DoE for final approval, and in particular to determine whether a public inquiry should be necessary. The Board's planning consultants appeared to have thought initially that consent would readily be forthcoming in view of GLC approval, but this was far from the case. In fact, the GLC had privately let it be known to the DoE that it was fundamentally opposed to the project but felt that it could not delay planning consent any further, in view of the stream of concessions wrought from the Board. Just as the GLC had delayed for so long over a scheme which proposed a big office block in a residential area, so the DoE in turn proved reluctant to allow such a scheme on similar grounds. At root it was simply not prepared to agree to such a departure from office location policy without a public inquiry. North Thames (by now a Region of the new Gas Corporation) heard of the likelihood of a public inquiry in January 1974. This presented a serious dilemma. Such an inquiry would certainly take from eighteen months to two years, with no certainty of final approval. At this stage the Department of Energy, which had strongly supported the Board's case throughout the negotiations, now suggested that yet a further modification to the plans, which would reduce the size of the building and hence obviate the need for an additional road, might persuade the DoE to agree to the scheme without any inquiry. North Thames accordingly submitted yet another and very substantially modified plan in February 1974. The building now covered only 179 000 sq ft and many departments, including Accounting and Finance, would have to be located elsewhere. All the procedures had to be gone through yet again. By June the plans had once more been approved by the London Boroughs and by the GLC, and in July 1974 the DoE once more was asked for planning consent. In the interim the Region had decided to explore other avenues in view of the many disappointments in the progress of the Pinner project. In February 1974 it heard of a promising development at Ealing on the Uxbridge Road and entered into preliminary negotiations with the developers. It now became even more urgent to get a final decision on the Pinner project if the Ealing site was not to be lost to another client. North Thames made every effort to persuade the DoE to agree to the modified plan. It enlisted support from 'its' Ministry, and Sir Jack Rampton, the Permanent Under-Secretary at the Department of Energy, Sir Arthur Hetherington, Chairman of the British Gas Corporation, and Peter Emery, Parliamentary Under-Secretary at the Department of Energy, all pressed North Thames's case. But to no avail. The DoE remained not only adamant but also unhurried. In October the DoE suggested to the Department of Energy that the project could be integrated with Harrow's embryonic proposal for a major City Centre shopping centre with offices, the time-scale for which, as John Barnes, the Secretary, told Cooper, 'is anyone's guess'. Not until 11 November 1974 was the Region finally informed that a public inquiry must be held, whereupon Cooper reluctantly but inevitably decided to abandon the Pinner project. The Chairman wrote later, 'It grieves me that one man sitting in the anonymity of Whitehall was able to make such a far-reaching decision and turn down the scheme on peripheral planning grounds. The whole life and tempo of North Thames would have been changed enormously

35 The Executive Committee at the new Regional Headquarters, Staines, January 1977. Left to right: Haydon Griffiths (Controller of Purchasing and Supplies), Derek Dutton (Head of PR), Reg Bloom (Secretary), Dr Ted Johnson (Management Services Director), Robert Evans (Deputy Chairman), Paul Dixon (Personnel Director), Jack Smith (BGC Deputy Chairman and guest of honour), Dennis Grimster (Customer Service Director), George Cooper (Chairman), Tony Clark (Head of Corporate Planning), Philip Sellers (Finance Director), George Holmes (Sales Director), Peter Shepherd (Deputy Director of Engineering).

for the better if we had had a new Chief Office early in our reorganisation.'

With the abandonment of the Pinner project, North Thames was effectively back where it had started. Unfortunately the Ealing plan had become too costly and the British Gas Corporation turned it down. In view of the urgency of the situation and the many disappointments with the planning authorities George Cooper now took the decision to look for suitable ready-built accommodation rather than go once more through the time-consuming and frustrating business of developing North Thames's own schemes. During 1975 various office blocks were examined, at Finchley, Wembley, Basildon, and Southend; but none proved suitable.

Then, by one of the rare strokes of good fortune George Cooper received during his chairmanship of North Thames, he was told at a social gathering by the wife of a colleague that a large office block at Staines was on the market. The ten-storey building had been started by Ready Mixed Concrete for their headquarters in 1974 but the company had been hard hit by the building recession and needed to sell. Cooper moved swiftly. The British Gas Corporation approved the terms and in February 1976 North Thames announced the decision to transfer its Regional Headquarters to Staines. Even now there were unexpected planning delays, but on 10 January 1977 the first staff were able to make the move, and in the following months about 1000 staff in Engineering, Finance, Secretarial and Legal, Sales, Customer Service, Management Service, Personnel, Corporate Planning and Public Relations took their places. The new building housed nearly all the headquarters departments, including the main computer unit. The main exceptions were Customer Acounting (which continued at Alperton and Ilford) and the Supplies and Transport Departments, which were located at Bromley-by-Bow. Success after such a long and frustrating search for a new headquarters opened a new era for North Thames. The move away from central London was a major psychological break with past traditions; the grouping of the various departments under one roof was a boost both for morale and efficiency, and the step, belated as it was, marked the final phase of Cooper's centralisation, planned as long ago as 1970.

9

The Staines Era: Renaissance and Reformation

It is tempting to see the decade 1976–86, spanning as it does the end of the conversion and the privatisation of British Gas, as something of a coda to earlier developments. The great themes of the past, Algerian natural gas, oil gasification, conversion, and the decline of manufacturing, had all come and gone. Now with the Staines headquarters, with tasks clarified and confined under the umbrella of British Gas, and with the Regions seemingly in the role of pawns to British Gas's Chairman Rooke, the scope for individuality among Regions was obviously diminished.

Yet tempting though this picture is, it conceals more than it reveals. In many ways the last decade has seen fundamental changes every bit as significant as in earlier times, while Regional identity has remained sharp and in some respects has even strengthened. In these years the Region's efficiency, morale, and general effectiveness have been transformed to an extent impossible to envisage in the early 1970s. The wounds, self-inflicted and otherwise, which had disfigured North Thames in the first half of the 1970s were not easy to heal. Customer confidence was at a low ebb. In 1977 a new Alan Bennett play raised nightly chuckles from West End audiences when one character, asked which totalitarian authorities he had suffered under, named the North Thames Gas Board as the worst. Sadly, it was not simply a totalitarian image that North Thames had to exorcise; it was that of a highly inefficient regime as well.

The period of transformation coincided almost exactly with the chairmanship of John Gadd, which began in April 1977 and lasted until January 1988, just over a year after privatisation. Gadd was thus the longest-serving Chairman of North Thames with the exception of Michael Milne-Watson, and Gadd's influence on the course of events was profound.

Like his predecessors, John Gadd had built his career in the gas industry. He started as a pupil engineer with Leighton Buzzard Gas Company as a sixteen-year-old in 1941. After various appointments in engineering and general management he became Personnel Manager of Southern Gas in 1962, Deputy Chairman there in 1969, and Chairman of

In 'The Old Country' North Thames Gas is named as a "totalitarian authority,"

GAS SHOWROOM

but in the New Gas Era North Thames Gas <u>tries</u> to make it's customers feel special.

NORTH THAMES GAS

36 North Thames's advertisment in the theatre programme for Alan Bennett's *The Old Country*, 1977: a quick response taken on the Chairman's initiative.

Eastern Gas in 1973. Gadd was thus well suited to take up what was generally regarded as the most exacting of the Regional chairmanships. His experience of the industry was deep and varied, and he had held leading executive positions during the critical years of conversion. Also, like George Cooper, he was an outsider to North Thames, and so immune from the Gas Light & Coke Company traditions which many (including Cooper) felt still haunted the Region. Perhaps of greatest significance was Gadd's spell as Personnel Manager at Southern, for it was in the area of industrial relations that the new Chairman was to make a particularly valuable contribution.

Both North Thames and the gas industry had undergone many fundamental changes in the decades prior to Gadd's arrival. North Thames Gas in 1949 was a dominant component of a minor industry. Thirty years later North Thames had a much reduced role in a now major energy industry. The transformation of the total energy market is best described by a few figures. In the space of only six years, between 1970 and 1976, gas went from bottom to leading position among major fuels in providing Britain's energy (defined as the amount of heat supplied to final users, excluding transport). In 1970 gas had contributed just 10 per cent of the total, but by 1976 it had overtaken electricity, coal, and finally oil, to assume the leading position with around 25 per cent of the market. Thereafter the popularity of gas has risen steadily, reaching nearly 45 per cent in 1986. At this latter date gas was supplying nearly 60 per cent of domestic energy and 35 per cent of non-domestic. Already in 1974 gas had replaced coal as the main provider of domestic energy, its share rising from only some 12 per cent in 1965 to 40 per cent a decade later, and in 1982 gas overtook oil as the main source of industrial energy, its share reaching 36 per cent in 1985 whereas in 1970 it had been barely 5 per cent.

It is worth emphasising that this truly dramatic rise of Britain's gas industry took place against a stagnant and even falling total energy market for much of the period. This is shown clearly in Table 9.1.

Table 9.1   British energy market, 1970–85 (million therms)

	1970	1979	1985
Coal	18.3	9.8	6.6
Oil	15.6	12.9	7.9
Electricity	6.3	7.8	7.8
Gas	5.7	16.4	17.7
Total	45.9	46.9	40.0

Source: Department of Energy.

As the arrival of natural gas enhanced the position of Britain's gas industry, so it helped reduce the roles of the individual Boards and Regions. The new hierarchy established in 1972 confirmed a process of centralisation and standardisation in evidence since the mid-1960s. The Regions ceased to manufacture gas, and became concerned essentially with distribution and customer-related activities. And they had to adjust to these changes with a work-force, and often an organisational structure, geared partly to a now defunct regime. Spare capacity in some sectors coincided with extreme pressure elsewhere. When we add to these changes the burdens of conversion, the revolution in consumer demand brought by new standards of central heating, the wholly new industrial and commercial applications for which natural gas was suited, and the rapidly changing technological environment brought by computerisation and other innovations, we can glimpse the challenges the various gas Regions had to confront in the 1970s. None had more challenges than North Thames: as the Region with more customers in each sector, domestic, commercial, and industrial, than any other in 1972, and with the largest central heating load in the country, pressures on customer service and accounting were often felt acutely.

The new role for North Thames which emerged during the 1970s was not simply that of a rather inefficient Region within a changed industry and organisational hierarchy. Other developments too were altering the place of North Thames within the national framework. In the domestic sector, for example, the relative saturation of the market, especially for cooking, meant that there was far greater opportunity for other Regions to expand their numbers of customers and sales of gas and appliances. National population movements and prosperity also influenced the overall balance, North Thames tending to have greater than average prosperity but a less than average growth of population within its area. Thus the total number of domestic customers served by North Thames was virtually the same, at around 1.8 million, in 1986 as it had been in 1972; yet the national total had risen by more than 3 million, adding over 25 per cent to the total. Gas sold by North Thames also rose in this period by less than the national average, though the difference was not so marked. As a result of these various changes North Thames slipped from first place among Regions in terms of numbers of customers to second in 1976 and third in 1982 (a position subsequently maintained). In terms of overall gas sales, North Thames improved its position from fourth to second, largely due to stagnating industrial sales in the 'industrial' Regions of the North and the Midlands after 1979.

In summary, North Thames in 1972 could still be ranked unequivocally as the leading Board, even if this dominance was neither as clear cut or all-embracing as it had been in the 1950s. North Thames still had more employees, a bigger wage bill, more domestic, industrial and commercial customers than any other Region, and was second only to the North West in total domestic gas sales. By 1979 North Thames could no longer rank as the leading Region by most of these counts, and at the time of privatisation in 1986 North Thames was only third in domestic sales, third in numbers of domestic customers and second in total

Table 9.2   North Thames's ranking among Regions, 1951–86 (figures at 31 March)

	1951	1973	1982	1986
Employees	1	1	1	2
Population served	2	3	3	4
Number of Customers	1	1	2	3
of which Domestic	1	2	3	3
Industrial	1	1	1	2
Commercial	1	1	1	1
Gas Sold	1	4	3	2
of which Domestic	1	2	3	3
Industrial	4	4	4	7
Commercial	1	1	1	1

Sources: North Thames Gas; British Gas Annual Reports.

employees (though the wage bill and salary bill, due in part to high London costs and a relatively large ratio of senior management, was still greater than elsewhere). Table 9.2 shows some of these changed rankings over the years.

As we have seen, in the new post-1972 era of natural gas much of the former independence of the Area Boards was ended, due, as the *Financial Times* rather colourfully put it, to 'the creation of the monarchy of British Gas from the lands of the warring Area Board barons'. But until privatisation in 1986, British Gas was very much a constitutional monarchy, subject to influence and interference from governments as well as from factors such as relative fuel prices and unforeseen supply difficulties. The national market environment in which North Thames and the other Regions were called upon to perform their new role was of fundamental significance to their operations, and needs to be explored in a little detail.

Natural gas permitted the enormous expansion of gas sales between the late 1960s and the mid-1970s. Expansion of gas sales was sustained by three factors: very favourable gas prices relative to other fuels, which not only enhanced sales to existing consumers but also encouraged development of new markets; aggressive marketing, especially the extension of industrial sales often at low contract prices; and the very rapid growth of the domestic central heating market. Price movements were fundamental. Over the period 1962–79 electricity charges rose by 415 per cent and solid fuel by 476 per cent, while gas prices rose by just 160 per cent. Fuel oil prices rose by 320 per cent in the years 1974–9 alone.

By 1975 the phase of rapid expansion had come to an end. Whereas in the five years after 1969–70 total national gas sales rose by 147 per cent and industrial sales rocketed by 411 per cent, in the five years following 1974–75 total gas sales rose by 29 per cent and industrial sales by only 10 per cent. And in the five year period following 1979–80, gas sales rose just 6.2 per cent while industrial sales actually fell by 8.4 per cent. This was the national backdrop, with its ramifications for customer-related activities, against which North Thames and the other Regions had to operate.

Now, how do we account for the radically slower pace of growth from the mid-1970s? Certainly the slower pace between 1975 and 1979 was neither unexpected, nor, for the Regions, unwelcome, giving as it did a breathing space as the conversion programmes came to a close. By 1975 the supplies of North Sea gas, planned as early as 1967, had been fully achieved more or less on target, and the rather frenzied period of expansion, marked by vast new industrial and domestic central heating loads, had come to an end. Already, in the year 1973–74, the Corporation had adopted a policy of not accepting major new industrial and commercial contracts, and in subsequent years new extensive commitments were very carefully monitored in line with anticipated supplies and peak load constraints.

To some extent, therefore, the slowdown of the gas market after 1975 must be seen as an anticipated result once the full supplies of North Sea gas commissioned in the late 1960s came on stream. Moreover the huge rates of growth achieved could obviously not be maintained. Indeed, as mentioned already, the decade of the 1970s was a time of overall stagnation in the energy market, while between 1979 and 1982 there was a sharp industrial recession and contracting industrial demand.

Slower gas sales were caused also by delays in new supplies of natural gas. Most serious was a full year's delay in the arrival of gas from the Frigg field, originally expected in the autumn of 1976, while gas from the Brent field, planned for 1979, did not arrive until May 1982.

Another important factor in slowing gas sales was the end of a long period of relatively cheap gas. Price increases, desired by the industry (in order to meet financial targets and to pay for new investment) had been held back by Government price restraints in the early 1970s at a time of rampant inflation. The oil crisis of 1973 and the miners' strikes of 1972 and 1974 had further encouraged the use of gas. But from late 1974 there began a series of tariff increases which lessened differences between competing fuels. The broad comparability of fuel prices received further impetus when the Government, in the wake of the second oil crisis of 1979, requested the Gas Corporation to increase its tariffs for the subsequent three years by 10 per cent more than the rate of inflation. Gas still remained highly competitive, and continued to increase its overall share of the energy market. Nevertheless, rapid price increases at more than the rate of inflation dampened demand, a process enhanced by continuing national and regional programmes of energy conservation.

A longer-term problem which emerged in these years was that by the late 1970s cheap gas from the southern North Sea fields was starting to run out, while new supplies from the northern fields and elsewhere could only be acquired at rising costs. In other words, gas costs were destined to rise in the 1980s, threatening to undermine the medium- and long-term competitive position of gas. This in turn made the reduction of non-gas costs (of which two-thirds consisted of labour costs) an absolute priority for the various Regions.

The second oil crisis of 1979, sparked by the revolution in Iran in July of that year, provided a sharp twist to the gas industry's fortunes. Sudden increases in oil prices, and fears about the future of oil supplies, led to an upsurge in demand for gas. There was, according to British Gas's *Annual Report*, 'a sudden and unprecedented increase in demand for gas amounting almost to a flight from oil'. The industry faced 'a virtual landslide of customers wanting to change to gas. New business increased dramatically in all markets'.

We might expect that a sudden increase in gas demand would result either in sharp price increases, or in greater supplies, or both. There were some price increases, of course, but they were controlled and staggered in line with Government policy. And, somewhat oddly, supply increased very little in view of comments about 'unprecedented demand' and 'dramatic increases'. Instead, the 'flight from oil' was countered largely by encouraging energy conservation and by severe restrictions imposed on supplying new customers. Restrictions included curbs on advertising for new business. In particular, the promotion and advertising of load-building domestic appliances ceased while new supplies to industrial and commercial customers and new connections to existing domestic premises were severely curtailed. There was also a limitation of new large-scale contracts, especially to industrial and commercial markets, a policy allied with certain Government-approved steps to ease supply obligations imposed under existing Acts of Parliament (later confirmed in the Gas Act, 1980).

As a result of these various factors and measures, total gas sales in 1979–80 increased by only 5 per cent compared with the previous year, a rate no greater than that achieved a year earlier and half the growth of the year before that.

The 1979 crisis ushered in several years of slow growth and stagnation for the gas industry. Stagnation was caused in part by the continuation of general economic recession and partly by the continuation of supply restrictions, not fully lifted until 1984. An interesting indication of the situation is provided by a comparison of the Corporation's own five-year forecasts of sales compared with the actual

Table 9.3   British Gas's five-year plan forecasts (billion therms)

5-year period	Target forecast	Sales at beginning of period	Actual sales at end year
1977–78 to 1982–83	18.1	15.2	17.3
1978–79 to 1983–84	19.5	15.9	17.3
1979–80 to 1984–85	19.3	16.7	17.7
1980–81 to 1985–86	19.6	16.4	18.7

Source: British Gas Annual Reports.

quantities eventually sold. These comparisons are shown in Table 9.3.

In other words, the forecast sales the Corporation felt able to predict for 1982–83 were not, in fact, achieved until the last year before privatisation. Earlier five-year forecasts, made in the mid-1970s, had predicted gas sales in 1980 of around 18 billion therms. In the light of these statistics the difficulties which the industry faced in meeting its 'landslide' demand in 1979–80 and the subsequent maintenance of restrictions seem something of a puzzle. Why did the industry find it so onerous to sell far less than the targeted supplies of gas in the early 1980s?

The answer, at least in part, was that the industry had underestimated its peak load requirements; this in turn put pressure not only on supply and transmission but also on storage to meet peak demands. The freezing winter of 1978–79, the coldest since 1962–63, showed clearly how the new central heating loads could cause embarrassingly large demands at peak times, with demand as much as five times that of a normal summer's day. A new factor raising peak demand, and hitherto ignored, was the coincidence of cold weather with strong winds. From this time onwards the 'wind chill' factor was built into peak load forecasts. From 1980 the Corporation undertook major new investment both in storage facilities to meet seasonal peaks (including new LNG storage tanks) and in SNG (substitute natural gas) plants to produce gas at peak times. Nevertheless, it was not until 1984 that the industry found itself with a better balance of total supply, total demand, and storage for peak demand. By this time, in any case, gas was operating in a more competitive and complex environment. Oil prices stabilised, and then tumbled in 1986. Electricity prices, aided by cheaper oil, also became more competitive, while the gas industry's own sales of appliances were challenged by the growth of competitive outlets.

In retrospect it is clear that the economic recession which retarded gas demand for much of the late 1970s and early 1980s was something of a blessing for an overstretched gas industry, both nationally and at the level of the Regions. But it was also a period of great anxiety and uncertainty. Above all, there was uncertainty about the role and nature of the industry within the public sector, for soon after the Conservative Government came to power in 1979 it became clear that not only was there the prospect of privatisation but that some Cabinet Ministers were in favour of splitting up the organisation into separate parts and reducing its activities. Thus, in 1980, the Government announced that British Gas would have to sell most of its large oil assets (such holdings occurred because gas and oil fields were normally found in association, and in a number of enterprises in which British Gas was involved oil interests were larger than gas). The necessary powers were contained in the Oil and Gas (Enterprise) Act of 1982, an important measure which curtailed British Gas's monopoly position in a number of respects and ushered in a period of intense public debate about the role and future of the Corporation. By 1984, most of the Corporation's oil assets had been sold, without compensation, on Government directive. This policy coincided with a major new tax, the Gas Levy, imposed after 1981, which further tightened the financial constraints under which the industry operated. In line with government anti-monopoly policy, the sole right of British Gas to purchase gas supplied from UK North Sea fields was ended in 1982. In putting forward this measure Nigel Lawson, the then Energy Secretary, was particularly critical of the Corporation's policy of rationing supplies to industry and blamed British Gas's monopoly of North Sea supplies and consequent low purchase prices for the low rate of new exploration and enterprise. Privatisation moved a step further in 1983 with the Queen's Speech promising that 'legislation will be introduced to prepare for the introduction of private finance into nationalised undertakings'.

Considerable general public concern arose from the question mark hanging over the showrooms and appliance business. This issue, was, of course, of particular significance to the Regions. In July 1980 came the long-awaited Report of the Monopolies and Mergers Commission into gas appliance sales, initiated in December 1977. The Report shocked the industry, arguing that the dominant position of British Gas in the appliance market was not in the public interest. British Gas should stop selling appliances altogether and its High Street presence should disappear. As a less radical alternative, the Report suggested that the appliance market should become more competitive, and the dominant position of British Gas reduced. A year later, in July 1981, the Government announced that the industry would be ordered to withdraw from appliance retailing and to sell off its showrooms over a five-year period, a threat which was later withdrawn.

These were trying years for British Gas. The Chairman, Sir Denis Rooke, upset by what he deemed 'incomprehensible and unfair' attacks on a successful industry, and fearful that British Gas would be dismembered prior to privatisation, publicly took issue with his critics. In the event, Sir Denis's views prevailed, and British Gas was to pass into private hands largely intact.

On 7 May 1985, the Energy Secretary, Peter Walker, outlined the long-awaited Government plans for the industry to the House of Commons. All the assets of the Corporation were to be transferred to a new company, whose shares would be sold to the public. Yet, under privatisation, the basic structure of the industry was to be left very much intact, with its gas production (though not its oil), its transmission and distribution facilities, its storage capacity (the future of the Canvey terminal had been called into question in 1980 on environmental grounds), its research stations, and its customer-related activities all linked in a single enterprise. A significant change, however, was the replacement of Regional Consumers' Councils by a single national body (though with some regional representation). Thus a North Thames Gas consumers' body, set up in 1949, was to disappear under the new legislation. The government Bill passed its second reading in the House of Commons in December 1985, and received its Royal Assent on 25 July 1986 (the Gas Act, 1986). Later that year, in December, British Gas was returned to private enterprise in a massive and historic exercise which was then the largest-ever company flotation in this or any other country. Some five million individuals applied for shares in the new company, and no less than 99 per cent of gas employees and pensioners were among the applicants.

The reasons for privatisation lie beyond the scope of the present story, but it may be emphasised that privatisation was not the result of any failure either by the Corporation or the individual Regions. Rather, the gas industry was widely recognised as one of the most efficient and effectively-led of the nationalised enterprises and the decision to privatise was part of a general Conservative programme whose objectives included reduction of the state sector, a belief in private enterprise, and a wish to extend public share ownership as widely as possible.

When we turn to the Region's performance in recent years, it is not surprising to find in broad terms a reflection of national trends. Thus an era of rapidly growing gas sales after 1967, especially to the industrial market, was followed by a period of much slower growth and the stagnation of industrial markets from the mid-1970s. Table 9.4, showing percentage growth over five-year periods, summarises these trends.

A number of interesting points emerge from Table 9.4. Most obvious is the great success achieved by North Thames in securing new industrial markets, especially before 1973. During 1971 industrial sales overtook commercial sales for the first time in North Thames's history and by 1974 were approaching 30 per cent of total sales. Equally striking

Table 9.4   North Thames: growth of gas sales (% change) over five-year periods

Period[1]	Domestic	Industrial	Commercial	Total	Average domestic consumption
1968–73	54	303	47	81	53
1973–78	33	51	65	44	36
1978–83	27	−25	18	11	24
1981–86	18	−11	18	12	13

[1]Year ending March 31.
Source: North Thames Gas.

was the later stagnation of industrial sales and the peak figure reached in 1977–78 was never subsequently matched. In 1980 commercial sales overtook industrial once more, and by March 1986 industrial sales accounted for only 16 per cent of the total, little more than on the eve of conversion.

Commercial sales have always been a major component of North Thames's sales, and North Thames has supplied more gas to such markets than any other Region. The heart of this market lies in London's many hotels, restaurants and cafés, shops and offices, and public buildings. The relatively slow growth of this sector in the early 1970s and more rapid growth between 1973 and 1978, shown in Table 9.4, was largely due to the timing of the conversion programme. Much of the commercial market lay in central areas of the capital which were among the last sectors to be converted to natural gas.

Another point of interest shown by Table 9.4 is the steady decline in the rate at which domestic households increased their average consumption. Many factors were at work here, including higher gas charges, more efficient gas appliances, and energy conservation. But most significant was the slower rate at which new customers adopted gas central heating, an inevitable development following the very rapid growth rates from the late 1960s. Nevertheless, the table shows how after 1978 domestic sales rose considerably faster than the Region's average total sales, confirming and strengthening North Thames's role as a 'domestic' Region.

Table 9.5 further confirms how the increased sales by North Thames after 1974 went largely to domestic customers. Average domestic consumption per domestic customer continued to rise steadily, from 279 therms in 1970–71 to 411 in 1975–76, and to 633 a decade later.

Accompanying the broad, long-term trends have been some quite dramatic changes within North Thames which have resulted in greatly improved efficiency and performance throughout the Region. The main developments took place in the wake of the events of 1979. As we have seen, the years 1979–83 were, throughout the gas industry, dominated

Table 9.5   Total gas sales (million therms)

	Domestic	Industrial	Commercial	Total	Average per domestic customer
1967–8	390	70	132	593	216
1970–71	506	107	159	772	279
1973–74	643	351	218	1216	355
1976–77	747	366	263	1376	423
1979–80	930	384	351	1665	517
1983–84	1079	329	380	1788	586
1985–86	1189	317	454	1960	633

Source: North Thames Gas.

by a rather curious crisis: first, in 1979, came a period when demand was rising (due to the oil crisis) but such demand could not be catered for (due to the underestimation of peak load requirements); second, thereafter came recession and competition which continued and enhanced the earlier self-imposed period of stagnant sales. The result was a critical period in which action, sometimes drastic action, to reduce costs had to be taken.

For North Thames the strains on capacity caused by the harsh winter of 1978–9 and consequent leap in peak demands were the more severe because they followed two exceptionally mild winters when, for the first time since 1963–64, the maximum daily sendout failed to set a new record. Table 9.6 illustrates just how massive the peak demands became at this time.

Table 9.6   North Thames's maximum daily sendouts (million therms)

1975 (Dec. 15)	7.90
1977 (Jan. 17)	7.40
1978 (Feb. 17)	7.78
1979 (Feb. 15)	9.03

Source: North Thames Gas.

Table 9.7 further puts the record sendout of 1979 in the context of other records set in various years, and it is notable how in very recent years North Thames has been able to expand its peak sendouts considerably.

A major problem faced by the Region in recent years has been falling sales of domestic appliances. Tables 9.8 and 9.9 show how appliance sales have deteriorated sharply from the early 1970s, leading to excess showroom capacity and underemployment among the customer service labour force.

Table 9.7   Selected record sendouts (million therms)

1962–63	(21 Jan. 1963)	2.13
1964–65	(2 Mar. 1965)	2.43
1969–70	(31 Dec. 1969)	4.02
1974–75	(19 Mar. 1975)	6.38
1978–79	(15 Feb. 1979)	9.03
1980–81	(8 Dec. 1980)	9.22
1985–86	(26 Feb. 1986)	11.97
1986–87	(13 Jan. 1987)	14.14

Source: North Thames Gas.

Table 9.8   Appliance sales, 1955–85 (000s)

Year (ending March 31)	Cookers	Water heaters	Space heaters
1955	149.2	64.6	10.1
1960	138.5	44.6	35.0
1965	113.6	42.2	97.4
1970	109.6	23.2	95.2
1975	71.3	20.1	66.9
1980	68.4	18.1	62.3
1985	56.3	14.0	40.8

Source: North Thames Gas.

Table 9.9   Sales of central heating boilers
(North Thames outlets)

Year (end March 31)	(000s)
1979	8.8
1980	8.7
1981	5.6
1982	6.2
1983	6.1
1984	6.7
1985	7.0
1986	8.7

Source: North Thames Gas.

The causes of sluggish appliance sales were complex and lay to some extent outside North Thames's control, as we have seen. Long-term factors included the slow growth of population and the number of households within the Region, and the 'saturation' of markets, especially for cookers and space heaters. Central heating sales and service were never a North Thames monopoly (on average only 20 per cent of boilers

in the Region were sold and serviced by North Thames) and even here
the total sales for 1972–73 of nearly 54 000 boilers was never subsequently matched. The oil crisis of 1979 and subsequent economic recession
also had a major impact on North Thames's appliance sales and service
workloads, just as it did for the industry generally. When advertising for
new products ceased, as British Gas endeavoured to damp down
demand, it was inevitable that competition from the private sector
should increase. However, the Report of the Monopolies and Mergers
Commission in 1980 and subsequent government pronouncements
boosted such competition beyond all expectation. In 1976 there were
only about ten retail outlets in the Region selling gas appliances outside
North Thames's own showrooms and authorised dealer network. Ten
years later the number was around five hundred. Table 9.10 shows how
the numbers of independent retailers selling gas appliances grew in
these years. They were mainly kitchen installers, but sales from large
discount retailers such as Comet and MFI also grew significantly.

Table 9.10   Independent gas appliance
retailers, North Thames Region

March 1979	13
January 1980	20
March 1981	111
January 1983	286
December 1984	410
March 1985	460

Source: North Thames Gas.

There were, in addition, various other factors tending to depress
North Thames's appliance sales. These included general economic
recession and low consumer spending-power; growing competition
from electricity as gas prices rose (gas charges more than doubled
between 1979 and 1983); and changing consumer demands which, for
example, increasingly sought integrated fitted kitchens combining both
electric and gas appliances, rather than the simple purchase of an
individual appliance from a limited range in a gas showroom.

It should be evident from what has been said so far that John Gadd
faced a number of very serious problems in the early years of his
chairmanship. In addition to low morale in the wake of George Cooper's
reorganisation and the still fragmented and inefficient structure which
the move to the new central headquarters could only gradually improve,
there was the fundamental dilemma of low growth of gas sales and
declining appliance markets. The crisis brought by stagnant gas sales
was severe. In 1982–83, in the wake of successive price rises, North
Thames sold less gas than in the previous year – the first time this had

happened since 1955. When we recall that gas sales were overwhelmingly the main source of North Thames's revenue and profits, and that gas costs were set inevitably to rise in the 1980s at a time when greater competition from electricity and oil might be expected, the urgent need to reduce non-gas costs, especially surplus labour capacity, becomes only too obvious. The overwhelming role of the gas account is shown by the fact that in 1985–86 gas sales totalled £697 million. Income from appliance sales was just £28 million, and from service work £27 million.

Gadd's revolution, for it was nothing less than that, was accomplished relatively quietly with nothing of the drama associated with his predecessor. Indeed, for the first two years after his arrival in 1977 the new Chairman made no fundamental changes, preferring, under the circumstances of previous internal and external reorganisation, to allow the Region a breathing space in which to digest the many earlier reforms. He was concerned above all to improve morale within the Region and to concentrate narrowly on small improvements rather than introducing sweeping changes on a broad front. In one of his first public statements the Chairman assured staff that no further major reorganisation would be undertaken in the near future. Another reason for caution was the unsettling effect of changes which took place within the Region's top management at this time. Gadd was particularly unlucky to lose his Deputy Chairman only a few months after arriving at Staines. Robert Evans left the Region in July 1977, after only two years at North Thames, to become Chairman at East Midlands. Donald Young, his successor, had already spent a year with the Region in 1974 on secondment from British Gas, but he too was to remain at Staines as Deputy only a short time, leaving in less than two years.

By 1979 circumstances had changed. The oil crisis, the bleak market situation, and improving morale within the Region heralded a new climate. In addition, there arrived in May 1979 a new Deputy Chairman, Tony Haynes, from the North Eastern Region. Haynes had already worked alongside John Gadd at Eastern Region and their earlier cooperation was a fruitful basis for the two to work closely together at North Thames. Haynes remained at North Thames until replacing Robert Evans as Chairman of East Midlands at the beginning of 1983. The combination was propitious for North Thames, for John Gass was the only North Thames Chairman able to carve out a satisfactory role for his deputy, and the two worked effectively together on the major problems facing the Region. Haynes's successor was Allan Sutcliffe, previously Deputy Chairman of West Midlands Gas. Sutcliffe was another effective Deputy Chairman, but he was soon seconded to British Gas in 1985 to head a Working Party dealing with the legislative aspects of the forthcoming privatisation.

As a result of a series of co-ordinated measures taken after 1979,

Gadd, his Deputies, and the Regional Management Committee were able to transform North Thames from probably the least efficient and cost-effective Region around 1976 to one of the most progressive a decade later. The improvements were undertaken in four main areas: reorganisation (again!); the slimming of the work-force in line with changes in workloads; rationalisation of property and land-holding, and better located and fewer showrooms; and the introduction throughout the Region of new computer-based technology.

Reorganisation (the term, for obvious reasons, was never used, it was called 'organisational development'), as we have seen, was not embarked upon at once. When John Gadd became Chairman of North Thames in 1977 the programme of centralisation started by his predecessor in 1971 was all but completed. This had given North Thames its five Area Headquarters, its centralised customer accounting, supplies and transport, and its new chief office. In Gadd's view this structure was excessively over-centralised, but reform could be neither swift nor far-reaching. For one thing, the Region needed time to recover from earlier upheavals; for another, any moves towards decentralisation needed strong management at local levels, and the new Chairman felt that time was needed to build up this strength in view of the many departures and reshuffles during reorganisation.

From the outset, though, Gadd felt that the appropriate unit of local management for customer service activities was a relatively small district, dealing ideally with less than 200 000 customers. In this way, the customer and organisation could be brought closer together. The Areas, by contrast, each covered on average some 400 000 consumers, and varied individually from 500 000 to little more than 200 000. The ideal, for Gadd, was a two-tier management structure based on headquarters and the district, whereas the inherited system had the additional tier of Areas with consequent multiplying of lines of responsibility and paperwork.

Not until 1986 did the Chairman feel able to introduce a two-tier district structure to North Thames, but from 1979 some steps towards decentralisation took place. Initially this involved strengthening the Area organisation. Area sales managers were appointed (in place of separate managers dealing with domestic, industrial and commercial sales) and they and the Area customer service managers were to be involved in their own budgeting and targets rather than being directed centrally from Staines. Co-ordination at Area level was to be achieved through a system of committees with an annually revolving chairmanship between the Area managers for sales, customer service, and engineering. There were also some further moves towards decentralisation with new Area appointments for personnel, transport, and stores.

Further changes were made in 1982 when the sales and service functions were brought together both at Area level and centrally. This move was prompted by growing competition from the private sector, and North Thames responded by a concerted effort to sell not only its appliances but also its service and experience. John Allan, hitherto Sales Director, became the new Director of Marketing, while at Area level new marketing managers were appointed.

In March 1984, customer accounting completed a major reorganisation, involving the closure of two offices (at Ilford and Pinner) and moves for 800 staff. Hitherto, all gas billing had been concentrated in the Ilford and Middlesex House centres, but with this reorganisation billing was made an Area responsibility in an effort to move customer accounting operations closer to the customer.

Finally, in April 1986, just months before privatisation, came the long-planned restructuring. On March 31 the former five Areas disappeared and were replaced by eleven districts. Each of the districts became a unit both for marketing (under a district manager) and engineering (under a district engineer). District boundaries were chosen to cover around 150 000 to 200 000 consumers and, as far as possible, to coincide with local authority boundaries. The objects of the reorganisation, in the Chairman's words, were 'to reduce costs, speed decision-making, and have those decisions made nearer the customer'.

The slow pace of reorganisation was prompted not simply by earlier upheavals and the availability of suitable management but also by lengthy negotiations which took place at all stages between management and unions. In many ways improved industrial relations were at the heart of North Thames' post-conversion renaissance, and already in 1980 Geoffrey Battison, Managing Editor of *Gas World*, singled out 'better human relations' as Gadd's major contribution to North Thames.

Alongside, and coupled with, reorganisation went quite drastic cuts in the labour force, especially after 1981, as Table 9.11 shows. The five-year period prior to March 1986 thus saw a fall in total employment of no less than 30 per cent, far more than ever experienced in a comparable period, more than that experienced by any other Region, and double the average for British Gas as a whole in this period. The result was a significant jump in efficiency and profitability. By the mid-1980s, North Thames was around midway among Regions in terms of profitability,

Table 9.11   Total employees 1976–86 (year ended 31 March)

Year	Total employees (000s)		Total
	Manual	Staff	
1976	5.4	8.9	14.3
1981	5.0	8.1	13.1
1986	3.2	6.0	9.2

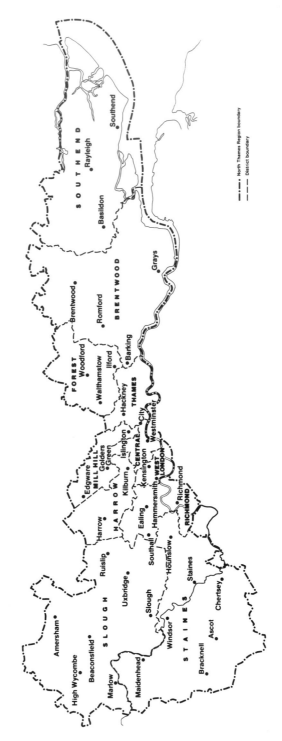

Figure 9.1 The eleven new Districts created by the restructuring of North Thames in 1986.

having been one of the least profitable a decade earlier, and projections suggested that the Region would move into second place by the early 1990s.

North Thames's success in trimming its labour force lay largely in Gadd's ability to isolate key areas which he tackled one at a time, and in his skill in negotiations with the unions involved. Gadd displayed both flexibility, where this was possible, and a refusal to yield on the essentials of the reforms.

The first, and most critical, sector to be dealt with in this way was customer service, where the establishment of a new marketing directorate in May 1982 was precipitated by a growing crisis in the sector. The crisis was not, as in the early 1970s, one of poor service and customer complaints, but a falling service workload, consequent overmanning, high costs, and low profitability. Indeed, in the year 1981–82 overall profitability per employee was the lowest since the price-freeze era of the early 1970s, while installation and appliance servicing recorded a series of heavy losses.

Falling workloads were caused by lower appliance sales (especially after 1979), the stagnant industrial market, growing competition, and a bold campaign by Gadd and Haynes to clamp down on a variety of practices which artificially inflated workloads (such as unnecessary service visits to contract customers). By the beginning of 1982, with workloads continuing to fall, the capacity of North Thames's service teams was already some 20 per cent in excess of demand.

In this new environment the Regional Management Committee took a number of steps. Most important, following the merger of sales and service, was to cut the number of posts, especially on the service side. As a result over 1000 workers were shed from the new directorate between 1982 and 1985. Another step was to revise and rationalise district organisations and working practices, reducing the numbers of service depots and showrooms and lowering the ratio of supervisory staff.

As part of a longer term plan the Chairman also improved customer service by strengthening the districts. In 1984 two pilot schemes for strong decentralised districts were established at Brentwood and Slough, and the success of this scheme led ultimately to the fundamental restructuring of the Region in 1986.

Such drastic changes could not take place without some friction and discord, but it is a tribute both to union realism and management negotiating skills that troubles were not more than they were. In these negotiations the skills and experience of Paul Dixon, Director of Personnel, were a major factor in the successful outcome. Paul Dixon had joined the Gas Light & Coke Company during the Second World War and had worked closely with George Cooper and Paul Rhodes during the major reorganisation of the 1970s. He became Personnel Director in 1971 and was consequently involved in all the complex and protracted industrial relations issues which arose in that period. Much was accomplished in a very short space of time. In little more than two years following the setting up of the new marketing directorate in 1982 the service workforce had been cut by around 1000, thirteen depots closed (and a further eleven by the middle of 1985) and the number of work zones reduced from fifty-four to thirty-seven. In 1977 there had been fifty-seven depots dealing with marketing operations; by the end of 1984 the number was down to thirty-eight, and by December 1986, only thirty-one. In addition, fifteen smaller showrooms were closed in the years 1977–84. As part of the labour cutback in customer service no more apprentices were recruited after 1981, and, once the last group of apprentices finished their training in 1984, all service apprentice training facilities were dismantled.

Early retirement, voluntary redundancy, and redeployment were all used as steps to cut the work-force, but it still proved necessary in the summer of 1983 to make some 275 service fitters effectively redundant (though all were offered other jobs, mostly as manual labourers in the distribution sector). A difficult period followed, with a number of depot stoppages and a five-week strike by service engineers in the Western Area.

Nevertheless, the changes brought perceptible gains in productivity and profitability, while standards of service to customers showed steady improvement. Moreover a more buoyant market environment after 1984, combined with successful campaigns to expand customer service, helped reverse the trend of falling service workloads.

Among other significant steps taken to improve working practices in these years involved the meter reading staff within the customer accounting division. Here a costly bonus scheme introduced in 1963 in the days when most meters were coin-in-the-slot, had become wholly inappropriate for credit customers and new meter-reading technology. Already, by mid-1974, less than half the Region's domestic customers had prepayment meters; by early 1984 the numbers of such meters were down to 300 000 and by the end of 1986 to under 150 000. The obsolete bonus scheme was successfully withdrawn in 1982, although to do so involved the termination of employment contracts for virtually all the outdoor meter-readers, and their re-employment under new terms. Once more a long period of complex and delicate negotiations was handled by both sides with a mixture of realism and skill.

The steady fall in the work-force coupled with early retirements brought a growing proportion of pensioners; indeed, during 1985 the numbers of pensioners exceeded the number of employees for the first time, since when the gap has widened substantially. It was a sign of the times than in 1975 North Thames decided to set up a Gas Retirement Fellowship (the first Region to do so) and by 1983 membership exceeded 3500. One consequence of the growing numbers of pensioners was the mounting cost of distributing the *Thames Gas* magazine, which had always been sent both to employees and pensioners. In August 1985, therefore, the magazine format came to an end, breaking a tradition which had lasted since 1911. Instead, a new newspaper for employees was introduced, while pensioners received a separate bulletin.

As mentioned previously, the early 1980s saw substantial rationalisation of retailing activities and the closure of a number of showrooms. Here, John Gadd's policy was threefold: to close small showrooms which could not carry the full range of appliances to offer the choice desired by modern consumers; to concentrate on a small number of large showrooms ('core showrooms') in major shopping centres and other prime locations; and to take such premises on short leases in order to gain maximum flexibility in relocating. The result of these policies was a considerable fall in the total number of showrooms (with the policy of rationalisation by no means ended at the time of privatisation), but also the opening of some very advanced centres with the benefits of up-to-date technology. Table 9.12 shows how the total number of showrooms at North Thames fell from its 1969 peak, and when the programme of closures is complete the Region will have well under half the numbers of showrooms which it had at that time.

Table 9.12   Number of showrooms, 1949–87

Year (end of year)	Number of showrooms
1949	87
1960	93
1969	95
1977	80
1983	72
1984	61
1987[1]	55

[1]Mid year.

Among major new showroom developments in recent years has been one at Ealing Broadway, established in 1984 and replacing one in the Broadway which had been opened by the Gas Light & Coke Company in 1928. This showroom was used as a pilot experiment prior to the introduction of large scale computer technology into showrooms. Another ultra-modern showroom, the largest in the Region, was opened at Basildon in 1985, and the following year North Thames replaced its

37 A new showroom in Hammersmith Shopping Centre, 1979.

showroom in Barkers of Kensington (opened in 1980) with a new one in Kensington High Street incorporating a great deal of the latest technology including desk-top computer links with the accounting department and central stores.

The introduction of new computer-based technology into showrooms was only one aspect of computerisation, which was one of the major themes of Gadd's chairmanship. The tentative steps towards computerisation taken by the Board following the installation of the first computer in 1966 were mentioned in an earlier chapter, but from around 1976 the pace quickened. With the end of conversion and the successful end to the search for a Chief Office, computers and computer-based technology have transformed the work of virtually every department in the Region. In June 1977 the computer centre at Peterborough Road, Fulham, was transferred to the Staines headquarters, the Region deciding to continue with ICL computers and to adopt the new ICL 2900 range, and from around this time North Thames changed its position as the most backward of the Regions to become one of the leading Regions in the introduction of computer technology. By 1983 the Region's computer staff numbered about 300, some 200 of them based at Staines, and by early 1986 the total staff had risen to around 380. The first visual display unit (VDU) to be installed in a showroom was in Kensington in 1975; by 1983 the ICL 2900 computers were supplying information to some 300 VDUs at more than sixty locations, while by the end of 1986 nearly 1500 VDUs were in operation, serving nearly every aspect of the Region's work and covering virtually the entire North Thames area. In 1986 the Region took the decision to change its computer suppliers and to adopt IBM mainframe computer processors. The ICL computers had proved in some respects unable to cope with the vast workloads of great complexity required by North Thames, and the first of the new IBM computers was installed in 1987.

Of particular significance, in view of their key role in customer relations and overall profitability, has been the adoption of vastly improved systems in customer accounting and customer service. In both areas the arrival of new technology has been combined with changes in organisation which together have promoted greater efficiency. In 1976 plans were started to replace the Region's complicated billing system of the ICL 1905 computers and in July 1980 the new system, termed CAMI (Customer Accounting Management Information System) was successfully inaugurated in the Eastern Area and extended subsequently to the rest of the Region. Customer services were greatly improved by the adoption of MASS (Multi-Area Service System) which was pioneered in the North Western Area in 1982 and adopted throughout the Region in 1984. Under this system, service workloads could be planned more efficiently with a minimum of form filling. A further innovation was the introduction of a Same Day Service System on minicomputers during 1984.

Among many other information technology developments may be mentioned improvements resulting from Optimal Mark Recognition, introduced in 1977 and 1978, which led to a 15 per cent speeding up in the time taken between meter reading and despatch of the customer's account. Greatly improved productivity also followed the full computerisation by 1976, using the Inventory Control and Analysis System (INCA), of the new Central Stores at Bromley-by-Bow.

A major development within the engineering and distribution departments took place in 1981 with the adoption of a new system (MINE) for storing information about the Region's distribution network. Already, by early 1982, the system had stored over one million items of information about the Region's 10 000 mains throughout its 60 000 streets, and in the following years it was extended to incorporate job instructions and was linked to other computer systems within the Region. The contribution of advanced technology to engineering problems was also seen with the introduction of the British Gas On-Line Inspection Vehicle, or 'intelligent pig'. The pig, first used in the Region in 1980, a moving vehicle with magnetic tape heads, was developed to 'inspect' pipes and record many thousands of items of information without disturbing or disconnecting them. In 1986 the pig made a major 50-mile survey of the Region's north orbital pipeline.

Yet another area where Gadd's policies have made a distinctive impact on the shape and functioning of the Region is in the rationalisation of its vast landholdings inherited from the Gas Light & Coke Company. North Thames, with its gasworks, holder stations, offices, depots, welfare facilities, and showrooms, has always been a substantial property owner. The prime locations of many of the properties and the large areas of land belonging to some of the works has meant that the asset value of North Thames's holdings has always been much higher than for Regions elsewhere in the country. The development and administration of this vast range of properties has formed a significant and continuing activity, but since the early 1970s the character of North Thames's property holdings has been largely transformed under the direction of the Property Committee, a body established originally by George Cooper and with a membership including the entire Regional Management Committee together with the Regional Surveyor (the only committee so constituted, and evidence of the importance attached to land and property holdings).

The transformation of property holdings has been stimulated by three main factors. First came the contraction and ultimate demise of manufacturing capacity; the need for land and its attendant plant, accommodation and facilities for staff was accordingly diminished (although most sites have continued to serve as holder stations and for various other purposes). The end of manufactured coal gas meant the finish of coal purchases and coke sales, and so of the enormous storage facilities hitherto required; and it meant too the closure of the Products Works, the end of the collier fleet and the shutting down of a host of related operations. Second, came centralisation: with the Staines and Area headquarters, the billing centres, the Bromley-by-Bow centralised stores and transport complex, and other large central units, there has been a corresponding decline in the need for many of the outlying offices, depots, and stores. And third, came a movement for rationalisation and economy, in evidence during the 1960s and gathering pace in the post-conversion era. In turn, this movement was fostered and reinforced by centralisation, the growing use of computers, and rationalisation of showrooms, depots, and warehouse facilities.

As a result of land disposals, North Thames now controls far less land and many fewer buildings than it did in the days of manufacturing. In the mid-1950s, for example, the Building and Property Maintenance Department looked after no fewer than 770 separate premises of various shapes and sizes, including offices, showrooms, warehouses, depots, stores, houses, and cottages. At the end of 1984 the figure stood at under 250, although some of the individual premises were, of course, very large. Formerly too, the Department maintained eleven sports grounds covering some 150 acres. The main grounds were at Acton in the west and East Ham in the east, with others at Iver Heath, Southall, Mill Hill, Beckton, Lea Bridge, Woodford, Brentford, Grays, and Southend. Now only Acton and East Ham remain, for the communities which once in their thousands supported such events as the Annual Galas at Beckton and Mill Hill have vanished.

Then there were the gas stations themselves, many of them vast. Largest was the colossal complex at Beckton where the gas plant, storage facilities and Products Works occupied a site of around 540 acres. By the mid-1970s, with the labour force reduced to a few hundred, desolate parts of the site were not infrequently used for film and television scenes, one director choosing Beckton for its 'eeriness', while another, Stanley Kubrick, recreated there in 1985 the war-torn Vietnamese city of Hue for his film *Full Metal Jacket*. Another large works was at Bromley-by-Bow, the site extending to 160 acres. Other works, such as Fulham and Brentford, occupied valuable central locations, the latter covering nearly nine acres on both sides of the High Street. Among this mass of property was much of historic interest. Fulham's No. 2 holder was scheduled as a historic structure in 1954; it was then the oldest working gas holder in the world, constructed in 1830 by the old City Gas Company. Another famous Fulham building was Sandford Manor House, supposedly built by Charles II for Nell Gwyn. Of similar

38 End of an era at Beckton, when three chimneys erected by the Gas Light &
Coke Co. c. 1930, and last used for gas making in 1969, were demolished on 15
July 1984.

antiquity is the Billericay showroom, the original meeting place of
the Billericay Independent Protestant Dissenters in 1672.

Since around 1970 land disposals have been substantial, and from
1976 the movement gathered pace as the end of conversion and the
opening of the Staines headquarters meant that land at the gas stations
and many London offices would be dispensed with. Already by the
end of 1973 the total area of land controlled by North Thames had
fallen to 1384 acres from its Vesting Day figure of some 1750 acres. By
the end of 1984 the area had fallen further to 1151 acres, and by
December 1986 to only 966 acres.

Major disposals in the earlier part of the period included the sale in
1971–72 of part of Beckton's Products Works site for redevelopment.

From 1981, substantial areas at both Beckton and Bromley-by-Bow were sold to the newly-formed London Docklands Development Corporation (LDDC). By 1984, as a result, the Beckton site had declined to 327 acres and Bromley-by-Bow to only 75 acres, the latter therefore becoming less than half its former size. A further massive sale to the LDDC in May 1986 of 130 acres at Beckton, and sales there for a new road system and river crossing reduced the Beckton site to under 180 acres.

These changes brought the end of many once-familiar landmarks, such as the last giant retort-house chimneys, felled at Beckton in 1984. Also gone is the old Nine Elms river site, once a bustling 20-acre works employing more than eight hundred people. The last sales here were made in 1980 when the British Gas Corporation bought the site for industrial development. This was the Corporation's first venture in such a development. Subsequently, housing development projects have been undertaken at former works' sites in Marlow and Fulham.

Several of the former head office buildings in central London have proved valuable assets. Indeed, the sale of 30 Kensington Church Street in 1978 and of the offices on Monck Street, Westminster (formerly the headquarters of the Engineering Department) in 1981, together realised a greater sum than the 100 acres or so disposed of at Bromley-by-Bow and Beckton in 1981 and 1982. The sale of much of the Fulham Works site also released valuable development land. Among other significant disposals have been the sites of the old central stores on the Great West Road and of the warehouses and offices at Haggerston, both in 1978; the Heston warehouses and offices, the first divisional headquarters of the Gas Light & Coke Company, in 1980; and part of Kensal Green site in 1985, the single most valuable disposal undertaken by the Region.

Rationalisation of property has also been seen in the policy of dismantling the Region's waterless gasholders, both unsightly and costly to run and maintain. Three such holders disappeared within twelve months in 1985–86, at Staines, Woodford, and South Harrow. The latter was a 240-ft monster erected by the Gas Light & Coke Company in 1931, and one of a pair with that of Kensal Green, already demolished in 1976. The holder at Brentford was also dismantled in 1987, leaving only two, at Battersea and Southall, still operational.

With the upheavals of conversion over after 1976, the Region was able to turn its attention to renewing and maintaining its 11 650 miles of distribution system. After 1978, increasingly sophisticated technology and materials enabled the Region to achieve a significant reduction in gas losses from leakage with a minimum of disturbance to traffic. This attention to distribution was in part a consequence of renewed public anxiety about the safety of natural gas at the beginning of 1977.

Fortunately, serious gas explosions have been something of a rarity in Britain's gas industry and a rarity too in the North Thames Region.

However, around New Year 1977 there occurred a cluster of explosions which led to the setting up of an independent inquiry under Dr Philip King, who had assisted Professor Morton in the earlier inquiry into gas safety. The King inquiry was set up in the wake of a series of explosions over the Christmas and New Year period. The King Report, published in June 1977, made a number of recommendations for improved safety, but it confirmed and emphasised the excellent safety record of the gas industry and the high quality of the safety precautions already undertaken in the various Regions. Natural gas had not resulted in an increase either in the numbers or in the severity of explosions.

The explosions examined by Dr King were those at Bristol, Brentford, Beckenham, and Bradford. The explosion at Brentford was in the North Thames area. The accident happened on 29 December at 9.40 a.m. in a men's outfitters' shop (the same day as the Bristol explosion, and the day after the one at Bradford). There were no fatalities, but thirty-eight were injured, six being detained in hospital. The cause of the explosion was a gas escape in a fractured 4-inch main outside the shop, the fracture probably caused by settlement damage due to heavy traffic. The mains itself, though laid in 1935, was found to be in good condition. There were no common causes in the four explosions, other than the presence of gas itself. In fact, at Brentford the police had been informed about a smell of gas the day before, but North Thames were not informed until the following morning – alerted by the occupants of an adjacent shop. North Thames engineers were actually in this shop when the explosion occurred.

The King Report laid particular emphasis on the damage which heavy traffic could cause to gas mains and noted that in 1975 and 1976 there had been two exceptionally hot and dry summers in succession which had caused a dry-out of the earth and consequent damage to a number of gas mains throughout the country.

One of the consequences of the King Report was that North Thames, in common with other Regions, laid great emphasis on repairing and re-laying distribution systems, making use of the most up-to-date technology. As a result of this and other safety measures the numbers of accidents in the North Thames Region continued to fall throughout the 1970s. In the year 1976–77, for example, the numbers of fires and explosions were one third lower than the average for the previous ten years.

Another issue of public concern in these years was anxiety about the possible unfortunate consequences of disconnecting gas and electricity supplied for unpaid bills. Attention was focused on the plight of the elderly, the unemployed, and other unfortunate individuals during a severe winter, and concern came to the fore in the winter of 1975–76. The gas industry's record in cases of genuine hardship has been a good one, and the industry had no difficulty complying with the announcement made by the Government in February 1976 that no 'pensioner households' would be disconnected before June of that year. Subsequently, in January 1977, the gas and electricity industries established a voluntary Code of Practice for dealing with cases of particular hardship. The operation of the Code, monitored by the National Gas Consumers' Council, followed existing gas industry practice, and the first report of the Consumers' Council, which included sample checks in the North Thames Region, found no cases where the Code had been contravened. Subsequent monitoring by the Regional Consumers' Council showed no violations of the Code by North Thames, where it was the practice to contact the Department of Health and Social Security before an entry warrant was sought. Although there were some fluctuations in the numbers of disconnections, the trend from the late 1970s was downwards (see Table 9.13).

Table 9.13   Disconnections of credit
customers, North Thames

1979–80	8050
1980–81	8243
1981–82	6688
1982–83	7574
1983–84	7123
1984–85	6958
1985–86	6188

Source: North Thames Gas.

Energy conservation has been yet another continuing theme for the gas industry during the 1970s and 1980s. North Thames has played a full part in efforts to conserve energy, in line with Government and Corporation policy after the first energy crisis of 1973, and pursued with even greater vigour after the second in 1979. In 1982 the Region set up a centre for Energy Management at Fulham to give advice and training on fuel conservation for industrial and commercial gas users. Conservation efforts have included campaigns to encourage energy conservation among all classes of consumers, internal schemes to cut down on wastage, and promotion of both Regional and National Gas Energy Management Awards (GEM) which were first introduced in 1976. These awards have been made jointly to the commercial or industrial enterprises making the largest energy savings, together with the Region on whose technical advice and experience such savings were made. In 1982 North Thames won the commercial GEM award for its work with Lloyds of London, the City insurance centre, where gas consumption was reduced by 74 per cent with a saving of some 100 000 therms annually.

The growing emphasis on energy conservation was symptomatic of the changed market environment which occurred from around the mid-1970s, as slow growth of gas sales succeeded the earlier phase of exceptionally rapid expansion. Nevertheless, the Region had still to look to the future and to secure new loads where possible; and there were some notable additions through large-scale contracts, especially after 1982 with the gradual easing of earlier restrictions.

The Region (like the Board prior to 1973) had of necessity to make supplying new housing developments, both local authority and private, very much a priority. Were gas not supplied at the outset, potential loads might be lost forever. For this reason, even in periods of the tightest restrictions, such contracts were always sought enthusiastically. The Region's record here continued to be a successful one, with virtually all local authority housing and over 80 per cent of new housing developments being supplied with gas. Some of the largest contracts were arranged with the London Docklands Development Corporation, supplying gas to the various schemes which began to mushroom on London's revived riverside after 1981. The development has given North Thames immense opportunities, over 80 per cent of the entire docklands redevelopment area lying within the Region's territory. The Central Area completed a major new pipeline to the Isle of Dogs in 1984 to carry gas to thousands of houses and new industrial estates. The Region's role in the docklands' development, the only major growth area in the Region's territory after 1980, was particularly close; as well as supplying fuel needs, the Region also, as we have seen, provided some of the land for redevelopment from its defunct sites at Beckton and Bromley-by-Bow, while in May 1986 a further 20 acres at Beckton was sold for the new East London River Crossing, due for completion in the 1990s.

Among other significant contracts in recent years was one signed in 1979 to supply nearly one million therms annually to Kew Gardens, and one in 1985 to supply more than five million therms annually to the Heathrow terminals, including some 800 000 therms to the new Terminal 4. Another big commercial contract was signed in the same year with the British Museum for the supply of over 500 000 therms. Industrial sales were boosted by several contracts with brewing firms, including one for 2 million therms annually, signed in 1985 with Truman's Brewery in east London. Another large interruptible load was negotiated in the same year with Kodak Ltd to supply around 10 million therms annually over a three-year period.

Table 9.14 shows the Region's major interruptible industrial contracts over the period 1977–86. What is striking is how dependent North

Table 9.14   Selected interruptible industrial sales, 1977–86 (million therms)

	1977–78	1981–82	1985–86
London Transport	71	63	64
Tate & Lyle	28	25	28
Slough Estates	37	25	37
Ford's Power Station	78	15	1
Thames Board Mills	33	9	8
Total of Above	247	137	138
Total Industrial	440	334	318

Source: North Thames Gas.

Thames has been on just a handful of major contracts; this, of course, reflects the economic character of the area served, which has few major industrial firms, and the consequence of the loss of one or two large customers can be serious for the Region. Sales to London Transport alone in 1985–86 were more than 20 per cent of the total industrial load.

New and renewed industrial and commercial contracts after the late 1970s were signed at considerably higher charges than those in the initial boom period before 1975. This changed policy reflected both the reduced need to expand loads at almost any cost, and the growing cost of gas itself as the cheaper southern North Sea fields became exhausted. As a result, although total industrial sales fell, as we have seen, their profitability to North Thames rose.

North Thames's progress in the decade before privatisation was substantial and wide-ranging. Terms such as 'resurgence' and 'revival' were commonly used to described the Region's fortunes in this period, and the success of John Gadd's policies was evident throughout the Region's activities. A noteworthy feature of the Region's growing strength was that once again North Thames began to be a supplier of personnel to key posts elsewhere in the industry, recalling the heyday of the old Board.

As a result of the bold steps taken after 1980 the Region's profitability improved, as the labour force was trimmed and rationalisation took effect. In 1985 the installation of appliances and contracting account moved into profit for the first time, reflecting greater efficiency on the part of the Region's fitters. Indeed, North Thames's data suggest a 50 per cent improvement in efficiency in the decade 1976–86. Total trading costs showed a steady decline in real terms after 1981. While the workforce declined, gas sales and total turnover rose. Thus gas sales per employee rose 27 per cent in the five-year period between 1977 and 1982, while the increase between 1982 and 1987 was no less than 68 per cent. In the same periods total turnover per employee increased by 45 per cent and 70 per cent respectively. Thus, as privatisation approached, efficiency not only improved perceptibly, but at an accelerating rate.

Further signs of progress came from traditional trouble spots. The number of working days between meter reading and despatch of accounts was around twenty-five days in September 1972. By June 1974, the delay was eleven days, and by 1980 it was down to three days. On the eve of privatisation it had fallen to under two and a half days. Outstanding correspondence at billing centres also showed dramatic improvement: 54 000 items in January 1972; 40 000 in September 1976, but only 6000 by September 1977. Despite considerable staff reductions and a growing work-load, the level of outstanding correspondence was still held at around 6000 items at the close of 1986.

Table 9.15   Complaints to North Thames Gas Consultative and Consumers' Councils, 1971–86

Subject	1971–72	1972–73	1973–74	1974–75	1975–76	1981–82	1985–86
Sales and Service	901	2151	1613	1721	1378	766	643
Conversion	1162	1643	750	545	156	–	–
Disputed Charges and Accounts	577	2978	1719	1140	1656	976	1002
Others	665	1733	1320	1298	1450	1053	1015
Total	3305	8505	5402	4704	4640	2795	2660

Source: North Thames Gas Consultative and Consumers' Councils.

Progress was also seen in the critical areas of customer relations and customer satisfaction. The very high levels of complaints seen at the height of conversion had declined considerably by 1980. Although numbers of complaints tended to oscillate from year to year, and there were a few periods of considerable strain, the overall trend was downwards, as shown in Table 9.15.

Table 9.16 shows the falling numbers of complaints received by letter to all central sources, the Consumers' Council, British Gas, the Regional Headquarters, and directly to the Chairman. In the decade 1976–86 complaints fell by half, while over the entire period shown in the Table the decline was more than threefold.

Recognition of improvement has come from British Gas Gold Flame awards for customer service operations, awarded to Regional service teams and held annually since 1973. The awards are based on market research among gas consumers, and so reflect the level of customer satisfaction. No North Thames district has ever won the coveted trophy for overall 'best service team', but several have received the somewhat

A MESSAGE FROM THE CHAIRMAN

"WE MUST **NOT** BE DEMORALISED"

We have been having a very difficult time during recent months, and the last few weeks have been particularly bad. You will all have seen the articles in the Evening Standard and many of you will also know of the bad press that we have been getting in many local newspapers and of the problems we have had with Members of Parliament in some parts of our area. Even 'Gas World' decided to have a go a⁺ its own special con⁺ sort of unconst informed criticis body any go or our ᵒ Kensington Court Hotel, on December 14th that I was aware of the tremendous pressures on us at the present time. We are tackling an extremely difficult job—nothing less than the conversion of up to 6 lion gas appliances t new fuel. We are the wa c

39 The Chairman's Christmas message to staff, December 1972. A bleak period and not much seasonal cheer.

double-edged award for the 'most improved' during the year. Essex Area was the first winner in this category when it was introduced in 1974. Subsequent successes were Thameside District (1978), Hackney District (1983), and Palace (Westminster) District in 1984. In 1984 only one other Region showed a greater overall improvement in customer service. In 1986 the Region had its best ever year in the national awards,

Table 9.16   Complaints by letter,
1974–87 (year ended March 31)

1974	11 950
1975	10 000
1976	8 600
1977	6 550
1978	6 400
1979	5 927
1980	5 334
1981	5 206
1982	4 777
1983	4 607
1984	5 115
1985	4 575
1986	4 196
1987	3 809

Source: North Thames Gas.

Redbridge (in the newly-formed Forest District) capturing the 'most improved' trophy, with five other North Thames teams in the top ten. And Colne (Staines District) achieved the highest-ever North Thames placing in the overall service league, 28th out of the 115 service units taking part.

The varied elements of the post-1976 revolution have seen the structure, climate, and visible appearance of North Thames change in striking fashion. The centre of gravity of the organisation has shifted from central London to Staines, and Staines itself is now part of a constellation firmly within the orbit of British Gas. The new and streamlined North Thames which has emerged has left little to remind one of the undertaking which started off some forty years ago, as bit by bit the legacies of the Gas Light & Coke Company have disappeared.

In retrospect, it is strikingly clear that in all essentials except name and ownership the Gas Light & Coke Company came to an end not in 1949 but in the early 1970s. Despite fears and forebodings at the time, nationalisation, in fact, made little difference to the way in which Londoners obtained their gas, how they were supplied, or where they were supplied from. The sea-change, in more than one sense, came with the advent of natural gas, for it was this event which ended gas manufacture and dictated increasing control from the centre.

Londoners can still see some links with the past, of course. The capital still retains some 1500 gas lamps, more than any other city in the world, while the old St Pancras holders, renovated and repainted in 1978 in their original vermilion, black and white, recall the days of the Imperial Gas Light & Coke Company which began life in 1824. It is gratifying also that the Region has established a historical museum of its

40 Official opening of the Historical Museum, Bromley-by-Bow, 1983. In the Memorial Gardens are, from the left, Alan Webster, Controller of Supplies and Transport; Edward Johnson, Director of Management Services; John Day, Director of Engineering; Ernie Fisher, formerly Engineer-in-Charge, Beckton; Don Coote, formerly Regional Design and Construction Engineer; Paul Dixon, Director of Personnel; 'Bertie' Moys; James Burns; Barry Reynolds, Director of Finance; Chairman John Gadd; Leslie Clark; Gilliam Gervase-Williams; Kenneth Gervase-Williams; Reg Bloom, Regional Secretary; and Derek Dutton, Head of Public Relations.

own at Bromley-by-Bow. This was officially opened in 1983 by the
former Chief Engineer and Deputy Chairman, Jim Burns, who donated
his own George Medal, awarded for bravery during an air attack on
Bromley in 1941. The museum will surely stand as a reminder of a
tradition of service to Londoners stretching back for more than 175
years, a tradition which links the England of the days of the early
Industrial Revolution to the new technological age in a way that no
other industry can match.

The successful privatisation of British Gas in December 1986 marked
the end of thirty-seven years of nationalisation, a milestone which in
many ways is an appropriate place to end the story of North Thames
Gas. The retirement of John Gadd shortly afterwards (January 1988) and
his replacement by Mr Arthur Dove, formerly chairman of South
Eastern, is another landmark, for Gadd's period of office witnessed so
many fundamental changes in the shape and structure of the Region.

Not that North Thames ended as a Region with the arrival of private
ownership. The organisation and procedures of British Gas remained
very much after privatisation as they did before, with Sir Denis Rooke
staying on as Chairman of the new British Gas plc and the existing
Regions remaining under their incumbent chairmen. So North Thames
passed into private ownership with John Gadd at the helm, just as in
1949 the North Thames Gas Board had emerged under Michael Milne-
Watson.

Such continuity in the midst of change seems to be a characteristic of
the gas industry. It is noteworthy, for example, that even the Regional
boundaries have remained virtually unchanged, despite the dramatically changed nature of gas enterprise and the major industry-wide
reorganisations of 1972 and 1986. Noteworthy particularly when one
reflects that these boundaries in turn were based upon a combination of
traditional private industry, municipal enterprise, and wartime civil
defence organisation. Continuity, and perhaps a deep-seated conser-
vatism, is seen also in the activities undertaken by the gas industry. The
industry has clung to its traditional tasks: acquiring, distributing, and
selling gas, and marketing gas appliances. Government efforts to hive
off parts of the industry have been resisted. Thus the industry has
remained essentially a *gas* industry, with little diversification into new
areas and with gas still fiercely competitive with, and independent
from, other energy industries. Whether the new era of private
enterprise will lead to substantial diversification, and so produce
fundamental changes in these areas, only time will tell.

A notable link between past and future, and a good note on which to
close this history, came with the decision to locate the new Thames
District headquarters at Beckton. The new office, opened on 1
December 1986, is to serve an area whose boundaries were drawn to

include the whole of the burgeoning docklands redevelopment scheme. Thus from a base established in 1868 by the Gas Light & Coke Company, and still recalling the name of Simon Adams Beck, North Thames will face its most exciting and challenging opportunities in the future.

Bibliographical Note

This book is based largely on the records of North Thames Gas located at its head office in Staines and also at the nearby district showroom. These records include Minute Books of the various committees, account books, and a wide range of correspondence, memorandums and miscellaneous information on particular subjects. Published material includes the *Annual Reports* of the North Thames Gas Board (1949–72); the *Thames Gas Magazine* (the house journal of North Thames, formerly the *Co-Partners' Magazine* of the Gas Light & Coke Company since 1911; the name was changed in April 1951); *News*, the sales and service magazine of the Board (1953–69); and a variety of other periodicals, special reports and pamphlets published by the Board and its successor on different subjects.

The sources for all the tables in the text, except where otherwise stated, derive from these North Thames materials and from information provided by various departments. Because so much of the unpublished data is uncatalogued, separate source references have not been given.

For those wishing to explore in depth particular aspects of the North Thames story, the *Thames Gas Magazine* and its predecessor are indispensable. The records of the Gas Light & Coke Company (before 1949) have been deposited at the GLC Record Office, while those of other constituent companies of North Thames Gas are held in regional record offices. The standard history of the company is by S. Everard, *The History of the Gas Light and Coke Company 1812–1949* (London, Ernest Benn, 1949). Some information relating to North Thames Gas can be found in various parliamentary inquiries and reports, especially the *Report from the Select Committee on Nationalised Industries: The Gas Industry* (HMSO, 1961), while the *Annual Reports* of the Gas Council and the British Gas Corporation contain much useful statistical data. A great deal of information on North Thames, and on all aspects of the gas industry, is contained in the trade press, especially *Gas World*. For details of gas conversion, see R. P. Rhodes. 'Conversion at Canvey', *Institution of Gas Engineers*, Communication 730 (1966); and R. P. Rhodes, F. A. Collins and J. D. Greene, 'The Conversion of Central London' *Institution of Gas Engineers*, Communication 935 (1974).

The best introduction to the history of Britain's gas industry is by T. I. Williams, *A History of the British Gas Industry* (Oxford: Oxford University Press, 1981), while the history of conversion is outlined in C. Elliott, *The History of Natural Gas Conversion in Great Britain* (Royston, Cambridge: Information and Research Services, 1980).

Appendix

CHAIRMEN AND DEPUTY CHAIRMEN OF NORTH THAMES GAS BOARD/REGION

Chairmen

M. Milne-Watson	18 January 1949–30 April 1964
R. S. Johnson	1 May 1964–19 May 1970
G. E. Cooper	20 May 1970–31 March 1977
J. Gadd	1 April 1977–31 January 1988
A. A. Dove	1 February 1988

Deputy Chairmen

F. M. Birks	18 January 1949–30 April 1956
R. N. B. D. Bruce	1 May 1956–31 December 1959
Dr J. Burns	1 January 1960–31 October 1962
J. A. Hepworth	1 November 1962–31 October 1964
L. J. Clark	1 November 1964–31 March 1967
L. W. Smith	1 April 1967–31 March 1972
R. P. Rhodes	1 January 1973–8 June 1975
R. Evans	9 June 1975–30 June 1977
D. A. Young	18 July 1977–20 March 1979
E. A. Haynes	1 May 1979–31 December 1982
A. Sutcliffe	23 May 1983–31 July 1986
A. McKay	1 August 1987–

NORTH THAMES GAS BOARD PART-TIME BOARD MEMBERS, 1949–72

E. V. Evans	18 January 1949–30 April 1953
L. C. Hansen	18 January 1949–30 April 1957
G. D. Dillon	17 January 1949–30 April 1966
Mrs I. T. Barclay	31 March 1949–30 April 1963
E. Bayliss	12 May 1949–11 May 1969
Lord Forrester, Earl of Verulam	9 August 1949–13 October 1960
Sir Henry Tizard	30 May 1952–30 April 1953
Sir Clifford Radcliffe	1 January 1955–31 December 1957
Air Chief Marshal Sir Arthur P. M. Sanders	8 November 1956–31 December 1964
W. D. Goss	16 May 1957–30 April 1961
Lord Collison	15 May 1961–31 December 1972
Earl of Halsbury	1 March 1962–31 December 1972
F. L. Levy	1 March 1963–28 February 1970
J. A. Buckley	1 November 1964–15 May 1966
Dr K. G. Denbigh	19 May 1966–31 December 1972
J. G. Beevor	1 September 1966–31 August 1969

E. J. Edwards	1 April 1967–30 April 1971
Sir Christopher Higgins	12 May 1969–31 December 1972
W. Hyde	17 March 1971–31 December 1972
R. P. Rhodes	1 May 1970–31 December 1972
Dr J. Burns	1 June 1959–1 January 1960

NORTH THAMES GAS BOARD AS AT 31 DECEMBER 1972

G. E. Cooper
L. W. Smith
R. P. Rhodes
Lord Collison
Dr K. G. Denbigh
Lord Halsbury
Sir Christopher Higgins
W. Hyde

CHAIRMAN'S MANAGEMENT COMMITTEE FROM 1964

R. S. Johnson	July 1964–May 1970
J. A. Hepworth	July 1964–October 1964
L. J. Clark	July 1964–March 1967
L. W. Smith	July 1964–December 1972
B. Wood	July 1964–July 1965
J. A. Buckley	July 1964–May 1966
H. W. Moys	July 1964–May 1966
A. D. L. Copp	July 1964–February 1966
G. H. W. Madge	October 1964–June 1971
E. J. Edwards	November 1964–April 1971
J. S. Barnes	July 1965–March 1976
L. H. Harden	December 1965–February 1969
A. R. Bovington	February 1966–March 1969
R. P. Rhodes	May 1966–June 1975
C. P. N. Cox	June 1966–October 1971
R. G. Bloom	April 1967–June 1983
A. J. Cross	March 1968–May 1971
A. J. Vinegrad	February 1969–September 1973
E. S. Milner	April 1969–April 1971
A. Green	June 1969–July 1971
P. A. Shepherd	October 1969–June 1971
G. E. Cooper	May 1970–March 1977
A. A. H. Clark	January 1971–October 1980
S. A. Mealey	May 1971–March 1976
R. G. Evans	May 1971–August 1973
P. D. Dixon	May 1971–January 1988
R. O. Emmony	July 1971–January 1978
Dr E. Johnson	July 1971–May 1985
D. R. Grimster	August 1971–May 1982
K. L. Pickthall	November 1972–August 1974

G. E. Holmes	November 1973–March 1978
H. J. Lorton	August 1974–March 1977
D. A. Young	January 1974–October 1974
	July 1977–March 1979
D. V. Dutton	January 1974–
C. E. Mills	March 1975–April 1975
R. Evans	June 1975–June 1977
P. Sellers	January 1976–June 1980
T. H. Griffiths	January 1976–December 1980
J. Gadd	April 1977–January 1988
J. F. Day	April 1978–August 1983
J. Allan	July 1978–January 1988
E. A. Haynes	May 1979–December 1982
B. J. Reynolds	July 1980–August 1985
A. G. Webster	March 1981–July 1986
A. Sutcliffe	May 1983–July 1986
M. J. Piper	August 1983–
D. Brooks	January 1984–August 1987
P. J. Smith	November 1985–

Note In January 1973 the Committee became the Management Committee. Members of the Committee were also members of the Executive Committee, which existed alongside the Management Committee from 1973 until 1977. In September 1987 both committees became the Executive Committee and in April 1982 the Regional Management Committee.

Index

Note: page numbers in **bold** type refer to illustrations.